The Battle of Olustee, 1864

ALSO BY ROBERT P. BROADWATER

*Chickamauga, Andersonville, Fort Sumter
and Guard Duty at Home: Four Civil War Diaries
by Pennsylvania Soldiers*
(McFarland, 2006)

*The Battle of Perryville, 1862:
Culmination of the Failed Kentucky Campaign*
(McFarland, 2005)

The Battle of Olustee, 1864

The Final Union Attempt to Seize Florida

ROBERT P. BROADWATER

McFarland & Company, Inc., Publishers
Jefferson, North Carolina, and London

LIBRARY OF CONGRESS CATALOGUING-IN-PUBLICATION DATA

Broadwater, Robert P., 1958–
    The Battle of Olustee, 1864 : the final Union attempt to seize Florida / Robert P. Broadwater.
        p.   cm.
    Includes bibliographical references and index.

    ISBN-13: 978-0-7864-2541-9
    (softcover : 50# alkaline paper) ∞

    1. Olustee, Battle of, Olustee, Fla., 1864. I. Title.
    E476.43.B76   2006
    973.7'36 — dc22   2006020495

British Library cataloguing data are available

©2006 Robert P. Broadwater. All rights reserved

No part of this book may be reproduced or transmitted in any form or by any means, electronic or mechanical, including photocopying or recording, or by any information storage and retrieval system, without permission in writing from the publisher.

On the cover: top: woodcut of Jacksonville under Union army occupation (courtesy United States Army Military History Institute); map is from Floridamemory.com

Manufactured in the United States of America

McFarland & Company, Inc., Publishers
  Box 611, Jefferson, North Carolina 28640
    www.mcfarlandpub.com

TABLE OF CONTENTS

Introduction   1

ONE • The War Comes to Florida   7
TWO • March to the Interior   34
THREE • Finegan Springs a Trap   72
FOUR • A Brave and Bloody Stand   105
FIVE • The Twilight of Battle   137
SIX • Flight to the Coast   153
SEVEN • Final Operations   171

Epilogue   181
Appendix I: The Opposing Armies   191
Appendix II: Casualties   193
Appendix III: Enlistment of Black Troops by State   196
Appendix IV: The Flag of the 2nd Florida Cavalry (Poetry)   197
Chapter Notes   201
Bibliography   209
Index   215

Introduction

The battle of Olustee capped the failed Union attempt to wrest the eastern and central portions of Florida away from Confederate control and thus deprive the Southern armies of the great stores of food and supplies that the state was providing for the Confederate cause. It also marked the end of the failed attempt to reorganize the state government and re-admit Florida into the Union, a goal that was important to the Lincoln administration.

Florida had been the third Southern state to vote for secession and leave the Union, but aside from the fact that it had been among the first to take steps to leave behind the old national government, the state held little importance, for either side, in the early years of the war. Florida's sparse population meant that there were few real cities, and the state held no strategic value so far as the Union was concerned. Northern activities were largely confined to occasional raids against coastal ports such as Fernandina, St. Augustine, and Jacksonville. From a Confederate viewpoint, the vast expanse of Florida's coastline made the state almost impossible to guard, as more troops would be needed to guard its coastal boundaries than it was judged the state was worth. Florida's defense was limited to a small home guard, scattered throughout the state, that operated more like partisan ranger units than like an army of defense.

By the end of 1863, both North and South acknowledged that Florida had attained a level of importance it had not held in the first two years of the war. The state had become strategically important to both sides, owing to the fact that it was now a crucial source of supplies

Introduction

for the Confederate armies, specifically General P.G.T. Beauregard's forces at Charleston and Savannah and General Braxton Bragg's Army of Tennessee. The Confederacy was running short on everything by the close of 1863. A large portion of its territory was in Federal hands, and the areas that were still under Confederate control had been strained to the breaking point to try to meet the demanding needs of the Southern armies in the field. By the end of 1863, the exports of Florida food had become crucial to the Confederate war effort. The chief commissary officers for South Carolina, Georgia, and General Bragg's army all stated that they could not maintain their armies were it not for Florida, the former officer stating: "We are almost entirely dependent on Florida.... We now have 40,000 troops and laborers to subsist. The supply of bacon on hand in this city (Charleston) is 20,000 pounds and the cattle furnished by this state is not one-tenth of what is required."[1]

Indeed, Florida was feeding the Confederacy, or at least its armies. It is estimated that by 1864, the state was providing 25,000 head of cattle and 10,000 head of hogs to the war effort annually. Florida had been elevated to a status of strategic importance to both sides. The Confederacy could not hope to supply its armies without the sustenance provided by the state, and that very dependence made Florida an important military target for the Union armies. If the North could cut off the supply of food coming out of Florida, it could seriously cripple the Confederacy's ability to make war.[2]

In the North, the desire to mount an excursion into Florida went far beyond the benefits that could be achieved in dealing a blow to the Confederate war effort, however. Strong political forces were at work, and the state was viewed as ripe for the picking by an administration that sought to reconstruct the local government and bring Florida back into the Union as a Republican supporter. President Lincoln was facing strong opposition, both from within his own party and from the Democrats, and it was hoped that an occupied and reconstructed Florida would send delegates who would be friendly to Lincoln's nomination for re-election to the national convention.

Both the military and political objectives that led the North to send an army to the shores of Florida, in the beginning of 1864, would

Introduction

be foiled by a hastily collected Confederate force, led by a general who did not possess the confidence of his commanding general. The two armies would meet at Olustee, or Ocean Pond, as it was referred to by the Southerners, in a battle that did not follow the plans of either commander on the field.

By comparison, Olustee would be one of the smaller battles of the war, with only approximately 10,000 men participating in it from both armies combined. It was not a stage for the tens of thousands of soldiers who fought in the better known engagements like Gettysburg, Chickamauga, or Shiloh, but for those who participated in it, it was as fierce a struggle as any fought on this continent during the four years of Civil War, and it produced results that equaled or exceeded those won on many larger fields of conflict. In a battle that lasted only about four hours, the casualty rates were appalling. The Confederate army suffered casualties of approximately 17½ percent of the force engaged, while the Union army sustained losses of 35 percent, greater than those suffered at Gettysburg or Chickamauga. Many veterans of Gettysburg, and other hotly contested fields of the Army of Northern Virginia, who fought at Olustee proclaimed that it was the hottest fight they had been involved in during the war.

The battle also showcased the fighting ability of the black troops who were in the invading army. Fully one-third of the Union force was made up of black soldiers, at a time when many in the military still doubted the black man's ability to serve as a soldier. Though black troops had already taken a conspicuous part in operations against Port Hudson, Chickasaw Bayou, and Battery Wagner, opinion in the military still tended to view black troops as good for nothing more than fatigue or guard duty, not as front line units who could help to stamp out the rebellion. The battle of Olustee gave the famed 54th Massachusetts another opportunity to prove its fighting mettle. It also gave the other two black regiments in the Union army a chance to show that they would fight, if given the chance, even though one of the regiments had been in the army for only about a month, had received very little training, and had not even been given proper instruction on the loading and firing of their muskets. Combined with the previous examples

Introduction

of the courage and dependability of black troops, Olustee served to fire the call for black enlistments, a call that would, by the end of the war, see over 180,000 black men don the Union uniform and fight to preserve the Union and their newly granted freedom under its banner.

The Confederate victory at Olustee ensured that the South could continue to depend on a steady stream of much needed products from within its borders. The loss was viewed as a disaster in the North, and the Lincoln administration was subjected to severe criticism for the failed effort, as well as for the obvious political reasons that had occasioned it. The Union army would continue to maintain a presence in the state till the end of the war; however, it would be limited to a few coastal garrisons that made infrequent raids into the interior. The battle of Olustee preserved the interior of Florida for the Confederacy, and by the end of the war, this region would be the largest tract of land that was still in Confederate hands and Tallahassee would be the only Southern state capitol in which a Confederate government still resided.

Though it was the largest land action to take place in Florida during the war, the battle of Olustee has been relegated almost to obscurity in the history of that war. Had it been fought in 1861, instead of 1864, the carnage that the battle exacted would have ensured that it eclipsed engagements like Wilson's Creek, Ball's Bluff, and many of the other battles that are better known, but not as costly. Another factor that contributed to the lack of attention the battle has received, over the years, is that it was fought largely by generals and troops who were not considered noteworthy. Union General Truman Seymour and Confederate General Joseph Finegan never achieved a stature of fame that would cause students of the war to study this battle as a part of their overall careers. In addition, there was a stigma attached to the battle that has only begun to be removed in recent decades concerning the men who fought the battle. Studies of black troops were not much in demand in the decades that followed the war. It has only been within the past few decades that interest in the contributions of black troops has begun to soar, making battles like Olustee, in which some of these units saw their first combat, a focus for students of the period.

The Battle of Olustee will present the story of the failed attempt

Introduction

to bring the Sunshine State back into the Union through use of force and of the desperate struggle that ended the campaign. Much of the story will be told through the words of the actual participants, so that the reader may gain a first-hand insight into this important, but often overlooked, campaign. The reader will discover the acts of heroism that took place on the ground, as the Fifty-fourth Massachusetts and Eighth United States Colored Troops endeavored to hold their ground against the gallant charge of Colquitt's seasoned veterans. They will also discover the atrocities that took place following the battle, when wounded black troops were murdered by some of the Confederate victors.

The Florida campaign combined the military and political aspects of the struggle as few other battles of the war did, and its history combines both the best and the worst of that era. Both sides were worthy of praise, and both were deserving of condemnation. One Confederate veteran of the battle would later write: "In giving my recollection of the battle following, known as that of Olustee or Ocean Pond, I would say that of all those fought during the war, I know of none presenting more peculiar features than this one, or one of more intensity, yet historians but rarely refer to it and then in only a passing word or two."[3] The battle of Olustee and the Florida campaign are important parts of the history of the Civil War, and the following pages will try to pay honor to the sacrifices that were made upon its bloody field. It is the purpose of this book to tell the story of this battle in more than just "a passing word or two."

In this book the reader will follow the Olustee campaign largely through the experiences and words of the men who participated in it. First person accounts have been widely used so that the reader may view the campaign through the eyes of the men who were there. In most cases, their quotes have been included just as they wrote them, accounting for some discrepancies in spelling and punctuation. By using their words, the author has tried to capture the emotion of the campaign and give the reader an opportunity to be guided through the campaign through the words of its participants.

ONE

THE WAR COMES TO FLORIDA

In the closing months of 1863, the state of Florida began to assume a position of importance, with both the Federal and Confederate governments, that it had not previously enjoyed. The eyes of both governments were cast upon the state for military as well as political reasons. Prior to that time, both sides had largely ignored the state. The Confederacy had stripped away almost all of the available manpower to serve in other theaters of the war, leaving only a scant defense force that was scattered throughout the state. In the North, the military and political powers did not deem the value of Florida to be sufficient to take advantage of its relatively defenseless condition, and to mount an effort to wrest it away from the Confederacy. To be sure, there had been several raids conducted by the Union army, and the military had established and maintained a presence in a few coast towns like St. Augustine, Fernandina, and Jacksonville, but there had been no concerted effort to take control of points in the interior. Available manpower was the chief reason why there were so few Confederate troops in Florida, as well as why the Union army did not avail itself of this obvious opportunity. The vast majority of the troops, on both sides, were needed for other arenas of war. Operations at Charleston, as well as those of the field armies under Confederate General Braxton Bragg and Union General William S. Rosecrans, took precedence over the defense, or capture, of Florida. There were simply not enough men on either side to worry about Florida, in the early years of the war. That situation had changed by the end of 1863, as both sides recognized the

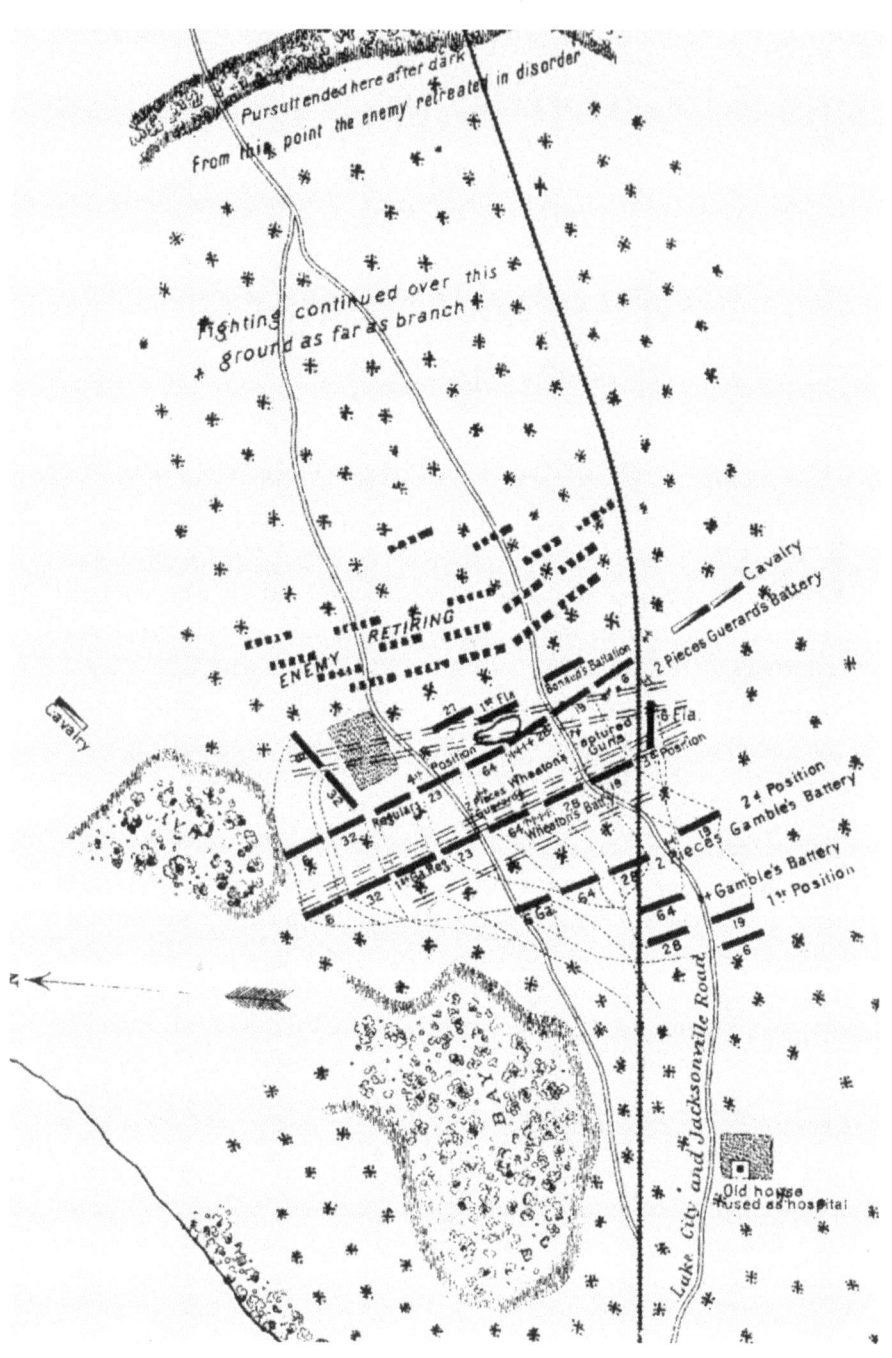

One • The War Comes to Florida

increased importance of the area, and each side steeled itself for the inevitable struggle that would come to control it.

In late 1863, a Confederate officer serving in Charleston wrote

> The stock of bacon and beef for the armies of the Confederate States is now exhausted.... Starvation stares the army in the face; the handwriting is on the wall.... From the best information I have the resources in food [meat] in both Tennessee and Virginia armies are exhausted. This remark now applies with equal force to South Carolina and Georgia.[1]

The food shortage in the South had become alarming, and the two main Southern armies in the South, under generals Beauregard and Bragg, were both looking to Florida to alleviate the hardships of their men, caused by shortages of food. In October of 1863, Colonel L.B. Northrup, Commissary General for the Confederacy, reported that the Confederacy was "completely exhausted of supplies," and had only enough meat rations for a few days. The Southern armies would be faced with severe hardships since Northrup estimated that it would be 48 days before the new crop was harvested in the deep south. North Carolina had been sending all of its surplus crop to Virginia, and Alabama and Florida had been providing supplies for Georgia and

```
         Confederate Forces
         Federal Forces
         Railroad
         Turnpike road
The ≡ ≡ ≡ lines mark the different positions occupied
by the Enemy, and from which they were driven.
The ........ lines mark the movements of our Regiments
from one position to another.
    Our forces are here represented in the four distinct positions
which they occupied, from the Road-Crossing near which the
fight opened, to where the Enemy's retrograde movement began;
from this point our whole line advanced in pursuit.
```

Opposite and above: Sketch of the battlefield of Olustee, showing the positions of the Union and Confederate forces on the field (magnified detail from the atlas in *Confederate Military History*).

The Battle of Olustee, 1864

South Carolina.[2] The middle counties of Florida, namely Alachua and Marion, were looked upon as a veritable commissary for the Confederate armies, with their vast surpluses of food, particularly cattle. In his report to the governor, at the end of 1862, the state comptroller for Florida reported that there were 658,609 cattle then within the state's borders. This estimate was probably far below the actual number of cattle in the state, as it was based on returns from 1860 to 1861. Large herds of cattle had been driven into Florida, from Georgia, after that date, to prevent their being captured by the Federals, and these numbers were not reflected in the comptroller's report. In December of 1863, Brigadier General D.P. Wood, commanding the District of Key West, stated, "Two thousand head of cattle are reported to be driven out of Florida every week for the rebel armies." Clearly, Florida had become the food-basket of the Southern portion of the Confederacy.[3] This increased importance of Florida to the Confederate war effort was not lost upon the Union military commanders of the region. The shortages in the Confederate army were well known to them, and the prospect of seizing the central region of Florida, and thereby cutting off these much needed supplies to the Confederacy, began to take shape in the minds of the Union leaders in the fall of 1863. By seizing control of the interior of the state, or by destroying the rail lines through a raid, the Union could disrupt the shipment of food from Florida to the rest of the Confederacy, an accomplishment that would be as important as a victory in battle.

Another reason for the Union to establish an active presence in the interior of Florida was the recruitment of black troops. The newspapers in New York City had been trumpeting the cause of black enlistment during most of 1863. One referred to an army of blacks as "a great volcano, about bursting, whose lava will burn, flow and destroy." Another called black troops "not a phantom, but the reality of servile insurrection."[4] Union enlistments were down during 1863, and the draft had to be invoked in many congressional districts. The recruitment of black troops was seen as a way to possibly avoid the hated conscription by giving the blacks an opportunity to aid the Federal government, and at the same time, help to win their freedom. Most of

One • *The War Comes to Florida*

the white officers and men in the ranks were still doubtful of the worth of black troops in combat. It was largely held that they would not fight and did not have the capacity to make good soldiers. Their recruitment was coveted largely from a desire to have them relieve white troops from guard and fatigue duty. These white troops could then be added to the men in the ranks, providing an increase of manpower in an indirect manner. Though black regiments had already seen service at Port Hudson, Chickasaw Bayou, and Battery Wagner, they were still considered to be an unknown quantity by most of the white officers in the Union army. The Florida campaign would do a great deal to influence a change in that thinking.

Regardless of the manner in which they would be employed, there was known to be a large population of blacks in the interior of Florida, working as slaves, and the Federal military viewed this population as a recruiting ground from which it could obtain large numbers of enlistments. At this time, authorities in Florida estimated that there were approximately 56,000 slaves in the state, with 40,000 of them residing in the middle counties.[5] Major General Quincy Gillmore, commanding the Federal army at Charleston, had applied to the government for additional troops in the fall of 1863, in order to be able to mount an expedition into Florida. He specifically requested to have some of the new black regiments that were being raised sent to his department so that he could replace some of his white units that were doing garrison duty, with it in mind that the white troops would then make up the expeditionary force. The response he received from Washington was that these troops were more sorely needed elsewhere, particularly in the Department of the Gulf. Gillmore's request to have existing regiments was denied, but he was granted authority to form all of the regiments of black troops that he could raise from within his military district, which stretched from Key West to Charleston and also encompassed Alabama. In recruiting these regiments, the slaves in Florida seemed to be the most logical place to begin, owing both to the numbers of slaves there and the sparse number of Confederate soldiers on hand to defend them. Once the regiments were raised, Gillmore was authorized to establish review boards to commission

The Battle of Olustee, 1864

The Union military hoped to enlist large numbers of blacks from Florida's slave population to serve in the army. Many slaves had been enlisted in South Carolina, like those pictured in this photograph (courtesy United States Army Military History Institute).

deserving white non-commissioned officers and enlisted men to lead them.[6]

Major General Quincy A. Gillmore was a West Point graduate in 1849, graduating first in his class. He was assigned to the coveted Engineer Corps. Gillmore had served as the engineering officer during the Port Royal Expedition, and had later won fame as the officer who reduced and captured Fort Pulaski, in Savannah Harbor. He was described by contemporaries as

> an excellent officer to manage a siege operation; but in leading troops in the field, as an independent and final authority he was too apt to be careful of the expenditure of life at too late a point in his operations. This was a common defect in our generals; they seemed to lose their nerve at the critical moment and shrank from possible slaughter.[7]

Political motivations were as strong as the military ones in forming the strategy to invade the interior of Florida with an expeditionary force. President Lincoln had only recently unveiled his ten percent plan

One • The War Comes to Florida

of reconstruction for the Southern states, and Florida was seen as a prime candidate to serve as a model of Lincoln's plan of reunion. Many Florida natives had expressed to the government the desire of the populace to rejoin the Federal government, and had implied that all that prevented such a move was the presence of the Confederate military in their state. The president was advised that Floridians would flock to the national banner if there was a Union army in the state to protect them from retaliation at the hands of the Confederates. The state was represented to be held hostage by the Confederate military, and it was promised that, if released from this bondage, the citizens of the state would rapidly form a loyal government that would pledge its allegiance to Washington and the Lincoln administration.

General Quincy A. Gillmore. The Florida expedition would take place under his departmental command, though he would not personally lead the invading army (courtesy United States Army Military History Institute).

Lincoln was facing a serious challenge to his bid for re-election in the 1864 campaign, both from the Democratic Party and from within his own party. The prospect of creating a loyal government in Florida, one that would send delegates to the national convention who would vote for Lincoln, appealed to the president and fueled his desire to see a military intervention in the state. On October 8, 1863, Lincoln was approached by Judge Philip Fraser, an exiled Floridian, who had been a Republican office holder before the war. Judge Fraser stated that "if forces are to be sent to Florida to be used as tools for political wire-pullers and speculators it were better not to send them at all. We want bold and earnest men to go down inspired by true purpose — the restoration of Florida to the Union as a free state. Political maneuvers may come after but not before." The prospect of establishing a military presence in Florida may have led to Lincoln's announcement of his Amnesty Proclamation, on December 8, 1863. This proclamation outlined Lincoln's plan for the reconstruction and re-admittance of Southern states in which ten percent of the voting population in the 1860 election would take the oath of allegiance and desire to be brought back into the Union. The situation in Florida seemed ideal to make it the first of the reconstructed states and a model for all that would follow.[8]

Secretary Salmon P. Chase, Abraham Lincoln's competition within the Republican Party for the presidential nomination in 1864. Lincoln's desire to obtain Florida's three electoral votes was a main reason for making the Florida expedition (courtesy United States Army Military History Institute).

The possibility of bringing Florida back into the Union before the end of the war was not merely wishful thinking on the part of the administration. Some years after the war, Confederate General Samuel Jones stated that he felt the plan to be entirely feasible.

> "Florida appeared to offer better prospects in such an undertaking than any other Southern State," he said. "Its great extent of

coastline and its intersection by a broad and deep river, navigable by vessels of war, exposed a great part of the State to the control of Union forces whenever it should be thought desirable to occupy it. The exigencies of the Confederate service had in a great measure stripped Florida of troops. If a column of Union troops could penetrate the country westward from Jacksonville, occupy a point in the interior, and break up communications between east, middle, and west Florida by the destruction of the railroad and bridges about the Suwannee River, the Southern Confederacy would not only be deprived of a large quantity of the food drawn from east and south Florida, but a point d' appui would be established for any of the inhabitants who might be disposed to attempt the organization of a State acknowledging allegiance to the United States."[9]

Truly, Florida appeared to be the best place for Lincoln to test his reconstruction plans for the Southern states.

Major John Lay, assistant adjutant general to Brigadier General Thomas Gordon, in Tallahassee, reported that the shortage of soldiers and the poor morale of those who were in the state was so severe that the military was not even able to sufficiently guard public property.

> There are here I ascertain upon accurate inquiry, $6,000,000, more than $300,000 in commissary stores, including, at least 125,000 lbs. of bacon and pork, large quantities of sugar and sirup, besides large and valuable amount of quartermaster's stores. For the removal of these stores no provision has been made, and there is no defense force here for adequate guards for public property.... The number of desertions is alarming. Col. Gamble, of this place, showed me a letter from Taylor Co[unty], in which the position of the organized deserters is represented as bold and dangerous. I can see nothing that can be done at present towards checking them. Mr. Houston and others reliable just from the neighborhood of Gainesville report the conduct of the enemy as conciliating in the extreme, not injuring persons or property, sending back negroes, and urging the continued cultivation of farms, bidding very strongly for the Union sentiment of the State....[10]

The Battle of Olustee, 1864

The Lincoln administration was being pressed by a number of prominent citizens who also wanted Florida to once more be brought under the Federal banner. In one way or another, all of them sought to acquire personal gain from the venture. In September of 1863, Eli Thayer approached Lincoln with a proposal to colonize Florida with blacks and Northern volunteers. He asked that he be appointed military governor of the state, and that Brigadier General James A. Garfield be given command of the Department of Florida, with a 30,000-man army to protect the colonists. Lincoln declined his support of the plan.[11]

A group of Northern businessmen, led by Marshall O. Roberts, were demanding that the government seize the Florida Railroad. These Northerners happened to be the majority stockholders in the railway, which had been controlled by the Southern stockholders since the commencement of the war. By invoking the articles of the two confiscation acts passed by Congress, as well as the Direct Tax Act, these men hoped to gain complete control of the Florida Railroad, once it was captured by the army. The railroad was important to the government, as well, but not for the reason of restoring ownership of it to these businessmen. Its importance lay in it being a means of conveyance to transport men and material to and from Florida. In the end, the Northern investors were blunted in their attempts to control the railroad. They had hired a Federal tax commissioner, L.D. Stickney, to look after their interests, and to keep the taxes paid on the railroad. Stickney was too busy pressing his own interest in becoming a Federal tax commissioner in Florida, and failed to pay the taxes. The line was then sold to other investors.[12]

The prospects of an expedition to Florida were discussed through the end of 1863. General Gillmore submitted a proposal for an expedition on December 22. On that same day, a group of exiled Florida Unionists set sail from Port Royal, South Carolina, for a meeting in St. Augustine. Stickney was among their number. They reported, upon reaching the city, that a mass meeting had been held there on December 19, at which the attendees had overwhelmingly voted for a reorganization of the state government as part of the United States, the abolition of slavery within state borders, the expulsion of Confederate

One • The War Comes to Florida

authorities, and the immediate resumption of relations with the Federal government. They declared the articles of secession to be null and void, and called for the election of state congressmen to a "loyal" legislature. The 24th Massachusetts Infantry was garrisoning the city, and it was reported that the officers of that regiment had already begun to prepare the blacks in the surrounding area for reconstruction. Before the end of December, a petition was sent to President Lincoln from the Unionist partisans in the city requesting immediate "armed occupation" of the entire state. It was signed, "many Union men."[13]

On January 13, 1864, President Lincoln wrote to General Gillmore, in Charleston:

> I understand an effort is being made by some worthy gentlemen to reconstruct a loyal state government in Florida. Florida is in your department, and it is not unlikely that you may be there in person. I have given Mr. Hay a commission of major and sent him to you with some blank books and other blanks to aid in the reconstruction. He will explain as to the manner of using the blanks, and also my general views on the subject. It is desirable for all to cooperate; but if irreconcilable differences of opinion shall arise, you are master. I wish the thing done in the speediest way possible, so that when done it will be within the range of the late proclamation on the subject. The detail labor, of course, will have to be done by others, but I shall be greatly obliged if you will give it such general supervision as you can find convenient with your more strictly military duties.[14]

The "Mr. Hay" that Lincoln referred to was John Hay, his personal secretary. The President was taking no chances on instructions for the reconstruction of Florida being misconstrued. He was sending one of his most trusted staff members along to make sure things were conducted according to his wishes. Hay had been commissioned as a major in the Union army, especially for this expedition. He was supplied with record books and certificates to be given to all who took the oath of allegiance to the Federal government. Hay had volunteered his services to Lincoln for this assignment. He would travel to Florida carrying a carefully prepared address to the citizens, to convince them to

The Battle of Olustee, 1864

pledge their support to the Union, once the Northern army had gained control of the region.[15]

On January 14, Gillmore informed Halleck of his intentions to land a force in Florida. It is curious that neither Edwin Stanton, the Secretary of War, nor Gideon Welles, the Secretary of the Navy, had been included in the planning stages of the expedition. Orders were coming directly from Lincoln to the commanders in the field, bypassing his top naval and military leaders in Washington. In his message to the general-in-chief, Gillmore stated: "Sir, Unless it will interfere with the views of the War Department, I shall occupy the west bank of the Saint John's River, in Florida, very soon, and establish small depots there preparatory to an advance west at an early day."[16]

On January 15, Gillmore wrote to Stanton, giving the Florida expedition as the reason why he had previously requested the transfer to his department of new black regiments that were being raised. It is possible Gillmore felt that if he stated the fact that he wanted the regiments to facilitate the move of an army to Florida, the War Secretary would reconsider his pre-

Major John Hay, Lincoln's personal secretary. Hay was sent along on the Florida expedition as Lincoln's personal representative and was to help facilitate the reconstruction of the state (courtesy United States Army Military History Institute).

vious refusal. Stanton stuck to his original assertion that the Gulf Department was in more urgent need of those troops, and Gillmore would have to recruit his own black regiments if he desired additional manpower. In the letter of the 15th, Gillmore also stated, "Moreover, I am obliged to mount some of my very best infantry, as my entire cavalry force is less than 300 effective men. My plan in a great measure depends upon getting these new colored regiments...."[17] The operation was in trouble right from the start. Stanton had no intention of releasing any of the new black regiments to Gillmore, and that officer would have to make do with the troops he already had on hand. It had been Gillmore's intention to use the black regiments to release veteran white ones from duty at Charleston, so that he could send an experienced and battle-tried force to Florida. Stanton's refusal to provide him with any additional regiments meant that much of the force he would be sending to Florida would have minimal experience in the army.

A message from General Halleck, dated January 22, informed Gillmore,

> In regard to your proposed operations in Florida, the Secretary replied that the matter had been left entirely to your judgment and discretion, with the means at your command. As the object of the expedition has not been explained, it is impossible to judge here of its advantages or practicability. If it is expected to give an outlet for cotton, or open a favorable field for the enlistment of colored troops, the advantages may be sufficient to justify the expense in money and troops. But simply as military operations I attach very little importance to such expeditions. If successful they merely absorb our troops in garrisons to occupy the places, but have little or no influence upon the progress of the war.[18]

Halleck's message to Gillmore seems to display a testiness and lack of cooperation arising from a sense of being bypassed, in the chain of command, by Lincoln dealing directly with Gillmore. Halleck voiced a tacit opposition to the project, and reiterated the War Secretary's platform that no additional troops would be sent to the area. This was as much as he could do to show his dissatisfaction. The Florida expedition was Lincoln's pet project, and as such, it would take place with or without Halleck's blessings.

Gillmore tried to plead his case to the general-in-chief.

> In reply to your letter of the 22nd instant I beg leave to state that the objects and advantages to be secured by the occupation of that portion of Florida within my reach, viz, the richest portions between the Suwannee and the Saint John's Rivers, are: First. To procure an outlet for cotton, lumber, timber, turpentine, and the other products of that State. Second. To cut off one of the enemy's sources of commissary supplies. He now draws largely upon the herds of Florida for his beef, and is making preparations to take up a large portion of the Fernandina and Saint Mark's Railroad for the purpose of connecting the road from Jacksonville to Tallahassee with Thomasville, on the Savannah, Albany and Gulf Railroad, and perhaps with Albany, on the Southwestern Railroad. Third. To obtain recruits for my colored regiments. Fourth. To inaugurate measures for the speedy restoration of Florida to her allegiance, in accordance with instructions I have received from the President by the hands of Maj. John Hay, assistant adjutant-general.
>
> I am expected to accomplish these objects with the means at my command. The only requisitions which I have made in excess of my ordinary wants to enable me to accomplish this work speedily are for 1,500 horses and 1,500 sets horse equipment, to enable me to mount some infantry. If the filling of these requisitions will occasion any embarrassment to the departments of supply they can be reduced 30 percent.[19]

Brigadier General Truman Seymour, commander of the District of Hilton Head, was selected to command the expedition. On February 4, Gillmore issued orders to Seymour to prepare to embark, the following day, with his expeditionary force, consisting of the Seventh Connecticut Infantry, Seventh New Hampshire Infantry, Eighth United States Colored Troops, Second South Carolina Infantry, Third United States Colored Troops, Fifty-fourth Massachusetts Infantry, Fortieth Massachusetts Mounted Infantry, Independent Battalion Massachusetts Cavalry, Langdon's Light Battery, Elder's Horse Battery and a

One • The War Comes to Florida

General Truman Seymour. A hero of Fort Sumter and veteran of operations in Charleston Harbor, he was Gillmore's choice to lead the Union army in the expedition (courtesy United States Army Military History Institute).

section of James's Rhode Island Battery. The men were to be instructed to have rations for six days, half of them being cooked, and they were to have no less than 60 rounds of ammunition per man.[20]

General Seymour was a 39-year-old minister's son and a West Point graduate in the class of 1846. A native of Vermont, Seymour had excelled at drawing at the Academy, so much so that he was given a position to instruct it. He had served, with distinction, in the Mexican War, and in the war against the Seminoles, in Florida. The outbreak of hostilities had found Seymour stationed in Charleston, at Fort Sumter. Upon the surrender of that fort, Seymour was brevetted a brigadier general for gallantry displayed in its defense, and was assigned to duty in the Washington defenses. He commanded a brigade in the Peninsula Campaign, Second Manassas, South Mountain, and Antietam, before being transferred back to Charleston in November of 1862.[21] It was Seymour's command, of which the Fifty-fourth Massachusetts was a part, that had made the disastrous assault on Battery Wagner in June of 1863, which gained everlasting fame for the Fifty-fourth, but which also inflicted extreme casualties on the assaulting regiments. On the morning following the assault, the entire brigade could muster but 700 men.[22] In making this assault, Seymour had been accused by the press of sending his black troops in ahead of his white ones so that they would draw the majority

The Battle of Olustee, 1864

of the Confederate fire away from the other troops. This allegation led to charges of prejudice, but both the allegation and the charges were unfounded. Quite the opposite was true. Seymour believed in giving the black troops an opportunity to prove themselves in battle, and that is why he had allowed the 54th Massachusetts to lead the charge. Seymour had himself been severely wounded in the second wave of that assault, when he was hit by a fragment of an exploding artillery shell. His wound had just healed sufficiently for him to return to duty in December of 1863, just prior to his being named as the expedition commander.[23]

In the ranks, the esteem with which General Seymour was held seems to vary greatly. Lieutenant Tully McCrea, of the First United States Artillery, and a former roommate of George Armstrong Custer at West Point, wrote in a letter:

> A large expedition is leaving here today. I think the destination is somewhere in Florida, but that remains for us to find out after we arrive there. There are a large number of vessels in the harbor waiting to load troops and I suppose we will start tomorrow. General Seymour, my favorite general here, is in command and if we have an opportunity there will be some hard fighting and someone will be hurt.[24]

A historian in the 7th Connecticut Infantry offers a differing opinion of Seymour.

> The Florida expedition was entrusted to the command of General Truman Seymour, considered by more than the rank and file, as an eccentric West Point crank who aped the only Napoleon in prowling around camps at night to watch the men on duty, but he lacked the genius of his prototype in the performance of his own duty.[25]

A friend of General George B. McClellan, Seymour was among the last of that clique to be on active duty in the beginning of 1864. McClellan was the leading candidate for the presidency, of the Democratic Party, and it was ironic that one of the few pro–McClellan officers still on active service would be responsible for leading an expedition to Florida that had among its objectives the establishment of a pro–Lincoln reconstructed state government.

The naval portion of the expedition would be under the supervision of Admiral John Dahlgren. Like Gillmore, Dahlgren was receiving his instructions directly from the president, and not by way of Gideon Welles, Secretary of the Navy. Dahlgren was to provide the force Gillmore was sending with adequate transports, furnish a suitable number of escort vessels to protect the convoy while en route, and give naval fire support, once the soldiers were ashore.

From the beginning, there were ominous signs that good fortune was not smiling on the expedition. The refusal of the War Department to transfer any new black regiments into the department meant that Gillmore would not have the opportunity to send an experienced, all-white force with Seymour. Several black regiments would have to make up the deficiency of numbers. Of these, the Fifty-fourth Massachusetts had the most experience in combat, and that was both limited and of a disparaging nature. On the surface, Seymour's white regiments were all veteran units, and as they made up two-thirds of the expeditionary force, they could be counted on as a steadying influence for the black units. But fate and timing had conspired to create a situation where Seymour's white units were no more experienced than the black ones. The terms of enlistment had been due to expire for most of these regiments, and the military had exerted all the influence it could, along with generous bounties from the Federal and state governments, to induce the men to re-enlist. As an added incentive, those who signed up for another enlistment were promised a 30-day furlough to go home and spend some time with their families. Large numbers of men were persuaded to re-enlist in all of the white regiments that were part of Seymour's army, and they were all granted their furloughs immediately, before the expedition was to get under way. As such, most of the white regiments were drastically understrength. What was worse than the decreased numbers in the ranks was the quality of those who remained. A large number of them were conscripts, bounty men, or substitutes, most of whom were relatively new to the service themselves, and all of whom were suspect, so far as their dependability was concerned.

In the Forty-eighth New York, approximately 300 of the veteran troops were on furlough. A similar number re-enlisted from the Seventh Connecticut Infantry. One of the remaining veterans, who did not sign up for another tour of duty, stated, "The veteran volunteers start North today for a thirty days furlough. Those left behind are mostly substitutes and recruits of the bounty jumping character." With the re-enlisted veterans gone, there were only 375 men remaining in the Seventh Connecticut. Battery C, Third Rhode Island Artillery, had 99 men re-enlist. So many men were missing, on furlough, that soldiers had to be assigned from infantry units to enable the battery to have the manpower to operate the guns. Conditions were much the same in all of the white regiments.[26]

The black regiments taking part in the expedition would also suffer from a shortage of men in the ranks. There were no veterans in the black regiments to be furloughed, and the units had seen only limited combat, with the exception of the Fifty-fourth Massachusetts, in which to sustain casualties, but the ranks had been thinned by disease. A large number of men from these regiments had been forced to remain in South Carolina, having contracted, or been exposed to, smallpox. In addition to the troops, one line officer and one medical officer from each regiment was left behind to look after the infected soldiers. Seymour's army would be thus under a handicap before it ever boarded ships to sail for Florida.[27]

On February 4, 1864, Seymour received his orders from Gillmore to embark his expeditionary force without delay. The original contingent of Union troops was to consist of the Seventh Connecticut Infantry, Seventh New Hampshire Infantry, Eighth United States Colored Troops, Second South Carolina Colored Troops, Third United States Colored Troops, Fifty-fourth Massachusetts Infantry, Fortieth Massachusetts Mounted Infantry, Independent Battalion Massachusetts Cavalry, Langdon's Light Artillery Battery, Elder's Horse Battery, and one section of James' Rhode Island Light Artillery. The men were directed to carry three days' cooked rations, as well as three days' uncooked rations. They were also to carry not less than 60 rounds of ammunition per man, as well as knapsacks, haversacks, and blankets. Seymour was authorized to take along two wagons for each regiment of infantry and one wagon for each mounted company, which was to carry six days' forage for the horses. It was decided that only a small amount of medical supplies would be sent with the expeditionary force. A hospital steamer, the *Cosmopolitan,* would follow the little army, fully stocked to deal with any expected casualties.[28]

Seymour boarded the troops and teamsters and put to sea before daybreak on February 5. The weather was cold, wet, and windy, prompting Major John Appleton, of the Fifty-fourth Massachusetts, to declare that it was "not a nice day for an excursion." There were 28 transports in the flotilla (some accounts place the number of ships as high as 35, but 28 seems to be the most widely accepted number) that would carry the Union army to the shores of Florida, and the gunboats *Ottawa* and *Norwich* were dispatched to escort the transports. Though some of the men experienced seasickness, it was generally reported that the troops had a pleasant voyage down the coast. At 8:50 A.M., on February 7, the *Maple Leaf* arrived at the mouth of the St. John's River. It was closely followed by 11 of the other transports, and the men aboard each ship cheered as they arrived and passed the other vessels of the flotilla. At noon, the gunboat *Ottawa* steamed up the St. John's, followed by the *Maple Leaf,* the *General Hunter,* and the rest of the fleet, on the 25-mile journey to Jacksonville. Along the way, the fleet passed by scenes that spoke of previous raids and occupations of the area. The shoreline was dotted with burned sawmills, deserted houses, and boat landings that had been abandoned and were falling down. There were also many deserted resort hotels, where, before the war, many Northerners had come for health reasons.[29]

A Union soldier left an impression of the city.

> This is a very productive country; rich in all the tropical fruits.... Jacksonville was very important as the point from whence all the products of this country were shipped for the north or Europe. It was a very important lumber mart. Eleven steam saw mills were in operation, till they were burned, since the war broke out. The

The Battle of Olustee, 1864

Period woodcut of Jacksonville, Florida, the way it looked at the time the Union army occupied the city prior to its march into the interior (courtesy United States Army Military History Institute).

> town looks more like a thriving New England town than any place I ever saw south ... I may remark that Jacksonville owes its prosperity to northern men and capital.[30]

When the vessels finally came in sight of Jacksonville, the men beheld a city that appeared to be in a state of ruins. The vignette offered by the soldier above seems to have been that of an optimist, one who saw the town for the grandeur it had previously contained, and not for the destruction that was now apparent. Before the war, Jacksonville had one of the most contemporary cities in Florida. Now, its gas works were destroyed, and burned sawmills and warehouses surrounded the city. The business district was a shambles, but the private residences and shops seemed to have escaped the devastation of war. As the ships came nearer the city, it was seen that a number of women and children had gathered along the waterfront, waving handkerchiefs and greeting the arriving soldiers. Several men were also spotted, but they seemed to be hanging back from the welcoming committee, as if they feared being fired upon by the fleet. A soldier in the 115th New York Infantry described the scene:

> The buildings along the banks were filled with gray-backs of all ages, but none of them appeared in the least warlike. Some of the ladies actually waved handkerchiefs and threw kisses; but the men skulked behind trees and old sheds, and attentively

viewed the proud Yankee fleet and the gay display of national bunting.... A guerrilla observing the expedition approaching swore that he would shoot the first man who set foot on the dock

and he patiently awaited his opportunity as the ships made their way to the port.[31]

General Gillmore was accompanying the expedition, and he reported to General Halleck, in Washington, that "upon our approach the enemy abandoned and sunk [sic] the steamer St. Mary's and burned 270 bales of cotton a few miles above Jacksonville." The scuttled *St. Mary's* proved to be a point of contention between the army and the navy. Gillmore claimed that the prize belonged to the army because the arrival of the Federal army had induced the Confederates to abandon the ship. Acting Master Frank B. Meriam, of the steamer *Norwich*, insisted that it was his picket boat that caused the Confederate ship to be left behind, as it could have escaped Gillmore's land forces had the picket boat not been there. As naval and military forces still practiced the prize system in regard to captured enemy vessels, the contention between the two sides was not a point of honor, but rather an argument to see who would reap the financial gains of the capture. No record was left as to which side prevailed.[32]

The *Norwich* sailed on past the city, while the *Maple Leaf* and the *General Hunter* prepared to dock at the wharf. The time was approximately 4:00 P.M. It was soon discovered that there was a handful of Confederate cavalry in the town, and Major John Appleton, of the Fifty-fourth Massachusetts, disembarked his men immediately to try to capture them. Shots rang out as the Confederate troopers opened fire on the vessels, and a mate on the *General Hunter* was wounded, as well as a black soldier in the Fifty-fifth Massachusetts Infantry. General Seymour ordered Major Appleton to "take his men and catch the Rebels." Appleton reported,

> I tried, but our men with knapsacks were not fleet enough. I had a dark overcoat on and was conspicuous. One "Johnny" took deliberate aim at me over a fence. I saw him just as he fired.

The Battle of Olustee, 1864

> The ball came quite close, but did not hit me. By orders I placed men in each street, and pushed the command to the outskirts of the town, with no casualties on our side. We took a few prisoners, civilians, etc. Porter of Company A shot a Rebel through his leg, and got him and his horse.

As Appleton was pushing the enemy, 20 troopers of the Independent Battalion of Massachusetts Cavalry disembarked, and the Northern horsemen now took up the pursuit. They chased the Confederates for three miles, over a rotten plank road, capturing a signal station and 11 prisoners before being recalled to the city.[33]

For the soldiers in the Fifty-fourth Massachusetts, the expedition to Florida must have been received with mixed emotions. The regiment had held a special celebration on January 1, to commemorate the first anniversary of the Emancipation Proclamation, and the day had been spent listening to eloquent speeches and orations. But the men of the Fifty-fourth had little of real consequence to celebrate. Congress was still refusing to grant equal pay for black troops. Many of the men in the Fifty-fourth were receiving heart-wrenching letters from home detailing the misery being caused by the inequality of the pay,

> in which the wives of the enlisted men describe their sufferings, and the sufferings of their families.... Children have died because they could not be supplied with proper food, and because the Doctor could not be paid, or medicines obtained from the Druggist ... wives have proven untrue to their husbands and abandoned their offspring. Mothers advise their sons to throw down the musket and come home, it being impossible for them to live longer without their support.

The refusal of the government to grant equal pay to black soldiers was becoming a source of increasing alarm to the officers in those regiments. Sentiments in the Fifty-fourth, in the ranks, led several officers to fear an open mutiny, and Colonel Hallowell reported that two men of the regiment had been slightly wounded when they displayed a disposition towards leading such a mutiny. There had been reason to question whether these soldiers would fight, once they arrived in Florida, but their obedience to orders in pursuing the Confederate troopers through the streets of Jacksonville quieted the fears of most of the officers.[34]

For the Forty-eighth New York Infantry and Seventh Connecticut Infantry, the trip to Florida signaled a return to familiar surroundings. Both regiments had been shattered in the assault on Battery Wagner in July of 1863. In fact, the assaulting force had been so used up that the brigade to which these regiments belonged could muster only about 700 men after it was over. General Gillmore ordered both regiments sent to Florida, and they departed during the end of July for St. Augustine, and a quiet stint of garrison duty. The town boasted a population of but 400 souls, and there was little social life, but the soldiers established their own theater group to break the monotony, as they reveled in the abundance of fresh food the area had to offer. The regiments remained in St. Augustine until October of 1863, when they were recalled to Hilton Head. At Hilton Head, the Seventh Connecticut received 109 replacements who had recently been recruited in the North. A veteran of the regiment said, "They were mainly Germans with limited knowledge of the English language." For most of the men in the Forty-eighth New York and Seventh Connecticut, this expedition was to be a homecoming, of sorts.[35]

While Seymour was landing his army in Jacksonville, a diversion was being mounted from Fernandina. Colonel Henry Guss, commander of the Ninety-seventh Pennsylvania Infantry, which was then garrisoning the city, was ordered to support the expedition. His regiment was assigned the task of impeding the ability of the Confederates to bring reinforcements to the area by tearing up the railroad tracks beyond Baldwin. The line was to be left intact, from Jacksonville to Baldwin, to be used to supply Seymour's men. As the Union forces had no locomotive at hand for that purpose, it was hoped that the landing force could capture one, or that one would be stranded within the area of Union occupation by the Ninety-seventh Pennsylvania's destruction of track.[36]

The action of the Ninety-seventh Pennsylvania was not the only

Union effort to distract and confuse the Confederate forces in the region. Owing to the War Department's refusal to dispatch additional forces to Charleston, General Gillmore was concerned over the possible repercussions his pulling so many men out of the line might have. If the Confederates became too soon aware of the moves the Federals were making, they would be able to shift reinforcements to Florida and off set any advantage Seymour's army might hope to gain. It was also possible that General Beauregard might see an opportunity to go on the offensive at Charleston when it was learned that so many regiments had been transferred away from the army there. Gillmore was quite right in his apprehension. As early as January 14, General Beauregard had reported to Adjutant General Samuel Cooper, in Richmond, that he suspected an eminent movement by the enemy, though he was not yet sure of their intended target. On February 8, the day after Seymour's flotilla landed at Jacksonville, Union forces in Charleston took measures to further distract the Confederate defenders there and keep them off balance. Brigadier General Alexander Schimmelfenig, with three brigades of infantry and six pieces of artillery, made his way to Kiawah and Seabrook Islands, on the South Carolina coast, to make a demonstration against Charleston. The following day, Schimmelfenig's force crossed the Haulover Cut to John's Island and engaged the Confederate defenders there, sustaining slight loss and capturing several prisoners. General Beauregard assumed that this was merely a distraction, but Schimmelfenig was reported as having 4,500 men, and a force that size had to be taken seriously. Beauregard ordered Brigadier General Alfred Colquitt's Brigade to be ready to support General H.A. Wise, who was facing Schimmelfenig. He also ordered that troops be concentrated from Sullivan and James Island, just in case they would be needed to fend off a Federal assault. From the Union standpoint, this demonstration was an immense success. It froze the Confederate forces in Charleston in place, for the time being, assuring that Seymour's expeditionary force would enjoy overwhelming numerical superiority in the opening phases of the campaign.[37]

    By this time, however, Beauregard had been informed of the arrival of Seymour's flotilla in Florida.

One • The War Comes to Florida

> On the 7th of February (received 8th), Brigadier General Finnegan reported by telegraph that five gunboats and two transports of the enemy had made their appearance in the St. Johns, within five miles of Jacksonville, and on the next day announced the arrival at Jacksonville of eighteen vessels — gunboats and transports — the landing of the enemy, presumed in large force, and the immediate advance on the night of the 7th February.

Beauregard immediately ordered Major General Jeremy Gilmer, commanding the District of Georgia, to forward to Finnegan the Sixty-fourth Georgia Infantry, the First Florida Battalion, and a section of artillery that had been being held in reserve for just such an emergency. Brigadier General William Gardner, commanding the District of Middle Florida, was instructed to send every man he could spare to Finnegan's support, and Colquitt's Brigade was transferred from Charleston to Savannah, just in case the situation demanded that it also be sent to Florida. Beauregard informed Finnegan of his actions and advised that he "do what he could with his means to hold the enemy at bay, and to prevent the capture of slaves."[38]

Beauregard found himself facing this new threat to Florida during a time when his available manpower was in a much reduced state. Some 5,000 troops of the South Carolina Militia had just recently been discharged in his department, making it difficult for the general to sufficiently garrison his primary strongholds of Charleston and Savannah. Though he had applied to the Confederate War Department for the transfer of other troops to take their place, no reinforcements had been forthcoming. Beauregard was sure that the objective of the enemy was the occupation of Florida, but it was with trepidation that he ordered Colquitt's Brigade south. It was possible that the Union force in Florida was the real diversion, not Schimmelfenig's force. The Federals could be feinting in Florida, in the hope that Beauregard would send off enough of his Charleston garrison to meet that threat that they could then make the real assault upon his reduced army there. Beauregard took steps to accept the challenge in Florida, but he continued to keep a cautious eye on the Union army at Charleston, just in case.[39]

Back in Jacksonville, General Seymour was organizing his force for a raid into the interior. He appointed Colonel Hallowell to be the military commandant of the city, with his Fifty-fourth Massachusetts to serve as the garrison force. For the residents of Jacksonville, being under the authority of a military commander was nothing new. This was the fourth time in the war, thus far, that the city had been occupied by the Federals.[40]

At this time, the expeditionary force enjoyed a tremendous advantage in numbers over the Confederate defenders of the area. Seymour had sailed with an army of some 7,000 men. To oppose this, General Finegan was frantically gathering together all available troops under his command. By February 10, he was only able to collect a force of 491 infantry, 110 cavalry, and two pieces of artillery. Outnumbered by more than ten to one, Finegan could do little more than harass the invading Federals, when they decided to move on his small command.[41]

Brigadier General Joseph Finegan had been born in Ireland in 1814. He had immigrated to Florida when he was in his early twenties, establishing himself first as a planter, then as the operator of a lumber mill. Finegan had served as a delegate to the secession convention, in 1861, and was subsequently placed in charge of the military affairs of the state by Governor Milton. In April of 1862 he was commissioned a brigadier general in the Confederate army and assigned to command of the District of Middle and Eastern Florida. Finegan had no military experience or training prior to his appointment in the Florida State forces, and he had little occasion to gain any during his time in department command. A few scattered Federal raiding parties constituted his encounters with the enemy thus far in the war. The Olustee campaign would serve as his first large-scale engagement of the war.[42]

General Beauregard was duly concerned over Finegan's lack of experience, and reluctant to trust the outcome of the campaign to the direction of such a relative novice. Beauregard's first thought was to go to Florida himself, but that would necessitate appointing an officer to command of the Charleston defenses. His choice for that assignment was Major General Daniel Harvey Hill, but when that officer was approached with the suggestion, he declined to assume the command. Beauregard then "directed Brigadier-General Taliaferro to proceed to

Florida and assume the command, "he being an officer in whose ability, field experience, and judgment I had high confidence." Unknown, at that time, to the department commander, Brigadier General William Gardner had returned from sick-leave, and was already on his way to join Finegan's force. Gardner was the senior officer in the region, and would naturally assume command once he arrived at the place where Finegan was concentrating his available forces. Gardner was a graduate of West Point, and had served in the Mexican War. He had led the Eighth Georgia Infantry at First Manassas, where his leg was so badly shattered by a cannon ball that he was maimed for life. Beauregard would have been relieved over the question of command in Florida, if he had known that Gardner was, at that time, en route to assume overall command of the Confederate forces there.[43]

While Beauregard was concerning himself with transferring reinforcements to Florida, and finding a suitable commander to lead them, he issued orders to Finegan that reveal concern both for the size of the force then in the state, as well as for its leadership. Finegan was informed of the actions his commanding officer had thus far taken, and was instructed to "maneuver" in an effort to "check or delay the enemy, but to avoid close quarters and the unnecessary loss of men." Beauregard did not want Finegan bringing about any pitched battles until his army there was reinforced and under new leadership.[44]

Finegan's instructions were quite clear. He was, for the moment, only to harass and delay the enemy, as best he could. There was to be no real fighting in Florida until the Confederate forces there were better suited to accept battle. But Finegan was not in control of the situation in Florida. General Seymour currently held all of the advantages, and seemed disposed to press the situation. By all appearances, he intended to move swiftly and force a resolution before any of Beauregard's plans could be brought to fruition. Finegan continued to gather to him all of the men he could find, watched the movements of Seymour's forces, and wondered if he could hold out until help arrived.

TWO

MARCH TO THE INTERIOR

After landing at Jacksonville, General Seymour seemed to be directing his expedition with firm resolve and lightning speed. Seymour had divided his army into four brigades for the campaign, three of infantry and one of cavalry. One interesting aspect of the campaign is that none of his brigades were led by a general, each of them, instead, being commanded by a colonel. Seymour formed a strike force, which he called his "Light Brigade," by placing together the Fortieth Massachusetts Mounted Infantry, the Independent Massachusetts Cavalry Battalion, and Elder's Horse Artillery, under the command of Colonel Guy V. Henry. This mobile force would have the ability to make swift raids into the interior, supported by the main body of infantry, in case of trouble. Colonel William Barton would command one of the infantry brigades, containing the Forty-seventh, Forty-eighth, and 115th New York regiments. Barton's former brigade, made up of the Seventh Connecticut and Seventh New Hampshire, would be commanded by Colonel John Hawley. The Eighth United States Colored Troops were added to this brigade, in an effort to bring it closer to actual brigade strength. Colonel James Montgomery commanded the last brigade, which included the Fifty-fourth Massachusetts and the First North Carolina Colored Infantry. The First North Carolina had just recently been redesignated as the Thirty-fifth United Stated Colored Troops, but for the duration of the campaign in Florida, they continued to use their original name.

Seymour wasted little time in Jacksonville. As soon as all of his troops were landed, he organized the army into three columns of march.

Two • *March to the Interior*

The Fifty-fourth Massachusetts was the most experienced of Seymour's black regiments attached to the expeditionary army. They had already gained national fame in their heroic assault on Battery Wagner, in Charleston Harbor, the previous summer. This period engraving shows the men of the Fifty-fourth gaining the parapets of Wagner (courtesy United States Army Military History Institute).

The Federals moved out, at sunset, each column marching on different roads that converged some three miles above Jacksonville. The Confederates had established Camp Finegan near the site of this road junction, and Seymour felt that he would make his first contact with the enemy at a small creek one mile before reaching that place. But no Confederates were to be found there. Once all three columns had arrived at the crossroads, it was determined that the infantry would bivouac there for the night. Henry's mounted column would push forward a few more miles, to see if they could make contact with the enemy. A correspondent of the *New York Times* accompanied Henry's force and left the following account of the events of that night:

The Battle of Olustee, 1864

> A night's ride, with the darkness so dense we could not see our horse's heads, through a hostile country which affords advantages for guerrillas, over a road the bridges of which the enemy had destroyed, and so forced our troops to ford the streams, would not be esteemed a pleasant adventure by our timid friends at the North. Every one, however, was in good spirits, and did not care how rapidly he rode, provided he could soon come up with the enemy.[1]

The troopers rode by an abandoned four-man picket post, and pushed forward until they came in view of the campfires lighting the site of the picket reserve position. The advance of the column did not wait for the main body to catch up, rushing right in among the Confederates, and capturing six of the Confederates who had been there. A brief respite was taken while the horses of the pickets were gathered up, then the column pushed forward again. They rode for 10 more minutes before coming in sight of Camp Finegan. Union scouts reported that there were approximately 200 Confederate cavalry in line of battle, awaiting the advance of Henry's men. The Confederates were a portion of the Second Florida Cavalry, under the command of Lieutenant Colonel Abner McCormick. Henry opted not to attack the waiting Confederates, choosing instead to bypass the position and try to strike an artillery camp that was thought to be at Twelve Mile Station, some four

General Joseph Finegan. Though he was not Beauregard's choice for command of the Confederate army in Florida, he performed the duties of command credibly and won the largest land battle to take place in Florida during the war (courtesy United States Army Military History Institute).

miles beyond. The way to the camp was through pine woods and heavy swamps, but the mounted column had the advantage of being led by local guides, loyal to the Union. One of these local loyalists was "Mr. Alsop, a man of Northern origin but for twenty years a resident of Florida." He was described as an "old and experienced lumberman" and actively volunteered his services from Jacksonville for twenty miles into the interior. With the aide of these guides, Henry was able to push forward rapidly.[2]

Colonel McCormick had previously been instructed by Finegan to "guard against being surprised," which that officer almost did in allowing Henry's mounted column to overtake his position. This, in large part, was not due to any fault of McCormick's, but to the stealth with which Henry's men had captured the pickets, before they could sound an alarm. McCormick had approximately 350 men with him at Camp Finegan and was badly outnumbered by Henry's column alone. It could not have hoped to withstand an attack from the supporting columns of Seymour's infantry. Henry's decision to bypass Camp Finegan allowed McCormick the time he needed to withdraw his men from the camp and march them westward, toward General Finegan, where the rest of the available forces in the region were concentrating. In his report, Finegan stated, "Their superior numbers deterred Lieutenant-Colonel McCormick, commanding, from attacking them, and in the darkness of the night he withdrew his command with caution and address and joined me at Camp Beauregard, near Ocean Pond, on the Olustee." It took McCormick several days to effect this junction with the rest of the Confederate forces, and he was not safely within Confederate lines until February 13.[3]

In the meantime, Henry's men, having bypassed McCormick's position, were rapidly bearing down on the artillery camp that the local guides had reported to be near Twelve Mile Station. This was their first action as mounted infantry, and thus far, they were performing splendidly. The regiment had received the first of their mounts only six weeks before, with many of the men having gotten their horses only a month before the campaign started. "Only those who have been through the process can understand and appreciate the pains and trials involved in breaking in a regiment, where both men and horses are ignorant of the first principles of the art," wrote one observer. "There is much vexation of spirit, and no little bodily anguish. I do not claim that the 40th are perfect, or even that they are average as good horsemen; but I do claim that in less than six weeks after the first man of them was mounted they participated, most efficiently, in a raid that involved great fatigue and accomplished important results."[4]

As at Camp Finegan, the troopers of the mounted spearhead gobbled up the pickets as they approached the artillery camp. Colonel Henry formed his men for the attack and ordered the bugler to sound the charge twice; then, turning to his men, he said: "If ever you yell in your lives, boys, yell now!" Henry would later write, "They charged with a yell that still lingers in the ears of those who heard it." "The rebel camp was nearly surrounded," stated the historian of the 115th New York Infantry, "when unfortunately, they became alarmed from some cause [undoubtedly the sounding of the bugle call to charge], and a large number of the rebel soldiers managed to escape to the swamps." The Union army immediately took possession of the camp, taking a large number of prisoners who had been sleeping when the Federal troopers rode in among them. They also captured "nine pieces of artillery, a wagon load of small arms, swords and sabers enough to arm a cavalry company, one flag and a considerable quantity of stores and ammunition." Other captured items in the camp attracted the attention of the soldiers in the ranks more than the military supplies.

> The rebel camp was filled with fat turkeys, chickens, ducks, and geese; and as soon as arms were stacked the order to charge the hen-coops was given, and the soldiers soon swept away all poultry from before them until feathers flew in all directions. Such a cackling and gobbling was never before heard in eastern Florida, and the rebels secreted in neighboring swamps must have enjoyed the midnight serenade.... We found hogs hanging up just dressed; kettles of beef steaming over the fire; plates of warm hominy and liver on the table; and papers and books strewn about in every direction. Rebel officers hardly stopped to dress, and left coats and swords behind for the dreaded Yankees.[5]

Two • *March to the Interior*

The Confederate camp contained a six-gun battery of Milton's Light Artillery. Sergeant William H. Trimmer, a member of the battery, described the attack on the camp from the Southern perspective.

> February 8, 1864, was a busy day moving our battery and stores from Camp Finegan to Picketts, on the railroad out from Jacksonville, as a raid on the camp was expected. I was quartermaster sergeant of Milton's Artillery, Company B; H.F. Abell captain. We had six guns, two brass howitzers and four Parrott rifles, battery wagon, forge, and about eighty horses. Many of our horses had distemper. At night we camped by the railroad ready to get aboard the train upon its arrival.
>
> I was detailed with six men to go back about two miles and bring to camp a disabled caisson that had been left with the men and four horses. We dragged the caisson out of the mud and near midnight arrived at camp. It was a cold, frosty night. We were eating and warming when we heard the tramp of cavalry, and in a few minutes a furious onslaught on the sleeping camp was made. As it was, I had to get away. Crossing the railroad into the pine timber away from the camp light, I witnessed the capture and total destruction of our camp. In less than an hour they captured battery, wagon, forge, the caisson we had brought in out of the mud, and two three-inch Parrott guns, set fire to the camp, and were gone.
>
> I could plainly hear the Yankee troopers, "Surrender, you damn Rebels!" and see them use their sabers. Rob Mum, from Apalachicola, had joined me, wounded by a sword on his forehead, which I bound up with a piece of shirt.
>
> When the raiders had gone, we walked to Baldwin, about ten miles along the railroad, arriving there before daylight. We went into the waiting room of the Askem House, and to my surprise, sitting by the fire was Captain Abell, who got away from the camp on his horse, which had been hitched by the tent, and without sword or saddle had ridden into a cypress swamp. His animal bogging down, he abandoned his horse. He was muddy from head to foot, without cap or sword, and very wet.
>
> Just at daybreak, some one called out; "Men, save yourselves! The Yankees are coming!"[6]

The Battle of Olustee, 1864

General Finegan reported the loss to his command, at Camp Finegan, to be not "more than 5 or 6 of our men." There were also two officers missing, who had been on sick leave and were supposed to have been captured by the Federals.[7]

By daybreak, Henry's force had reached Baldwin, some 20 miles west of Jacksonville. Though one would not know it to look at the place, it was strategically important to the outcome of the campaign. The town was on a railroad junction that connected Jacksonville to Georgia, and Fernandina to central and western Florida. The Confederacy had been using the town as a supply depot, and the Federals sought to take and hold it for the same purpose. As Henry's men approached the town, the alarm that Sergeant Trimmer had heard was echoed throughout the hamlet. Trimmer stated,

> It took but a minute to empty that room. I ran through the village of Baldwin as they charged us on their horses, firing their carbines and calling "Surrender!" In the palmetto, I threw myself down and they rode by me. By 10 A.M. all was quiet again in the village, but I lay in the palmetto within twenty yards of the railroad until late in the evening. In the meantime the Yankees found a pen of cattle in the woods, which they turned loose, driving them on their horses and shooting them down for sport. They came very close to me, and would have ridden over me but for the palmetto. At dark I heard bugles sounding, and very soon found myself surrounded by cavalry.

Trimmer was captured at this time, adding another prisoner to the huge cache that had already fallen into the Federals' hands.[8]

The railroad warehouse was found to be filled with stores and provisions for the Confederate army. Henry's force captured cannon, camp equipment, accoutrements, forage, cotton, thread, cotton sheeting, rice, molasses, blankets, hides, salt, flour, sugar, turpentine, along with 40 horses and mules. Any items that were not of use to the Federals, or could not be transported, were destroyed. General Seymour estimated the value of the stores captured to be $500,000. Neither side reported the loss of any men during the Federal occupation of the town,

Two • *March to the Interior*

and it is possible that Trimmer is the only Confederate who did not make good his escape. Other than the well-stocked warehouse, Baldwin looked to be a desolate little town. There were less than two dozen little wooden buildings, and they spoke of hard times and the poor people who inhabited them. "Yes sir," said one resident to an observing Yankee, "Baldwin is a dreadful poor city with right smart poor people in it." The trooper saw nothing in his scan of the town to make him doubt the statement.[9]

William Trimmer later recalled his capture, and being taken before General Seymour:

> I was at once taken before General Seymour, he with his staff occupying the hotel we had left so hurriedly. Good evening Colonel, who have you there asked the General. Why only one of those damned Florida swamp foxes, replied the Colonel, my men have just burnt out. The General then asked what I was doing hid away in the grass. I told him how his troopers had captured our camp and how I got away. He said are you hungry. I told him I was but wanted water, he told one of the guard to give me some. Sergeant he said, seeing the places where chevrons had been, what battery do you belong to? I told him. He replied yes it was some of your damned gunners that killed my men at the brick church. Continuing he said about how many men has General Finegan and told me that his troopers had captured four of your battery. Where are the other two? After more questions, Sergeant you seem to be an intelligent fellow. If you will take the oath I will turn you loose. I replied I am no fellow General, our negroes are fellows. Well, said he, you are an intelligent man. Here take the oath. I have taken an oath to support and defend the Confederacy, surely you do not wish me to violate that. Well, he said, I shall send you North. This closed the interview. Take this incorrigible rebel Corporal and put him with the other prisoners.[10]

While Henry's force was pushing forward, the infantry had stopped to bivouac for the night. The army ended its march at Camp Finegan. An officer with the infantry described the march:

The Battle of Olustee, 1864

> The ground traversed was largely cedar slough; that is a cedar forest overflowed with stagnant water from 3 to 10 inches deep. The intertwining roots made a hard but very rough bottom. It was soon so dark in the timber that I had to light matches to see my compass which was the only guide I had. My pistol holster being unfastened to render it easy to draw, a stumble of my horse threw the pistol out but I dismounted and groped around in the water til I found it.[11]

Colonel McCormick's men were still in the camp, and the Federal infantry surrounded them and threatened to bag the whole lot. The pickets were captured before they could sound an alarm. "We made a hard march," one of the Union soldiers later remembered, "mostly on a double-quick through swamps and woods, fording creeks and scaling piles of logs and brush, until the point of attack was just ahead." Somehow, the Confederate camp became aware of the presence of the Yankees, however, and most of the Rebels were able to escape into the swamps. Once in possession of the camp, a heavy picket line was established by Seymour's men before arms were stacked and the soldiers laid down to rest, at about 2:00 A.M. But the Federals were not to be permitted a peaceful night. Shortly after the troops had bedded down, the pickets were attacked by Confederate guerrillas. The men were called to arms, but by the time they had taken their muskets from the stacks and formed ranks, the pickets had driven off the attackers.[12]

On the morning of February 9, while Henry's men were seizing Baldwin, the rest of the army was occupied in scouring the swamps and woods around Camp Finegan, searching for Confederate stragglers. Several prisoners were taken, and a soldier in the 115th New York said that "they appeared to be perfectly panic-stricken, and a large number of them surrendered without firing a gun or making the least resistance."[13]

Though several of the Confederate prisoners were taken without firing their muskets, a soldier in the 115th New York was facing execution for discharging his musket, contrary to orders. The man was arrested, as soon as his musket fired, and was sentenced to be shot within three hours of the infraction.

Two • March to the Interior

The Provost Marshal General came up to the man, and in a solemn tone asked him if he was ready to die. The poor fellow was completely overcome, as he realized that he was under sentence of death, and the big tears started from his eyes. The Provost marshal continued; "Sir, get your affairs ready, for you die within three hours!" The last words sounded the death-knell in his ear, and the tears froze on his cheeks. He asked if there was no hope — no chance to escape the fearful doom?

Ah, yes; there is always hope while there is life. He was a good soldier, and his officers interceded for him, and in a short time presented him the joyful tidings that he was pardoned — snatched from the grave. Tears of thankfulness rolled down his cheeks, and he resolved to be a better man.[14]

Another soldier took a chicken from a poor widow, when he knew that he was disobeying orders. For that, he too was sentenced to be shot, but was pardoned for reason that he had always been a good soldier.[15]

On the morning of February 9, General Seymour sent word to General Gillmore, who was still in Jacksonville, conveying news of the capture of both Camp Finegan and Baldwin. Seymour expressed his concern over the ability to supply his army by wagon train and stated his belief that unless a railroad engine could be brought to that place from Fernandina, he would not be able to advance beyond Baldwin. The activity of the Ninety-seventh Pennsylvania, in tearing up the track, had not had the desired effect of trapping a Confederate engine within the sphere of Union operations. Seymour also told Gillmore, "If you want to see what Florida is good for come out to Baldwin." The commanding officer accepted the invitation, and joined Seymour at that place later in the day.[16]

Before leaving Jacksonville, Gillmore had set in motion another diversion intended to keep the Confederate forces in the area off balance and prevent reinforcements from being sent to Finegan's force, in front of Seymour. Major Galusha Pennypacker, with 290 men of the Ninety-seventh Pennsylvania Infantry, was ordered out from Fernandina to attack Confederate Camp Cooper, located some 25 miles from Fernandina. Gillmore planned a two-pronged assault, with another 25

The Battle of Olustee, 1864

men of the regiment, under the command of Captain DeWitt C. Lewis, a detachment of sailors, and two howitzers loaded on the brig *Perry* and the steamer *Island City* to sail up the Nassau River and cooperate in the attack. Pennypacker reached the camp in the early morning hours of February 10, and he deployed his men to attack it from three sides. The assault was scheduled for dawn, but when the Union lines went forward they found the camp to be deserted, except for a few guards. Gillmore's diversion was too late to accomplish its objective. Major Robert Harrison, and the three companies of the 2nd Florida Cavalry that he commanded, had vacated the camp two days earlier, and were already on their way to join forces with General Finegan.[17]

The mission almost ended in disaster for the Federals. Pennypacker sent two of his companies to make contact with the ships and inform them that the camp was empty, and the mission was cancelled. Many of the Union soldiers had attired themselves in captured Confederate clothing, as a lark, and when the ships spotted the gray-clad soldiers coming toward them, the crews prepared to defend against what they perceived to be an enemy attack. The mistake was discovered before the guns of the ships opened fire, however, and tragedy was averted. Both forces then returned to Fernandina.[18]

Major Harrison's cavalry were not the only reinforcements hastening toward Finegan. Aide from Beauregard was on its way, the only question being if it would arrive in time. Sergeant W.H. Andrews, of the First Georgia Regulars, remembered that on

> February 8, orders came for the Regulars and the 28th Battalion to move in the direction of Lake City, as the enemy had captured Jacksonville and was advancing on Tallahassee. The troops were soon on the march, leaving camps sometime during the night. As we marched by Rev. Brother Talley's, think every man must have been calling hogs. On passing his house, saw his yard fence lined with hog skins, so he must have been right about losing his hogs. But the boys swear they will kill any man's hog that tries to bite them.
> We marched 13 miles towards Quincy and bivouacked for the night. The boys amused themselves singing "Maj. Bonaud," to

the tune of "Billy Barlow." Don't expect the major likes it much, but says nothing. February 9 arrived at Quincy at about 1:00 P.M. and at 5:00 P.M. took the cars for Gen. Finegan's Command at Lake City. Between Madison and Lake City a serious accident happened. We were riding on flat cars which became uncoupled and ran into one another, badly injuring five men.[19]

A member of the Sixth Georgia described passing through Madison, Florida, on their way to join Finegan, and the reception they received from the ladies of the town.

> Learning that we were en route for the defense of the "Land of Flowers," and parry the threatened blow now aimed at their homes, and that we would pass through their town, they had prepared for us a sumptuous dinner of such viands as they knew would be heartily relished by hungry soldiers. After dinner, in behalf of our command, the accomplished Bennett Stewart, of Company "G" of our Regiment, tendered the thanks of the command to the ladies for this manifestation of their appreciation of our services in their behalf. He assured them that their homes should be protected at all hazards, and the enemy driven from their State.[20]

The main body of the Union army was also heading toward Finegan's position. On the morning of February 9, the infantry set out from Camp Finegan, in the direction of Baldwin, arriving at that place at 4 P.M., where a junction was made with Henry's mounted men. Captain Gustavus Dana, chief signal officer on Seymour's staff, relates an incident of the Federal officer's stay in the town.

> The officers ordered supper at the only tavern and it required considerable persuasion to get it for the landlord was afraid the rebels would hang him for it as they made a practice of doing in that section for like offences. The charge for supper was quite moderate, only $5.00 each, but on tendering greenbacks he was more scared than ever and nothing but rebel currency would do. One of the staff said "Hold on gentlemen I'll attend to that," and shortly after came in with a pocket full of rebel money with

> which he paid the bill. The next day he [the tavern owner] would take only greenbacks but had come down to 50 cents. We stayed at Baldwin Wed the 10th while Col. Henry reconnoitered up to the South Fork of the St. Mary's River. Gen. Gillmore, comdg. dept., reached us on the night we arrived at Baldwin and talked all night with Gen. Seymour, keeping us poor staff who were trying to catch 40 winks on the floor with our saddles, awake. I judged by what I heard that neither general had much faith in the success of the expedition and that it was purely a political move, intending to drive the rebels to the west side of the Suwannee River, giving us the whole east part of the state which was to be protected by gunboats patrolling the Suwannee & St. Mary's river, and thus enabling the larger part of the state to have a vote in the coming presidential election.[21]

A correspondent for the *Boston Herald* noted that a vote in the coming election was not what was foremost on the minds of the people of Florida, as Seymour's army marched within the borders of the state. Many locals were flocking to the Union army, prompted to do so by a presidential decree, not a presidential election. "The President's Proclamation of Emancipation is in great demand among the refugees," he wrote. "It is posted in and around Jacksonville, and is liberally distributed among the people in the line of march taken by the troops. Many refugees arrive daily and hourly. All are anxious to return to the Union; they express distrust and fear, like previous occupations of their country by the national forces, this one will be temporary. Against this fear they are becoming fortified by seeing the immense force now brought hither. It is certain at the rate which we have hitherto advanced a sufficient number of native Floridians will soon become emancipated from the tyrannical Richmond usurpers to reinstate their commonwealth among the fair sisterhood of the Union."[22]

But the advance of the Union army was not a liberating host for all of the Floridians along its path.

> Loud cries of a woman in dire distress broke the stillness of the Florida woods, a few days before the battle of Olustee. When met at the bars, a short distance from the road, she complained,

between her sobs and groans, of four colored soldiers who had just passed down the road. "They downed me and did what they pleased to me, and that's rather hard to take!"

After a short pursuit, the four were caught and arrested. They were found to be members of the Fifty-fifth Massachusetts. Captain Jack Hamilton, a judge-advocate, along with a military commission, including two officers from black regiments, heard testimony concerning the case all the next night, and found three of the soldiers to be guilty of rape, largely based on their own admission of guilt. General Seymour had issued strict orders to protect the civilian population, and accordingly, the three were sentenced to be hanged for the crime, with the execution of the sentence taking place as soon as gallows could be constructed. An onlooker who witnessed the scene said that "none of them got any sympathy."[23]

On the morning of February 10, Colonel Henry resumed the advance with his mounted men, departing the town at 9 A.M. The push to Baldwin had been a rapid one, making it possible for the Federals to catch the troops at Camp Finegan and the artillery camp off-guard and unprepared. This advance was conducted with a great deal more caution, however. The Union force had spent an entire day in Baldwin, giving the Rebels an opportunity to make preparations to give them a warm reception further down the line. Henry's march forward was slower, more deliberate, as the column anticipated being ambushed at any time along the way. The troopers followed the rail line west, and continued to gather in government stores that the Confederates had been forced to leave behind, in their haste to make a concentration of their forces. Four miles from Baldwin, they found 13 bales of cotton, ready for shipment. Further on, close to Barber's, they found 1,000 barrels of turpentine and 500 pounds of bacon, warehoused in a building next to the tracks. At 11:00 A.M., the spearhead reached Barber's, where Henry took the precaution of forming the column in a hollow square, in case of attack. He sent a scouting party of four men forward to the South Fork of the St. Mary's River, to reconnoiter for the Confederates he was sure were in the area. As the four men approached the river, they were caught in an ambush, having one man killed and two wounded. The lone unscathed man rode back to Henry to report that the detail had indeed made contact with the Confederates.[24]

The Southern force, dug in along the river bank, was the two companies of the Second Florida Cavalry, under the command of Major Harrison, that Pennypacker's raid had been too late to prevent leaving Camp Cooper. A correspondent of the *Boston Herald*, traveling with the army, left the following report of the engagement at the St. Mary's River:

> The bugle sounded the call to mount, and the advance of the Massachusetts battalion, under Major Stevens, started forward and entered a small defile leading through thick, impenetrable underbrush and pine trees to the bridge across the St. Mary's. The platoon of four men of the cavalry which had the advance had just passed a sharp turn in the road, and had approached close on the bridge, without anticipating an attack, when a half dozen reports were heard, and three of the four fell from their saddles, shot by a rebel force ambuscaded in a strong position beyond the stream.
>
> The column immediately came to a halt when the presence of the enemy was made known by the explosions of their guns, and the advance company pushed forward, under Captain Webster, to feel them and ascertain their position.
>
> It was received with a sharp volley of musketry, which dropped out of their saddles several brave men. The fire was instantly returned, with but little effect, and the enemy was concealed behind bushes and stumps, from which they could use their guns with deadly effect. The company, and the next behind it, was still pushed forward, and they were soon under a hot fire, which seemed to be concentrated on the advance with effect. On approaching the stream it was discovered that the bridge had been removed, and that the enemy was in strong force on the other side. The advance fell back, by order of Col. Henry, until he ordered up another company, when all charged down the road and attempted to ford the stream. As the ford could not be found just then, they fell back, and two companies of the 40th Mass-

achusetts were dismounted and ordered forward, with one company of the 1st Massachusetts battalion, as skirmishers. Leaving their horses in charge of the proper number of men, the dismounted men quickly advanced as skirmishers, and pushed down towards the river, and engaged the enemy sharply and effectively.

Meanwhile, as the force of the rebels was unknown to us, Elder's battery was placed in position on the crest on a little hill in front of Barber's house, which gently sloped down to the river bank, and the cavalry and mounted infantry were placed on either side of the line of battle to support it. Efforts were made to throw a force of cavalry across the stream on the left of the rebel position; but it was discovered that the river at that point was not fordable, and the attempt was relinquished. A company of dismounted men was, however, thrown down the stream, and placed in a fine position where the river makes a sudden turn, and where our rifles enfiladed the rebel front. A few volleys, which did considerable damage to the rebels in men and material, induced them to break and run in the most unceremonious manner, leaving two dead on the field, several wounded and about fifty or sixty horses, most of which were uninjured.

As soon as the enemy broke the cavalry dashed across the ford in front of the position just left by the rebels, and captured some four or five prisoners. The battery and mounted men were soon in column and across the river. We halted on the other side and made preparations for instant pursuit of the fleeing rebels. Those whom we found on the ground wounded and those picked up by some of the cavalry near the field pretended for the most part to have been Union men, conscripts in the service, and serving against their will.

Henry's force lost five killed and seven seriously wounded in the engagement. Several more were slightly wounded.[25]

The Federals need not have been overly concerned about the enemy it was facing at the St. Mary's crossing. The Second Florida Cavalry was in a deplorable condition and, as a unit, was hardly fit for field service. Their horses were in a jaded and broken state, a situation that was compounded by the fact that many of the saddles were in such a poor state of repair that they injured the animals. There was a shortage

The Battle of Olustee, 1864

of rifles and pistols in the command, and one company is listed as having only sabers with which to arm themselves. Cartridges were in short supply, for the troopers who did have firearms. That Harrison made a stand at all, with his command badly outnumbered, and in far less than fighting trim, was an example of bravery and determination that bordered on being foolhardy.[26]

Henry continued forward, toward Sanderson, some 14 miles further west, while the supporting infantry made its way to Barber's and the St. Mary's River crossing. General Seymour reported to Gillmore, who had gone to Jacksonville, preparatory to returning to Charleston, that

> The backbone of rebeldom is not here, and Florida will not cast its lot until more important successes elsewhere are assured. I believe that I have good ground for this faith, and as much has been done here already, and handsome trophies can be shown of success, I would advise that the force be withdrawn at once from the interior, that Jacksonville alone be held, and that Palatka be also held, which will permit as many Union people, &c., to come in as will join us voluntarily. This movement is in opposition to sound strategy, and is not directed, I understand, by General Halleck, who would doubtless have not advised it. Many more men than you have here now will be required to support its operation which has not been matured, as should have been done.[27]

It would appear that Seymour was beginning to lose control of the operation, as well as his confidence in himself. Gillmore would later testify that in their meeting, in Baldwin, he had instructed the general not to move further inland, but to fortify that town, instead. According to Gillmore's testimony, Seymour was advancing on his own initiative, and now that he had done so, it seems that he was beginning to lose his nerve. His army was pushing forward farther than it had been ordered to do, and now Seymour wanted permission to withdraw it back to Jacksonville, fearing that a numerically superior Confederate force was about to overwhelm him.

Two • March to the Interior

In the meantime, Henry's mounted column had reached Sanderson. General Finegan had ordered the removal of all Confederate stores from that place, and all had been gotten away, except for 1,500 bushels of corn. These were ordered to be destroyed before the Southerners evacuated the town, and the Union troopers took possession of the place amid the smoke and smell of the burning forage. Thus far, despite Seymour's apparent lack of confidence, the expedition had been a huge success. His army had captured Jacksonville, penetrated the interior of the state, scattered the small enemy forces that opposed them, and seized large quantities of military stores and supplies. When Henry's 1,400-man spearhead rode west from Sanderson, making contact with Finegan's main body of some 600 men, just east of Lake City, the Federal army stood on the verge of delivering the knock-out punch that could have captured the whole of central Florida and taken the state out of the war. The Union force had made contact with the Confederates some three miles from the city, drawn up in a line of battle that was estimated to be a mile in length. Henry's men approached this line in a fog that allowed them to get within 75 yards of the position before either side could clearly see the other. Heavy firing was commenced by both sides, but a company of the Fortieth Massachusetts Mounted Infantry was able to break through the left of the Confederate line. At this critical moment, Henry determined that his force was not strong enough to take the Confederate position without additional infantry support, from Seymour, and he ordered an end to the attack. The Union troopers retreated from the field, at a walk, covered by the Massachusetts Independent Battalion, as Henry withdrew his men in the direction of Sanderson. Flushed with success, and with all of the advantages in their favor, both Henry and Seymour allowed the opportunity for decisive action to slip through their fingers. Up to this point, the Federal army had penetrated some 50 miles into the interior of Florida. It had met Confederate resistance at three places and had brushed it aside while capturing a score of prisoners. Confederate property seized and destroyed amounted to some 1,000,000 dollars in value. Upon reaching Finegan's defensive works, Henry balked at attacking them, after brief development of the position, inaccurately estimating that it was held by a force larger than his own, and he returned to Sanderson to await the arrival there of Seymour's main body. A member of Seymour's main body described the scene as he

> just at twilight reached the hamlet of Sanderson. The flames of burning supplies — corn and turpentine — fired by the retiring Confederate cavalry lit up the group of houses near the railway station. At the "hotel" a dozen women gathered. "They were inclined to welcome us because they thought we would be able to prevent the spread of the destructive element." ... "They were nervous and fidgety but managed to assure us of their sympathy with the rebel cause.... Their features are sharpened and pinched as if the gaunt wolf famine had already been on the threshold of their dwellings."

Another soldier reported that the Confederates

> had taken warning at our approach and burned all their depots of supplies, half an acre of corn-cribs, and immense quantities of salt. They set the woods on fire so as to obstruct our onward march, but it was "no go." So far we had surmounted all difficulties and carried terror to the hearts of the traitors.... We camped in the streets of the town at night, and the rain fell in torrents. I awoke at three o'clock in the morning and found six inches of water under my blanket, and myself wet to the skin and numb with cold. Several of us stood around a fire and shivered until daylight. Three of the Johnnies, being rather "hard up" for grub, and not very bitter advocates of treason, came to the edge of a piece of woods and waved a couple of white rags as token of peace. Some of the boys went up to them, took away their guns, and escorted them to camp, where they took the oath of allegiance.[28]

Finegan reported that

> At 9:30 the enemy [Col. Henry's force] advanced upon us with a force estimated to be 1,400 mounted infantry and five pieces of artillery. Here they opened upon us, fighting as infantry, and skirmished heavily with my advance line. Discovering my position

and its strength and probably presuming my force larger than it was, they retreated to Sanderson, thence to Barber's on the east side of the St. Mary's river, where they constructed field works and concentrated their whole force for a final movement on Lake City.

A member of the First Georgia Regulars described the fight in more detail:

> February 11 about 9:00 A.M., the enemy's cavalry dismounted and attacked our skirmish line. Our line of battle was in the woods where a lot of rails had lately been split, and while our skirmish line was being driven back, busied ourselves piling up the rails for a breastwork to shoot from behind. We could see our boys and the yankees as they fought from tree to tree, flanking first on one side and then on the other. The zip of the minie balls sounded very familiar to the old soldiers who paid but little attention to them, but we had some new recruits who had never smelt powder before. One fellow in my company by the name of Walker, a tall gawky-looking man, was the worst-scared fellow I had seen in a long time. At one time as I walked up with a turn of rails on my shoulder, he was lying at full length on the ground with his rifle cocked and pointing over the rails and trembling like a leaf. The first thing I knew I was looking down the barrel of his gun. I told him to get up from there or I would break his cowardly back with a rail. The poor devil was so badly scared I was afraid he would shoot me for a yankee. When within 300 yards of us, the enemy retreated, carrying their wounded with them. No one hurt on our side.

Seymour was, at this time, already planning a retrograde movement to Barber's, and possibly Jacksonville. The crisis of the campaign had come to Confederate arms, and bluff and bravado had prevailed. Finegan was unaware that Seymour was planning to retreat even further, and that he was going to be allowed to have the time to amass an army that would be capable of meeting the Federals in open combat. The momentum in the Florida campaign was about to change.[29]

General Gillmore had instructed Seymour that he was not to "risk a repulse in advancing on Lake City but hold Sanderson unless there are reasons for falling back, which I don't know. Please inform me how your command is distributed between here and South Fork of the St. Mary. Please report by telegraph from Baldwin frequently." This latest order was contrary to Gillmore's previous directive to "push forward as far as you can toward the Suwannee River." It is unknown why Gillmore reversed himself at this time. Admiral Dahlgren had advised him that day that the majority of the naval vessels were being withdrawn from Florida, but the three gunboats the admiral was leaving behind should have been more than sufficient to cover the needs of the army. For whatever reason, Gillmore, in orders, was changing the immediate objectives of the campaign, and his subordinate was more than willing not only to comply, but to expand upon the new strategic thinking at hand.[30]

On February 11, Seymour responded to Gillmore's telegraph with the following:

> I am convinced that a movement upon Lake City is not, in the present condition of transportation, admissible, and indeed what has been said of the desire of Florida to come back now is a delusion.... As far as I can learn yet, Lake City will be defended by more infantry and artillery than I have with me. To be thwarted, defeated, will be a sad termination to a project, brilliant thus far, but for which you could not answer, in case of mishap, to your military superiors, and Stickney and others have misinformed you. The Union cause would have been far more benefited by Jeff Davis having removed this railroad to Virginia than by any trivial and non-strategic success you may meet, because victories must be decisive elsewhere before Florida can be won back by hearty devotion. By all means, therefore, fall back to Jacksonville.[31]

Seymour was proposing the evacuation of all of the territory that his army had already captured, in the interior of Florida, and the removal of his army to Jacksonville. His statements about a possible defeat, in front of Lake City, are redundant, in light of his superior's previous telegram, and a thinly veiled effort, on his part, to try to use his commander's own words to gain permission for the evacuation. Gillmore's intention was for the army to be concentrated in the vicinity of Baldwin. He had forwarded Colonel Montgomery's Colored Brigade to Seymour's support, and with these additional regiments, he felt sure that the expeditionary force could consolidate its position and hold against any Confederate force in the area. Both sides, at this point of the campaign, were wildly overestimating the strength of the other. Seymour was crediting the Confederates at Lake City as having more infantry and artillery than he did, though the actual number of Confederates then at that place was less than Colonel Henry had in his force alone. In the Confederate army, rumors circulated that the Federals had from 15,000 to 40,000 men, a force that, if the rumors were true, the Southerners could not hope to mount a successful defense against.[32]

Major John Hay, President Lincoln's personal liaison with the expeditionary force, was growing weary of Seymour's constantly changing assessments of the situation in Florida. In correspondence, he noted,

> Seymour has seemed very unsteady and queer since the beginning of the campaign. He has been subject to violent alternations of timidity and rashness, now declaring Florida loyalty was all bosh, now lauding it as the purest article extant, now insisting Beauregard was in front with the whole Confederacy & now asserting that he could whip all the rebels in Florida with a good brigade.

To be sure, Seymour was falling victim to uncertainty, in himself or in his mission, and probably a little of both. His actions were at times brash and over-confident, and at others he hesitated and showed a tendency to vacillate.[33]

On the morning of February 12, the Federal army left Sanderson and retraced its steps back to Barber's. There it would be reinforced by Colonel Montgomery's regiments. On the march, a Confederate cavalryman was found in the woods, and he was ordered to surrender. Instead, the Rebel jumped from his horse and threw away his weapons before making good his escape into the swamp. Another bold Rebel rode up to a Union cavalryman and impudently asked "when the Yankee infantry were coming along?" His audacious act complete, he wheeled his horse around and galloped for a nearby wooded area, closely pursued by the Yankee. The Union trooper overtook him, and knocking him from the saddle, took him prisoner.[34]

February 13 witnessed an event that would have far-reaching effects in the coming campaign. On that date, one half of the Seventh New Hampshire Infantry was ordered to exchange their new Spencer repeating rifles with the Fortieth Massachusetts Mounted Infantry. What they received, in return, were "old and much-abused Springfield rifled muskets." The regimental historian stated:

> Regarding the condition of those old muskets, we can only say that there was not a bayonet amongst them all; and in one company, I think, thirty were reported unfit for service, while in another company, D, to our personal knowledge, there were nineteen of them deficient in either lock, hammer, or rammer, and consequently were of no more use to our soldiers than an equal number of fence stakes.

The men of the Seventh New Hampshire did not hold the troopers of the mounted infantry responsible for the deplorable condition of the muskets, "for they had been roughing it ... along with the cavalry since the commencement of the campaign, and had hardly been allowed time to scrape the mud from their arms and equipments." The men did, however, hold their brigade commander, General Hawley, responsible for the exchange, and resented the fact that he had selected their regiment, instead of his old command, the Seventh Connecticut. "This transaction had the effect of dampening the ardor of the whole battalion of the Seventh," a member of the regiment stated. More than three hundred of the men in the Seventh New Hampshire were recruits, and they had only received a minimum of training with the carbines. They had never been drilled with a Springfield, but drilling was all that many of the weapons they had been given were suited for. Seymour's directive ensured that his mounted spearhead would have maximum firepower in any future actions, but it also ensured that the Seventh New Hampshire would be operating under a severe handicap, should they be called upon to assume a major role in the coming operations.[35]

Seymour's forces were concentrating at Barber's on February 13. Colonel Henry, with the Fortieth Massachusetts Mounted Infantry, was sent south, in the direction of Gainsville. On the 15th, Captain George Marshall, with a portion of the Fortieth, was attacked by Captain John "Dixie" Dickison and a detachment of the Second Florida Cavalry. Marshall was able to repulse the attack, even though he was outnumbered by the Confederate force. The Spencer repeaters had seen their first combat with the mounted force and had proven effective.[36]

Captain Dickison had already become a famous, or infamous, personality in the central counties of Florida prior to the Olustee campaign. He and his small cavalry band had been conducting an irregular guerrilla war against the Northern invaders that in some ways excelled even the exploits of the famed partisan leader Colonel John S. Mosby. While Mosby was noted for operating behind enemy lines, Dickison's fame came from the fact that he was able to maintain Confederate control of the center of Florida, despite the fact that he was often heavily outnumbered. Dickison's hard-hitting guerrilla tactics were so effective that he was commonly referred to as "Dixie" Dickison by his enemies, and the region of central Florida in which he operated was known as "Dixie's Land." His repulse, by Captain Marshall, was a rare occurrence during the war.

General Finegan was also in the process of changing his position and receiving reinforcements. By the 13th, he had managed to gather some 2,000 men and began a march toward Sanderson, selecting a site near Olustee, where he ordered the men to construct a strong line of field works. One of the Confederates laboring on the works stated, "If the enemy should ever get close enough to see our features, they will think they are fighting colored troops, as we are smoked as black as Negroes over our pine knot fires." Finegan was receiving crucial information about the Federal force from General Beauregard, and he was conducting himself accordingly. A number of dispatches from General Gillmore to General Alfred Terry had been captured, in Charleston, providing Beauregard with both the numbers and intentions of the

The Battle of Olustee, 1864

Federal expeditionary force. With this information in hand, the department commander felt justified to strip his garrisons elsewhere to meet the threat in Florida.[37]

Beauregard also intuitively realized something about the Federal campaign that even the Union leaders had not noticed. He wired General Gilmer, at Charleston, that it was probable that the enemy would advance across Florida from both the Atlantic and Gulf sides, making Tallahassee their target, and he informed General Gardner that he needed to know if "the enemy made a landing in force ... on the Gulf Coast of Florida." Beauregard saw, at once, the danger of a two-pronged attack, and the almost untenable position it would place his defensive forces in. Regrettably, for the North, top Union officers were not as quick to grasp the overall picture. The state of Florida lay within the jurisdiction of two Federal military departments: the Department of the South, Under General Gillmore, and the Department of the Gulf, under the command of Brigadier General Alexander Asboth. The two department commanders were not working together, in regard to the expedition, and Asboth's troops were conducting a "business as usual" approach to affairs within their sphere of influence. General Asboth would later write: "In my humble opinion, a combined movement toward

General Pierre G.T. Beauregard. Though his headquarters were in Charleston, Beauregard was responsible for protecting Florida from the Federal expeditionary force, as the state was part of his military district (courtesy United States Army Military History Institute).

Two • March to the Interior

The Confederates were forced to shift troops from other parts of the department to counter the Union threat in Florida. A large portion of them came from the defenses of Charleston. These Southern troops are captured in a rare camp picture in Charleston (courtesy United States Army Military History Institute).

Tallahassee from the Atlantic via Jacksonville and Lake City, and from the Gulf via Saint Mark's, would have proved more disastrous for the rebels." It is a mystery, both why the coordination between the departments did not take place, and whose responsibility it was for the failure to do so. Gillmore would have been out of place in ordering Asboth's cooperation, though he most certainly would have been given the freedom to do so from the Lincoln administration. It is probable that Gillmore felt that the project at hand could be accomplished by the soldiers of his department, alone, and did not think that the involvement of the Department of the Gulf was necessary. As both Halleck and Stanton had been excluded by Lincoln in the planning stages of the expedition, it is also probable that neither the Secretary of War nor the General-in-Chief became involved in any of the operational phases of the expedition. Indeed, Halleck, in his telegrams to both Gillmore and

The Battle of Olustee, 1864

The Union army, in Florida, was confined to footholds along the coast for the majority of the war. Fort Marion, the old Spanish fortress the Castillo de San Marcos, was a Federally held base for most of the war (courtesy United States Army Military History Institute).

Seymour, seemed to evince an attitude showing that he had little faith in the project or interest in its objectives. In any event, the coordinated operation that Beauregard feared was not taking place. Gillmore's department would be assuming full responsibility for the operations in Florida.

On February 12, Seymour had sent a telegram to Gillmore that he had ordered Colonel Henry's force to fall back to Sanderson, and he suggested that Colonel Charles Fribley's Eighth United States Colored Troops be sent to permanently garrison the town of Palatka. On that same day, Gillmore instructed Seymour to concentrate all of his forces at Baldwin "without delay" because of reports that the Confederates had a large mounted force moving down the St. Mary's that posed a danger to the right flank of the expeditionary force. Gillmore also ordered the Third United States Colored Troops, already at Baldwin, to send out scouts as far as the ford of the St. Mary's River to ascertain the validity of the reports. Seymour's telegrams to Gillmore had caused the latter officer to assume that the Confederates in the area outnumbered Seymour's force, and he was acting accordingly. In response to Seymour's request to have the Eighth U.S.C.T. garrison Palatka, Gillmore replied that that regiment should stay with Seymour's main body. Instead, he would order Colonel Francis Osborn's Twenty-fourth Connecticut, then stationed at St. Augustine, to undertake that duty.[38]

Gillmore was receiving a very confusing appraisal of the situation in Florida. Seymour seems to have lost his nerve somewhat in the time that he was telegramming his superior and informing him of his actions. The return of Henry's mounted column seems to have restored his confidence, however, and he once more entertained thoughts of a grand offensive in the area. Informing Gillmore that several of his officers were in agreement with his plans, he requested permission to position his forces at the South Fork of the St. Mary's, as well as at Callahan, while a third portion, under Henry, was sent on a raid to Gainesville. He further requested that troops be sent to seize the bridge at Middleburg and that the naval ships at Fernandina destroy all of the ferry boats they could reach, up the St. Mary's River, and that a demonstration be made against Savannah, Georgia, to assist in keeping Confederate forces there frozen in place. If all went as Seymour requested, his forces would end up holding a line that went from Fernandina, through Baldwin and Palatka, to St. Augustine.[39]

Seymour's request for a diversion at Savannah had already been superseded by the actions of Confederate General Beauregard. The rebel commander took the initiative by ordering all of his batteries bearing on Morris Island, in Charleston, to open fire on the night of the 11th, as if preparing the way for an infantry assault. The result was the withdrawal of the Union forces from Morris Island to Kiawah, which allowed Beauregard to finally release Colonel Alfred Colquitt's brigade and the Chatham Artillery for assignment in Florida. It would now be a race to see who reached Finegan's position first: his own reinforcements or the Union army.[40]

On February 13, the day that the exchange of weapons took place

The Battle of Olustee, 1864

between the Seventh New Hampshire and the Fortieth Massachusetts Mounted Infantry, Colonel Henry received his orders to move against Gainesville with a mounted column for the purpose of destroying, or capturing, any trains that might be in the vicinity. He was instructed that "all public property that cannot be removed will be destroyed, but private property will be scrupulously respected." By maintaining a strict regard for the property of private citizens, they hoped that the citizens would greet the Union army as liberators, not as invaders, and that the goal of the reinstatement of Florida into the Federal Union could be preserved. After the strike on Gainesville was completed, the force was to return to Baldwin while leaving a small detachment to guard the bridge at Middleburg. Captain G. E. Marshall was assigned to command the strike force, which was made up of 49 hand-picked men from companies G, H, and K of the regiment. Marshall's force was hard-pressed by the Confederates from the time the raid first began and was forced to engage in skirmishing during the entire march to Gainesville. The town was an important supply depot for the Confederates, and the Southerners planned to defend it. Upon reaching the town, Marshall learned from a local black man that there was a large force of enemy cavalry in the vicinity. This was Company C, Second Florida Cavalry, under the command of Captain W.E. Chambers. Chambers was approaching the town, and his force was a little more than a half-hour away when Marshall received the warning. The Union troopers were immediately put to work constructing a hasty defensive position out of 167 bales of cotton that were found in the town. They were assisted in their work by a number of black men from the area. As Chambers's cavalry approached the town, it was joined by Lieutenant Colonel Louis G. Pyles, who commanded a home guard unit made up of old men and young boys. The two officers determined to attack the town on different roads, but Pyles's militia never showed up at their appointed position. Chambers launched the attack alone and was repulsed by the superior firepower of the Union troopers with their new Spencer repeaters. The Confederates retreated and did not again attempt to enter the town until the Union force vacated it the following morning. One of the troopers in the Second Florida said, "We had in Chambers's command about one hundred and twenty of as good soldiers as there are in the army and the Yankees had about fifty all told. The outcome was anything but credible to the officer in command of the Confederate forces." The raid, and the subsequent repulse of the Second Florida troopers, had a good effect on the morale of the expeditionary force, but it did little to further the overall objectives of the campaign. Raids and excursions of this sort were harassing to the Confederates, but they did not bring Finegan's army to battle for a decisive engagement. The failure to do so was allowing the Southerners to assemble a force capable of defending the region against Seymour's invaders.[41]

Reinforcements from Beauregard had begun arriving at Finegan's position as early as February 10. A member of the First Georgia Regulars remembered that they "arrived at Lake City and was reviewed by Gen. Finegan." He stated that "the citizens of Lake City was glad to see the Regulars and had a long table spread with a bountiful dinner for the boys.... In the evening, the 1st and 28th [Georgia] marched out three miles east of the city and formed a line of battle."[42]

Over the next few days, Colquitt's Brigade, as well as other reinforcements, continued to stream into camp, swelling Finegan's numbers until his army was comparable in size to that of the Federals. On February 13, Finegan ordered a move that would place his army on ground he felt to be suited for a defensive position. That day

> the troops marched out of the works and formed by the side of the railroad where we waited for the arrival of a train to carry us to Olustee Station some 15 miles towards Jacksonville.... The cars soon arrived and the troops boarded for Olustee or Ocean Pond. On our arrival, formed line of battle, our left opposite Ocean Pond, the right extending across the railroad. Worked all night throwing up breastworks. During the night we were reinforced by the 32nd Ga. Regiment, 6th Florida, and Chatham's Artillery.

A line of field works had been completed by the following day, and the Confederates settled back to await the attack that was certain to come.[43]

The Battle of Olustee, 1864

William Frederick Penniman, of the Fourth Georgia Cavalry, left a description of the Confederate build-up taking place at Olustee:

> By Riding All day and half the night, the second night galloping we were pushed through to the little railroad station of Olustee, some twenty five or thirty miles east of Lake City, and went into camp to await results.
>
> We had started with three days cooked rations of cornbread and a bit of bacon, and being without wagons, not a cooking utensil in the whole command. The rations were consumed and the lean country offered a poor opportunity for foraging, but from some source corn in the shuck was obtained for our horses and a small amount of unbolted corn meal was divided among the troops. We had neither salt or meat, but necessity discovered to us a means of cooking what we did have, for in shucking the corn we could carefully set aside the best of the shucks, then mixing the meal with water, would place the batter inside the shucks, tie them up and thrust them in the hot ashes to bake. When they were withdrawn the "bread" so baked was the facsimile of an ear of corn, having assumed all the impressions of the former occupant of the shuck, and to the eye was an alluring appetizer to half starved men, but the absence of any salt made it a most uninviting temptation to ones taste.
>
> The following day train load after train load of infantry began to arrive, which proved to be largely Colquitt's Georgia Brigade, who were veteran soldiers just from Virginia, where their experience had been bought upon many bloody battle fields, whilst this was to prove our very first experience.
>
> I could not help but notice that the entire brigade seemed to be composed of mere youths, the majority doubtless being under twenty one years of age, certainly under twenty five. They seemed to be such a "devil may care" set as a whole, that to me they were a curiosity, realizing as I did the renown they had already earned as a fighting brigade.
>
> This brigade with the First Georgia Regulars, some Florida Cavalry and our own men, as nearly as I recall, made up the defendant army, together with a battery or two, all told some six thousand men Vs thirty thousand.[44]

Two • March to the Interior

(Penniman wrote his reminiscences in 1901, some forty years after the battle. Even then, he was convinced that Seymour's army was several times its actual strength.)

The concentration of the Confederate forces achieved at Ocean Pond was nothing short of amazing when one considers the different places they had been drawn from and the distance they had to traverse. Colquitt's men had left Savannah on the morning of February 16 aboard the Florida, Atlantic, and Gulf Coast Railroad, arriving at Station Number 9 that night. From there, they marched cross-country toward Madison, taking no baggage with them except for some cooking utensils the men could carry in their knapsacks. On the evening of February 17, Colquitt's force had camped for the night at a river some 12 miles from Madison, where he received an urgent message from Finegan requesting him to move with all possible dispatch, as Seymour's army was advancing rapidly upon his position. Colquitt immediately got his men under way, and sunrise on the 18th found them at Madison, where they boarded trains bound for Ocean Pond. In 24 hours they had marched 30 miles without leaving one straggler from the command behind. The brigade reached Olustee Station on the evening of February 18, only to learn that a battle was not quite as eminent as Finegan had believed, and that the advance of the Union army he had reported to Colquitt was nothing more than Seymour's cavalry advance.[45]

The arrival of Colquitt's Brigade was a cause for optimism throughout Florida. The "Tallahassee Floridian" celebrated Colquitt's arrival by telling "the people of Florida to be of good cheer. Don't give up in despair. Don't lend a credulous ear to false or exaggerated rumors. Rally to the defense of your country. Every man should have his arms and equipment in readiness for immediate use." The newspaper felt that with the Georgia Brigade now on the scene, the situation in Florida was secure.[46]

The position selected by Finegan would allow the Confederates to use the local terrain as an ally in the upcoming engagement. The Rebel left flank rested on Ocean Pond, an imposing body of water four miles long and two and a half miles wide, that emptied into the Okefenokee Swamp. By using this natural obstacle as an anchor for his left flank, Finegan was trying to ensure that the Federals would be unable to turn that portion of the line. The right of his line was anchored on another, smaller, pond. A third pond was in front of his line, on the left hand side, and there was a swampy bay in front to the right, which was only passable two hundred yards to the right, or south of the railroad. In front, the ground was covered by open pine forests, free from any underbrush that could conceal the movements of an enemy. The position was one of strength, provided Seymour acted as Finegan expected him to and made a frontal assault against his works. If all went according to plan, the Union forces would find themselves in the open, unable to maneuver right or left, and they would be forced to batter themselves to pieces in attacking Finegan's stronghold.[47]

Finegan had his men construct breastworks of logs covered with earth, having parapets that were six feet high and approximately four and one-half feet wide. Finegan supervised the construction himself, there being no engineering officer present with his command. That changed on February 17, when Lieutenant M.B. Grant arrived from Savannah to take charge of the construction. Grant collected what tools he could find from the neighboring plantations, about a dozen axes and two dozen spades and set a detail of men to work strengthening the works Finegan had already begun. Grant seems to have been impressed with the advantages of the position, as attested in his report:

> The left of the line as laid out rested upon Ocean Pond, a sheet of water some 4 miles long by 2 to 2½ miles wide, this furnishing a secure protection on that flank. In front of this line and to the left of the railroad an open pond, averaging 250 yards in width, extended to within 300 yards of Ocean Pond. This ground was entirely impracticable, adding greatly to the strength of this portion of the line. To the right of the railroad, and at an average distance of 400 yards in advance of our line, there extended a thick bay, impassable except within 200 yards on the right of the railroad. This bay continued ... with but one crossing at the road between bay and pond. Intervening between this bay and our line was an open field over which the enemy would have to advance in approaching the works. The right of the line, though not so well covered as the left, was still very much

strengthened by the large pond which continued some 2 miles on the right, for which distance it was only practicable for infantry at a few points, and would have proven very strong against a direct attack, but was liable to the same difficulty which presents itself in the occupation of any position in this country, viz, the practicability of turning it by a detour of a few miles.

Clearly, Finegan had selected a position of great natural strength, one that could be turned into an entrenched camp and supply depot for all further operations in the region. If Seymour could be induced into attacking him here, Finegan felt that a great victory could be gained over the invading Yankees. As his breastworks took shape, so did the army with which he would defend them. Reinforcements had been trickling in ever since the Union expeditionary force had landed in Florida. Now they were coming in large numbers. All seemed to be in readiness for Finegan to spring a trap and undo all that the Yankees had thus far gained in Florida.[48]

The following listing is a breakdown of the reported unit strengths of Finegan's regiments on the eve of the battle:

Colquitt's Brigade

Sixth Georgia: ten companies, 618 men
Nineteenth Georgia: ten companies, 591 men
Twenty-third Georgia: ten companies, 590 men
Twenty-seventh Georgia: ten companies, 605 men
Twenty-eighth Georgia: ten companies, 538 men
Sixth Florida Battalion: unreported

Harrison's Brigade

Thirty-second Georgia: ten companies, 1,036 men
Sixty-fourth Georgia: ten companies, 746 men
First Georgia Regulars: ten companies, 800 men
First Florida Battalion: unreported
Guerard's Battery: one company, 104 men

The Battle of Olustee, 1864

Reserves

Fourth Georgia Cavalry: ten companies, 933 men
Second Florida Cavalry: unreported
Leon Florida Light Artillery: unreported
Chatham Artillery: one company, 111 men
Milton Florida Light Artillery: unreported

In addition to these, the Fifth Florida Cavalry arrived at Ocean Pond on the 20th, badly used up from a forced march from Gainsville. They would see limited action at the end of the fight. The Fifth Georgia Cavalry and Captain Dickison's company of the Second Florida Cavalry would both arrive on the battlefield after the fighting had already concluded, but were available to participate in the pursuit of the Federal army.[49]

Finegan and Seymour had each adopted a strategy for their troops, but, as so often happens in war, chance and circumstance would serve as the real commanders of both armies. The coming battle would not adhere to the plans of either general, and each would be forced to adapt to the changing situation as best they could. As the opposing forces neared the contact that was sure to touch off a general engagement, Finegan's men continued to strengthen and fortify a position that would never be defended against a foe.

Seymour's advance, toward Lake City, came as a surprise to General Gillmore. Seymour was once again changing his opinion of the situation in Florida, and was taking the initiative without first consulting his commanding officer. In his official report of the incident, Gillmore wrote:

> On the 18th, I was greatly surprised at receiving a letter from General Seymour, dated the 17th, stating that he intended to advance without supplies in order to destroy the railroad near the Suwannee River, 100 miles from Jacksonville. I at once dispatched General Turner (my chief of staff) to Jacksonville to stop the movement. He was the bearer of a letter to General Seymour. Upon arriving at Jacksonville, after considerable delay, due to the inclemency of the weather, he learned that General

Two • March to the Interior

Seymour was engaged with the enemy in front, near Olustee. When I left Jacksonville on the 15th instant I was entirely satisfied with the success of our operations up to that time. I briefly communicated my plans with regard to Florida in my letter of February 13, from which I extract as follows, viz: General Seymour's advance has been within 4 miles of Lake City, but as his instructions were not to risk a repulse or make an attack when there was a prospect of incurring much loss, he has taken up a position at Baldwin, the junction of the railroad from Jacksonville with the one from Fernandina. He holds also the crossing of the Saint Mary's, South Fork, about 12 miles west of Baldwin. I intend to construct small works capable of resisting a coup de main at Jacksonville, Baldwin, Palatka, and perhaps one or two other important points so strong that 200 or 300 men will be sufficient at each point. Twenty-five hundred men, in addition to the two regiments that have been permanently stationed in this State (one at Saint Augustine and one at Fernandina) ought to be ample for Florida. The artillery captured here will suffice for such defensive works as may be deemed necessary. I desire to see the lumber and turpentine trade on the Saint John's River revived by loyal men, and for that purpose, and to give assurance that our occupation of this river is intended to be permanent, I have written to the Secretary of the Treasury recommending that the port of Jacksonville be declared open.[50]

From Gillmore's report, it seems clear that the commanding general had considered the offensive portion of the expedition concluded before Seymour decided to advance his force farther into the interior. Gillmore's plans were to consolidate their gains, fortify against a possible attack, and reinstate commercial activity in the region. The Union army had seized a large piece of Florida, and Gillmore believed that this was sufficient for the political and economic purposes for which the expedition had been mounted. He realized that further operations in the interior could result in a military setback that could undo all that had been accomplished and jeopardize the entire mission, and he advised Seymour to go no farther west. Instead, he was to strengthen his positions in the already occupied areas, securing them as the nucleus for the loyal government of Florida that would be formed there. When

The Battle of Olustee, 1864

Seymour decided to march for Lake City, it was on his own initiative and contrary to the wishes and orders of his commanding officer, and Gillmore would be unable to prevent the move before the critical battle of the campaign would be fought at Olustee.

In Seymour's behalf, it was reported that he had received information regarding the whereabouts and intentions of the Confederates on the night of February 18–19 that caused him to believe that by pushing his force forward he could defeat the Confederates and seize important military advantages. The exact nature of this intelligence was not revealed; however, it seems as if it was either unreliable or that Seymour acted upon it hastily.[51]

Seymour may have been persuaded in his thinking by what he had been hearing from the Florida residents his army came in contact with ever since it had arrived in the state. With an invading army at their doorstep, it seems as if most Floridians became immediate Union supporters, denouncing the Confederacy and affirming their longtime support of the Federal government. One observer commented on the residents, and from his words, it is easy to understand how Seymour might have felt that he had the support of the people and that the information he had received was legitimate.

> The refugees are unanimous in asserting that the secessionists cabal had never a very strong grasp in Florida. In proof of this, they cite the ill repute of the paper money issued by the confederacy. This, they assert, never passed at par. Those who had gold or silver at the commencement of the Rebellion have held on to it, only selling occasionally a little at an enormous rate of premium to blockade. The latest sale was the 5th of February, the day before we landed, when $100 in gold brought $2400 in Confederate money.
>
> The Floridian refugees declare that there always has been a majority for the Union among the population of the State. When the election was held for delegates to a State Convention, called to consider the propriety of seceding from the Union, the "rich," i.e. the slaveholders, used the most shameless and inconcealed intimidation, declaring boldly no Union candidate should ever be nominated! Thus a majority of the legal voters were deprived

of their just rights; delegates were elected against whom there was a majority of voters, if not votes. All they desire is permanence of rule under the Union authorities. They all deprecate the idea of the Union army being withdrawn.

Of the prisoners captured, about one-half take the oath of allegiance. To all the President's proclamation of amnesty is read and explained.

Seymour may well have been convinced that the loyalty of the residents was with the Union, and his army, when he sallied forth to meet Finegan's Confederates in battle, but the actions of these residents did not correspond with their verbal proclamations. There had been precious few who joined the ranks, or who supported the North in any other way. Most who could had sent away, or hidden, livestock and property to safeguard it from the invading Yankees, and several of those who were pledging their allegiance were at the same time sending valuable information concerning the size and intentions of Seymour's army to Finegan.[52]

Major John Hay, Lincoln's personal representative with the expedition, was becoming frustrated with the persecution of the campaign and losing faith in the idea of it gaining any fruitful objectives. In particular, he was losing faith in Seymour's handling of the army and responses to the situation in Florida. On the eve of the decisive action in the campaign, Hay seemed less than confident in the man to whom command of the army had been entrusted.[53]

THREE

FINEGAN SPRINGS A TRAP

Saturday, February 20, dawned bright and cool, as soldiers in the Union encampments arose and hurriedly prepared their breakfasts, hoping to get one good meal before another long, footsore day of plodding along the sandy ground of Florida's interior. At 6:30 A.M., Seymour's army began its march from Baldwin. Abraham Palmer, a soldier in the Forty-eighth New York Infantry, described the advance of Seymour's troops toward Olustee:

> The march to and from Olustee was a terrible one, the roads often running through swamps where the water was knee-deep; yet there were recompenses, for the day was clear and beautiful ... and often the sandy roads ran through pine forests, and the resinous odors of the trees gave a balmy fragrance to the air, and such was the brave spirit of the men that the anticipation of meeting the enemy on an open battle-field, where they hoped at last to conquer them, cheered and quickened their weary steps.

In the Fifty-fourth Massachusetts, it was stated that the damp, spongy ground put spring in the men's step, causing many of the men to break out in song. "We're Bound for Tallahassee in the Morning" and "Old Folks at Home" were two of the popular selections that hastened the Massachusetts troops along. In fact, one soldier in the Fifty-fourth remembered,

> The day was a most delightful one. The springs and rivulets along the line of march reminded us of the cool, refreshing waters at home.... You can see nothing but pine woods, marsh, and every five or ten miles a cluster of dilapidated, deserted huts, with no

signs of agricultural thriftiness. But immense tracts of the pine-woods land are prepared for the collection of pitch.[1]

Another soldier in Seymour's army disagreed with the Palmer's assessment of the march and the fighting spirit of the troops. He stated that the route had been "over a road of loose sand, or boggy turf, or covered knee-deep with mud or water" and expressed the conviction that instead of being in brave spirits to meet the enemy, the army was "weary, exhausted, faint, hungry, and ill-conditioned" to offer battle to the foe. Though the army had stopped for brief rest periods every hour, the men were not rested and had had little opportunity to eat more "than a mouthful of food."[2]

Lieutenant James Clark, the historian of the 115th New York Infantry, also declared that the march to Olustee, through Barber's, was hard on the men.

> The men were all tired out, our feet were bleeding, and every soldier declared that they could not go a single inch further.... It was a terrible tramp to say the least, and will never be forgotten by those who took part in it. We were obliged to ford creeks and rivers in the cold and thick darkness, and the only way the men could see was by the aid of large fires kindled by a guard sent in advance.... Our march had been so rapid, that the cavalry and artillery horses were worn out, and many had dropped down dead along the road.

Though he described the march as a horror, Clark did agree that "our march had been so triumphant through Florida that we began to think the rebels would offer no serious resistance."[3]

One Confederate regiment was sustaining heavy losses, even before the Union army reached the Ocean Pond area. Approximately 80 members of the First Georgia Regulars had gone home on a 30-day furlough because of their re-enlistment for another term of service. General Beauregard had given the officers of the regiment permission to grant this leave to any soldiers who signed papers for another tour of duty. On the eve of the battle, a dozen more members of the First

The Battle of Olustee, 1864

Georgia Regulars decided to take advantage of the offer and go home before the fighting. In passing through Tallahassee, they had seen the recently passed Confederate Conscription Law posted on a bulletin board, which stated that soldiers were conscripted by the government to remain in the companies and regiments in which they then served, effectively voiding the expiration of their current enlistments. These last members of the First Georgia to re-enlist presented their papers to General Finegan, who approved their furloughs, even though he knew about the Conscription Law that had already gone into effect, based on the offer that Beauregard had made them. At midnight on the night before the battle, these men had left for Lake City to seek rail transportation home. The result of these re-enlistments was that the First Georgia Regulars would be lacking about 100 men in the ranks the following morning when Seymour's army came to call.[4]

General Finegan's plan of battle was to have Colonel Colquitt, with two of his regiments, engage the enemy in advance of his works. Colquitt was to put up a good fight before retiring back toward the main Confederate position. Finegan felt sure that Seymour would pursue Colquitt's retreating force and be drawn right into his trap, forced to assail strong works, and would batter his army to pieces in trying to

General Alfred Colquitt. The arrival of Colquitt's Brigade put Finegan's army on a level of numerical parity with the Federals and allowed the Confederates to offer battle to Seymour's army (courtesy United States Army Military History Institute).

take them. On paper, the plan was a good one. Finegan's defensive position was definitely strong, and he was aided immensely by the natural barriers that served as his allies in the fight: the bodies of water on which his flanks were anchored. Everything depended on Seymour acting as he expected him to.

Initially, it seemed as if Seymour's army would do exactly what Finegan expected it to. Colonel Guy Henry's mounted brigade was in advance of the Union forces, and it was driving hard, outdistancing its infantry supports, in a race to cover enemy ground. It seemed as if Henry had no idea that there was any appreciable Confederate force in the area, as his march was based upon speed, with no regard to security. Indeed, most of the artillery and many of the muskets in the Union advance force were not even loaded. The Confederates had yet to mount any sort of a determined defense against Seymour's army. The Union troopers had become used to seeing the enemy's advance guard retreat before them ever since they had left Jacksonville. "Our policy had been to dash after them, and capture and scatter as many as possible. We had met with no repulse and few casualties. Our successes had unfortunately inspired us with a contempt for our foes."[5]

Colonel Henry's mounted column led the advance of the Union army. It was followed by Hawley's Brigade, Barton's Brigade, the supply train and medical vehicles, and finally by Montgomery's Brigade. It is indeed strange that they proceeded in column of march, with no flankers being thrown out to protect their movements. The *Boston Herald* correspondent noted that it was certainly a military oversight to "move a column of troops without the proper flankers through any portion of the enemy's country, even if positive information had been obtained that the enemy himself was a long distance off." In this instance, no such positive information concerning the absence of the enemy was in hand. "The road from Barber's to Lake City lies parallel with the railroad, crossing it at intervals on the average of five miles." Colonel Henry's column first made contact with the Confederates at one of these crossings, two miles east of Olustee.

> The head of the column reached this point at 2 P.M. The men had not rested from the time that they left Barber's, at 7 A.M.... Thus, after a tedious march of sixteen miles over a road of loose sand or boggy turf, or covered knee deep with muddy water, the troops, weary, exhausted, faint, hungry and ill-conditioned, were suddenly attacked by a large force of the enemy, who had concealed himself behind a thick wood, waiting with complacent satisfaction the entry of our men into his ambush.

Five mounted Confederates were noticed behind an old deserted mill, a little to the left of a stand of woods. They were obviously scouting the Union advance, and when Henry's men opened fire on them, they retreated back toward their main body. Henry's troopers then took up positions around the mill and waited for Hawley's brigade of infantry to catch up to them. The battle of Olustee was about to begin.[6]

The force that Henry encountered was Carroway Smith's Confederate cavalry screen, strengthened by two regiments of Colonel Colquitt's infantry, the Sixty-fourth Georgia and a portion of the Thirty-second Georgia, sent forward by Finegan to engage the Federals and draw them into the trap. The appearance of Henry's mounted column caused Finegan to alter his original plan somewhat, and he issued orders to Colquitt to add the Sixth and Twenty-eighth Georgia regiments, the Sixth Florida Battalion, and a two-gun section of Gamble's Florida Battery to his advanced force and drive away the Federal cavalry from the railroad. As Colquitt was taking charge of the additional troops, another order arrived directing that the remainder of the Thirty-second Georgia, the First Georgia Regulars, the Twenty-third Georgia, and the Chatham Artillery, under the command of Colonel Harrison, also be moved to the front. Finegan was committing the bulk of his command to a movement outside of his carefully prepared defensive works. Intelligence he had received led him to believe that Henry's troopers were supported by only three regiments of infantry. Finegan felt that this small force would not be apt to attack his fortified position, and if the Union force was really that small, his regiments could easily eliminate it in the open woods in front of his entrenchments.

Three • Finegan Springs a Trap

One Confederate soldier claims credit for drawing the first shot of the battle, at about this time.

> "I here make claim," wrote Corporal William Penniman, of the Fourth Georgia Cavalry, "that Col. Smith of the Second Florida Cavalry and myself jointly drew the first shot of the battle of Olustee. In some way, forgotten now, I found myself accompanying him quite a distance in front of our cavalry vidette lines, in a reconnaissance. We fastened our horses in a pine sapling thicket close by the railway, which here had an embankment of some five or six feet, and mounted the railroad bed. He was looking through his glasses in one direction and I happened to be looking in a different one, and thought I saw troops moving some ten to twelve hundred yards off in a bay gall. Calling his attention to the spot, he looked through his glasses and exclaimed, 'Its the Yankees sure enough and they seem to be niggers.' We waited looking at them advancing rapidly for probably ten minutes, when happening to look in another direction again I distinctly saw quite a body in heavy skirmish order advancing within three to four hundred yards of us. I called to Col. S. to get down from the railroad quick or we would draw their fire. The words were scarce out of my mouth before we received quite a volley, one shot piercing the side of Col. S's horse, from which the blood was freely flowing, but we mounted and got back to cavalry front before his horse succumbed. It was but a few minutes before the enemy were up to and pressing our front."[7]

As the fight was building up, one Confederate unit, the Second Florida Cavalry, received a fiery speech from its commander, Lieutenant Colonel A.H. McCormick, intended to inflame the men and make them fight like demons.

> Just as we were going into the fight Col. McCormick ordered halt! right about face! He rode down to about the middle of the Regiment and faced us; he pulled off his hat, raised himself as high as he could in his stirrups and spoke very loud and distinctly, saying: "Comrades and soldiers of the 2nd Florida

Cavalry, we are going into this fight to win. Although we are fighting five or six to one, we will die, but never surrender. General Seamore's [sic] Army is made up largely of negroes from Georgia and South Carolina, who have come to steal, pillage, run over the state and murder. Kill and rape our wives, daughters and sweethearts. Let's teach them a lesson. I shall not take any negro prisoners in this fight."

The presence of a large number of black troops in Seymour's army incited anger in other parts of the Confederate army, as well, and before the day was over, McCormick and many of his comrades in arms would make good their threat to teach the Negroes a lesson.[8]

When Colonel Colquitt reached the front he found the Sixty-fourth Georgia formed into a square to the rear of a point where a wagon road crossed the railroad. The Sixty-fourth was a new regiment that had never been in combat before. Its commander, Colonel J.W. Evans, had formed the regiment into a square in preparation to resist a mounted attack by Henry's troopers. Carroway Smith's cavalry was retiring down the wagon road, pursued by Henry's Federal troopers. Colquitt ordered Colonel Evans to reform the regiment in line of battle, to the left of the road. He then placed Gamble's Battery to the right of the Sixty-fourth, and extended the line by positioning the Nineteenth Georgia to the right of the guns. The Sixth and Twenty-eighth Georgia regiments extended the line to the left of the Sixty-fourth. Smith was ordered to cover the flanks with his cavalry, and he accordingly placed the Second Florida Cavalry on the right and the Fourth Georgia Cavalry on the left. Lieutenant Drury Rambo, Company A, Milton Light Artillery, had a 30-pounder Parrott gun aboard a railroad flatcar, and was ordered to proceed down the track to take up a supporting position for Colquitt's infantry. A little before 2 P.M., he reported to Colquitt that his big gun was in place and ready for action.[9]

Once Hawley's Brigade had caught up to Henry's mounted force, General Seymour directed that the Seventh Connecticut send forward a skirmish line to develop the enemy's position. Two companies were sent to the left of the railroad, and one to the right, with the remainder of the regiment following at supporting distance. The skirmish line was under the overall command of Captain Skinner. The footsore troops of the Seventh Connecticut "needed no gift of prophecy to foretell 'business ahead.'" The Union line of skirmishers was one and one-half miles long, with the men having five paces between one another. As it surged forward, the Confederate skirmishers fell back toward their main position, the line being formed by Colquitt. In a letter to his wife, one soldier in the skirmish line described the action:

> As we advanced, the enemy retired, keeping just in sight. Whenever we could get near enough to stand any chance of doing execution we would blaze away at them and they returned fire in a way that showed that they were good marksmen, for their shots came plenty near enough, although none of us were hit.

General Hoseph Hawley. His brigade made the first contact with the Confederates at Olustee and opened the battle (courtesy United States Army Military History Institute).

The Confederate position which

> greatly outnumbered our troops, was posted at a right angle to the railroad, the flank resting on swampy ground or lakes, and the front partially protected by logs. Our main force approached in three columns by the flank, left in front, the artillery in the road, and the infantry on each side among the pines. It was now about two P.M. and the situation as it appeared to Hawley's brigade was this: Our skirmish line was checked and rallied on

the reserve.... The Seventh promptly formed line on the center of the field about our regimental front from the railroad north side. Some of the other troops coming under fire while marching by the flank left in front, attempted to form in line of battle between our right and the railroad....[10]

William Penniman noted how the Union battle line had been drawn into the fight, precisely according to the wishes of General Finegan.

On the drill grounds of previous days it had always been a hard matter to make the boys keep proper alignment, but in the skirmish which at once began, they excelled in any drill attempt ever made previously. We were just scared enough to do what we were told to do and the best we knew how.... Our whole regiment, in fact the Second Florida also, moved like clock work, falling back in [echelon] movement, towing the Yankees directly back to where Colquitt's brigade lay in the wire grass, until when within a few hundred yards of them, we at the trot quickly moved by the flank, leaving the two armies opposite each other. In making this flank movement, not understanding the nature of the swamp called Ocean Pond, the larger part of our regiment went too far in and the horses sank to their bellies in the soft morass, causing us to lose a large number during the fight.[11]

Jerome Tourtellotte, a private in the Seventh Connecticut, noted the severe reduction of men in the ranks caused by the furloughs, but he did not believe that the additional manpower would have much improved the regiment's position. He stated that every

intelligent private well knew that the attacking party needed at least three to one when the attack was to be made against a foe fighting on his own dunghill and upon selected ground. The fighting would have had terrific attachments if the re-enlisted veterans, on furlough in the North, had been on the firing line, but the result could not have been different except in casualties.

Tourtelotte felt that of greater concern than the lack of soldiers in the ranks was the diminished number of commissioned officers that were with the regiment, noting that several companies were severely lacking in officers to lead them.[12]

As the Seventh Connecticut was making contact with the enemy, Hawley deployed the remainder of his brigade, placing the Seventh New Hampshire on their right and the Eighth United States Colored Troops on their left. This regiment had reported to him only a couple days before the battle, and its officers and men were largely unknown to their commander. The troops of the Eighth U.S.C.T. were accompanied by their mascot, an "old white dog" named Lion, who had been with the regiment ever since it had been mustered in at Camp William Penn, back in Pennsylvania. One member of the ranks noted that the dog raced alongside of the men and had "no objection to being among black soldiers." Langdon's and Elder's Union batteries were placed on either side of the road, in the center of the line, and Hamilton's Battery was placed on the left of the line, to be supported by the Eighth U.S.C.T. These dispositions were completed while the skirmish line of the Seventh Connecticut was still trying to develop the strength and position of the Confederates. It is doubtful if either officer knew who faced them across the field, at the time, but Hawley and Colquitt had been good friends in the old army, in the years prior to the war. Now they were preparing to face one another across a field of battle. Once Hawley had his regiments in line, Elder's Battery fired a shot in the direction of the Confederate line, hoping to draw a reply, but none was immediately forthcoming. He ran his guns up close to the center of the Confederate line and opened with a mixture of shell, solid shot, grape and canister. Confederate artillery now roared into action in response to Elder's move, and rebel sharpshooters began to pick off officers and artillerists. One observer noted, "The Rebel fire was quite low, so that our men were wounded in the feet and legs a good deal, but they were brought down and disabled as effectually as though shot in the head, and they toppled over with most disheartening frequency." The engagement now became general on both sides. "The rattling of musketry, the roar of artillery, the shrieks of wounded horses, the groans of dying men, the defiant shouts of those engaged in the combat, the dense smoke lighted up with flashes from the belching guns — these were the characteristic of the four hours' scene which followed."[13]

Captain Elder had run his guns too close to the Confederates, and his command was in extreme danger in its advanced position. Elder had planned ahead for this emergency, and ordered that his limbers be backed up, instead of reversing them, as was the common practice, so that he could withdraw to a safer position before the Confederates had time to recover from the shock of his initial bombardment and loose a deadly fire upon his command.[14]

The Seventh Connecticut, undersized from combat and re-enlistment furloughs, was armed with seven-shot Spencer repeating rifles, and thus was able to deliver a firepower that belied its small size. In fact, the ranks of the regiment had been so depleted that its ten companies had been consolidated into four, containing 365 men. The situation in the officer corps was even more extreme, there being only ten commissioned officers in the entire regiment, including the quartermaster, adjutant, and surgeon. "At last the enemy formed for a charge and came forward in solid column by regiments directly in front of the Seventh Connecticut and raised their battle cry, while their artillery redoubled its fire upon our ranks which lay quietly awaiting the word of command."[15]

The historian of the Seventh Connecticut remembered,

> As the smoke lifted at intervals we could see their long wavering lines. Their flags floating in the breeze and their mounted officers in the rear urging them on. Shouts and yells accompanied every movement of their lines. Our brave little band stood like a stone wall in the center of the field.[16]
>
> When their column approached near enough to give us a good shot Colonel Hawley said: "Now boys, give them the seven shooters." The little band sprang to their feet and pumped the bullets out of those rifles with astonishing rapidity and constancy. Their aim was good and the fire told. First from the flank the approaching column began to break, then from the center, and before the repeating volleys ceased the entire column had broken in confusion and retreated in disorder to their lines leaving their path strewn with dead and wounded.

Three • Finegan Springs a Trap

>By this time our ammunition was exhausted and A.A. [Acting Assistant] Adjutant General Moore was sent back to find the wagon and order it forward. His curb rein broke and his horse made for the rear in an undignified manner, but he got there just the same.
>
>He found the ammunition wagon in charge of Private Bogart of Company G, who on receiving the word drove rapidly forward to the line of battle and served out the ammunition.
>
>Colonel Hawley and his staff remained with the line and mounted during the whole fight. The colonel got a bullet in his saddle, one of his aids was wounded, and the horse of one of his orderlies was shot.[17]

Captain B.F. Skinner, commanding the regiment, left the following account of the fight:

>After moving up 200 or 300 yards I found the enemy drawn up in line to receive us in position to support their battery, the enemy here showing a front of five regiments, flanked on the right and left by cavalry, which made occasional demonstrations upon our flanks, but were easily turned back in disorder.
>
>After a few moments' attention from our seven shooters, supposing that support was close at hand, I pushed forward, firing rapidly as I went, which caused the enemy to give ground to us, I should judge, 200 yards, in some confusion, but firing as they withdrew. Here I discovered that the enemy were intrenched and delivered well-directed volleys of musketry. I found also that my ammunition was very nearly expended (some of my men being entirely out), there was no support in sight, I had already pushed so far in the enemy's center that my line formed a semicircle and that I was receiving the enemy's fire from three sides. At this juncture I decided to withdraw and save my command, which was done at the proper time, for had I remained there five minutes longer my whole command would have been swallowed up in the enemy's advance. My men withdrew rapidly. Those who had ammunition fired as they withdrew and divided to the right and left in order to unmask the Seventh Regiment New Hampshire Volunteers, who approached.[18]

The Battle of Olustee, 1864

During the confusion of the fighting and withdrawal, a personal matter of vengeance took place in the ranks of the Seventh Connecticut. Two substitutes in the regiment stopped fighting the Confederates long enough to settle a personal altercation. Jerome Dupoy had been shot in the head and killed, and it was widely rumored that it had been done by John Rowley, a comrade in arms. Dupoy and Rowley had previously been involved in a serious argument that ended when Dupoy cut Rowley with a knife. Rowley swore revenge, and many of the men in the ranks were sure that the bullet that killed Dupoy was his and not a Confederate's. When Captain Skinner investigated the incident, there was not enough evidence to charge Rowley with the shooting, so he was allowed to go free. Members of the company were convinced of his guilt, however, and he was at length arrested and placed in the guardhouse. During his confinement, Rowley "could not sleep, saw ghosts and at last confessed that he shot Dupoy purposely."[19]

The Connecticut boys were holding their own against the Confederates on their part of the line. Indeed, the rebels were stunned by the rapidity of the fire from their repeating rifles, and the accuracy of their volleys had been thinning the gray ranks in alarming fashion. The Sixty-fourth Georgia and Gamble's Battery were receiving the brunt of the Union fire, with all of the field officers of the former unit being shot down early in the engagement. The Sixty-fourth, being an inexperienced regiment, the loss of its officers caused considerable confusion that bordered on panic among the men. Only the presence of the veteran Twenty-eighth Georgia, on its flank, prevented the men of the Sixty-fourth from breaking and making for the rear. Colquitt threw the Nineteenth Georgia and the Sixth Florida Battalion into the fight to the right of the Sixty-fourth Georgia. The two units deployed in line of battle under a heavy fire from the six guns of Langdon's and Elder's batteries, located at the road. Both sides were fairly joined now, as more and more troops engaged in the conflict. As the numbers were fairly even, between the two armies, and as the battle was being fought on open ground, without advantage to either side, it was still pretty much anyone's fight to win. In the initial contact, it would indeed seem as if any advantage rested with the Union and the seven-shot repeaters of the Seventh Connecticut, but the regiment had paid dearly in holding its ground against the Confederates, with 69 of its officers and men falling as casualties. They had held their ground for 45 minutes, allowing the remainder of Hawley's Brigade time to get into position. If the other Federal regiments could hold as well, Seymour's ill-advised advance could be turned into a crowning victory for the Union, and all of Florida would be open to invasion and occupation.[20]

Corporal William Penniman held a different view of the stand made by the Seventh Connecticut. To him, the Union regiment had been completely bested on the field. He had watched the action unfold from his position in the swamp, as the Confederate troopers tried to extricate their horses from the mire. They had been a perfect target for the Seventh Connecticut's advance, in this exposed and vulnerable position, and for a time, it seemed as if they would all be captured. "The very atmosphere breathed of parrot shelles and bullets," he wrote, "but orders were given to a regiment, the Sixth Georgia I think, to move to the left and make a counter charge, which was instantly done, saving our whole command from capture, and from the work they accomplished in this counter charge, as I saw its results after the fight was over, must have almost annihilated the 7th Conn."[21]

A letter from a private in the Thirty-second Georgia, who identified himself only as "H.W.B.," echoed Penniman's sentiments and related how the fight soon opened and

> all the troops were brought forward. The enemy's first line in which all the known tribes were represented, negroes included, after some resistance was broken. The fight was now conducted in Indian style, both sides availing themselves of the protection of pine trees of which kind there was plenty. Our men continued to advance, never halting, making in the meantime the woods ring with the terrible rebel yell, and as a negro or a Yankee run from tree to tree muskets enough were generally leveled at them to stop their career.... On the following morning I rode over the field and was surprised to find so many killed, as the fighting had been most altogether a running one.[22]

The Battle of Olustee, 1864

Now that the battle was joined, it would seem as if General Finegan still wished to employ his plan of luring the Federals into attacking his prepared earthworks and desired Colonel Colquitt to withdraw his command, causing the Yankees to follow him into the trap. One Confederate solder related how "Col. Hopkins told me that Gen. Finegan ordered Gen. Colquitt to fall back during the fight but Colquitt sent him word it was no time to fall back and told him to send him more men, which he did." Colquitt saw an opportunity in the engagement he was now fighting, and he also realized that it would be difficult for him to extricate his command from the field, being as closely pressed as he was.[23]

To the right of the Seventh Connecticut, the Seventh New Hampshire was going into line. The Confederates in their front occupied a position around the railroad bed, or dump, which was a few feet higher than the surrounding ground, and formed a ready breastworks in case they were driven back by the Federals. The curvature of the railroad, at this place, formed nearly a semi-circle around the New Hampshire men. Southern artillery was shelling the Granite State troops as they formed, but their "artillery fire was very inaccurate and elevated, cutting and slashing the tops of the tall pine trees in the open woods through which we were then hurrying to the front, amidst the danger to us from falling branches and tree tops."

As the Seventh New Hampshire arrived at the front

> the firing was now beginning in earnest, as it was the work of a few minutes only to get the artillery into battery front. The particular position of the writer, at this moment, was on the left of the Seventh New Hampshire, Company D being the tenth company, which was then marching by flank, left in front. When within two hundred yards of the enemy's works, the order was given by our brigade commander, General* Hawley, to form column by companies, the order from Colonel Abbott being, "By company into line," which was rapidly executed, the company commanders repeating the order; our regiment occupying a

---

*Hawley was a colonel at the time but had been promoted to general before the quoted work was written.

Three • Finegan Springs a Trap

position at this time immediately on the right of the artillery, while the brigade of colored troops was attempting to form a line on the left of our batteries. An order was given by General Hawley, to "Deploy column on the fifth company," which was the color company. Colonel Abbott, repeating the order clearly and distinctly, ordered the battalion to face to the right and left, when General Hawley, finding himself wrong, said, "On your eighth company, Colonel Abbott!" when again seeing his mistake, the General said, "On your tenth company, sir!" All the companies, except the tenth, having already faced to the right and left, were marching to get into line as though deploying on the fifth company and under the successive change of orders the companies who were trying to deploy into line became badly embarrassed, and being under a terrific fire from the artillery and infantry of the enemy, and the wrong orders having been given and obeyed upon the instant, and the maneuver having been partially executed before the correct order reached them, the battalion had become so badly mixed that it could not be reformed.[24]

The evolution of command that Hawley wished for the regiment to perform was clear in his mind and had been performed by the men of the command on many a toilsome drill field, but, in the heat of battle, what Hawley wanted was not what he said. It was a simple mistake, a small error, and on the drill field could have been easily sorted out. However, this was on the battlefield, not the drill field, and the regiment was under fire. Some accounts allege that a portion of the regiment misunderstood the command and began to execute an improper movement, but the accounts of the members of the Seventh New Hampshire, who were on the field, all tend to support the contention that the failure lay in the orders given, not in the execution. Hawley had ordered the Eighth U.S.C.T. to leave the railroad along which they were marching and change direction to the right, moving nearer to the Lake City and Jacksonville Road, where they were to go into line with their right resting on a pond and their left making contact with Hamilton's Battery. The evolution he intended for the Seventh New Hampshire to make would have continued that line by placing their left flank on the end, to the right of the Eighth U.S.C.T. The Seventh Connecticut was giving way in front of the line Hawley was trying to form, falling back to the right and left of the New Hampshire regiment, and thus unmasked the unit to the full fire of the enemy, just as the companies were jumbled and facing every which direction. The resulting confusion was intensified by the severe fire the regiment was taking. In an effort to establish some sort of a defense, the men faced to the front and attempted to fight as best they could. The tenth company, on the left, was the only one that was able to form on the line that Hawley had intended. The rest were forced to stand and fight where they were.[25]

Sergeant Otis A. Merrill placed the blame completely on General Hawley, and not upon any failure of the regiment to execute his orders. He stated that the regiment had been under the direct command of Hawley for over a hundred yards prior to forming the line of battle, and the men had simply obeyed the orders as given. Confederate artillery was still firing high, but heavy casualties were being inflicted by small arms fire, and Merrill noted that "the bullets came faster from the rear than from the front." The situation on the left of the New Hampshire line was becoming particularly critical. The left of the line contained those companies that had been forced to trade in their Spencers for the unserviceable Springfields that Henry's mounted column had been using. As previously noted, most of the weapons were in a sorry state of repair, many completely useless. Jumbled and confused by the contradictory orders, and unable to fight back with the weapons they had been given, the companies on the left started to melt away, and the whole line began to make for the rear. Seymour's decision to increase the firepower of his mounted brigade was now proving to be a costly error in the infantry contest. The only exception to this was the tenth company, on the far left, the only one that had been able to assume its intended position in the line. This company held firm, and left the field only after the other companies had been driven off, leaving it on the field without support.[26]

Most of the officers of the regiment retired with the men, trying to rally them to turn and face the foe. Colonel Abbott and Lieutenant Van Keuren, one of Hawley's staff officers, were, with the help of the cavalry, able to stop some 200 of them and get them into position on the field, where they remained until ordered to retreat. For all intents and purposes, however, the right of Hawley's line had ceased to exist. The Seventh New Hampshire would serve under a cloud of criticism after the battle, for fleeing the field in the manner in which it did, but it would seem as if the criticism was unwarranted and unfair. To begin with, the confusion caused by the conflicting orders put the regiment in an untenable position right from the start. Add to that the fact that most of the veteran members of the regiment were home on re-enlistment furlough and had been replaced with new recruits, unaccustomed to being under fire. Lastly, there is the controversy over the exchanging of weapons. It can only be speculated what the difference might have been if the left wing of the regiment had gone into the fight with their Spencer repeaters, instead of the worn out Springfields with which they were armed. One can only point to the effective service rendered by the Seventh Connecticut, who still retained their repeaters, and assume that the additional firepower would have helped to stabilize the line and allow the regiment time to realign in its proper formation. Instead, the majority of the regiment was falling back toward the rear, exposing the Federal artillery and the Eighth U.S.C.T. on its left. The Seventh New Hampshire had taken a pounding during its short time on the front line, having 209 officers and men fall as casualties.[27]

One New Hampshire veteran later argued that the regiment had done all it could, given the circumstances.

> Some two months ago our regiment was furnished with Spencer Carbines with the expectation of being mounted. The horses had not been furnished at the time we left St. Helena for this expedition, the 40th Massachusetts were mounted and supplied with Springfield rifles. A few days before this engagement by order of the officer in command [General Seymour], half of our men were obliged to exchange their favorite pieces for the old guns of that regiment, many of which were so damaged as to be perfectly useless. I counted more than twenty in our company that were entirely useless. Many of them had no ramrods and

others had no locks. By this our entire regiment was disheartened. To be drawn up in line of battle to be shot down by the enemy and no effective weapon in their hands was truly discouraging. It should be stated that they had no bayonets, that most important part of the weapon having been thrown away by the mounted men as useless and cumbersome. In addition to this it should be remembered that we have over three hundred recruits, many of whom were never before under fire, and had not been sufficiently drilled for that position. Many of our recruits cannot understand or speak a word of the English language, having come from the Canada French settlements and Germany but a short time ago to be caught up by sharpers and thrown upon our hands as substitutes. In this condition our regiment went into the fight and did all they could. It is very easy to imagine how any men must feel when ordered up in front of the enemy with no weapon in his hand. It would be very natural for him to feel that he was useless in the struggle, and self-preservation would occur to him very soon. His reasoning would be, I am of no use, and why should I stand here for the sole purpose of being shot?

It has been stated that the 7th New Hampshire did not do all that was expected of them, and if they did not, the above important reasons should be taken into account. The conduct of our field officers is spoken of in the highest terms by all officers and men who were on the field. Col. Abbott was in the hottest part of the engagement, laboring with all his energies to keep the regiment in its place and make it most effective, without a thought to his own personal danger, while the missiles of death were flying like hail around him; and so of the others.[28]

The Eighth United States Colored Troops now found themselves almost alone on the battlefield, holding what had been the Federal left. The men had never seen battle, and in fact "had been recruited but a few weeks." The regiment filed onto the field amid a terrific fire of musketry and artillery and was directed by General Seymour to advance toward the railroad. Colonel Charles Fribley obediently followed the directive, even though his men were still in marching order and not ready for a fight. None of the men had had time to drop their knapsacks,

Three • *Finegan Springs a Trap*

and their muskets were unloaded. The regiment went forward at the double-quick and attempted to form a line 200 yards from the enemy, unable to respond with their empty weapons to the fire they were taking. One veteran of the battle described that portion of the field as "a place which was sufficiently hot to make the oldest and most field-worn veterans tremble; and yet these men, who had never heard the sound of cannon before, rushed in where they commenced dropping like grass before the sickle."[29]

Lieutenant Oliver Norton, of the Eighth U.S.C.T., in a letter to his sister said,

> Military men say it takes veteran troops to maneuver under fire, but our regiment with knapsacks on and unloaded pieces, after a run of half a mile, formed a line under the most destructive fire I ever knew. [Quite a statement for a soldier who had served with the 83rd Pennsylvania on Little Round Top, at Gettysburg.] We were not more than two hundred yards from the enemy, concealed in pits and behind trees, and what did the regiment do? At first they were stunned, bewildered, and knew not what to do. They curled to the ground, and as men fell around them they seemed terribly scared, but gradually they recovered their senses and commenced firing. And here was the great trouble — they could not use their arms to advantage. We have had very little practice in firing, and, though they could stand and be killed, they could not kill a concealed enemy fast enough to satisfy my feelings.[30]

The lack of expertise in handling their muskets was proving a huge handicap for the soldiers in the regiment. They had had almost no practice in loading and firing their weapons, and most of them being ex-slaves, they had no previous experience with firearms. "Colonel Fribley had applied time and time again for permission to practice his regiment in target firing, and been always refused." It is unknown why Fribley's efforts to properly train his men always met with a rejection, but the result of this oversight was evident on the field of battle, where his men fumbled and experimented, in the face of a withering fire, to defend themselves. Veteran units might have faltered, due to the killing fire that was being poured into the ranks, and green troops would most likely have broke and run at the first volley. Why then did the black soldiers of the Eighth U.S.C.T. stand to be shot down? The answer can probably be found in the fact that these were ex-slaves, participating in one of the early battles in which blacks were committed to combat. The South had made it quite clear what their intentions were concerning the use of black troops and had issued broadsides and newspaper reports that had found wide circulation in the North. Black troops, captured in battle, were to be returned to slavery. White officers, leading those troops, when captured, were to be executed for inciting servile insurrection. For the blacks in the Eighth U.S.C.T., losing was not an option. According to official Confederate policy, there would be no exchanges, no prison camps for them. Their options were: victory, death, or slavery. For many, death was preferable to a return to bondage.

To make matters worse, Colonel Fribley was killed shortly after engaging the enemy.

> After seeing his men murdered as long as flesh and blood could endure it, Colonel Fribley ordered the regiment to fall back slowly, firing as they went. As the men fell back they gathered in groups like frightened sheep, and it was almost impossible to keep them from doing so. Into these groups the rebels poured the deadliest fire, almost every bullet hitting some one. Color bearer after color bearer was shot down and the colors seized by another. Behind us was a battery that was wretchedly managed. They had but little ammunition, but after firing that, they made no effort to get away with their pieces, but busied themselves in trying to keep us in front of them. Lieutenant Lewis seized the colors and planted them by a gun and tried to rally his men round them, but forgetting them for a moment, they were left there, and the battery was captured and our colors with it.
>
> Colonel Fribley was killed soon after his order to fall back, and Major Burritt had both legs broken. We were without a commander, and every officer was doing his best to do something, he knew not what exactly. There was no leader, Seymour might better have been in his grave than there.[31]

Three • *Finegan Springs a Trap*

When Colonel Fribley received his mortal wound, he was placed on the footboard of one of the artillery limbers. By the time Captain Hamilton saw him there he "saw him dead, and directed one of his officers to take him off, as I had to use the limber to get off one of my guns. He was placed about twenty-five feet to the right and rear of my right piece, where I think he was left." Fribley's body was indeed left on the battlefield when the line withdrew, and fell into the hands of the Confederates.[32]

The battery that Lt. Norton mentions was Captain John Hamilton's Battery E, Third U.S. Artillery. Surviving members of that battery would later claim that their guns were lost because the men of the Eighth U.S.C.T. were cowardly and refused to defend them. This accusation was unfair in the extreme. The brigade commander, in talking of the plight of the Eighth U.S.C.T. stated, "Old troops finding themselves so greatly overmatched would have run a little ... with or without orders." Green, untrained, outnumbered, and without leadership, the regiment can not be blamed for failing to protect Hamilton's guns. By the same token, Norton's evaluation of the mismanagement of Hamilton's Battery is unfair and unfounded. The battery had been exposed to the same murderous fire as had the black troops and had been decimated by it. The battery had gone into the fight with 86 men and 50 horses. A section of the Third Rhode Island Artillery, under Lieutenant H. Myrick, had been attached to Hamilton and made up part of his command. In the short space of 20 minutes, 49 men, including all four officers, and 40 of the horses had been shot. The guns could not be removed simply because the horses to remove them had all been shot down. Two of the cannon had to be left to the Confederates, because there was not the means with which to save them, and the position was so exposed to enemy fire that to stay and protect them meant almost certain death.[33]

Lieutenant George E. Eddy, of the Third Rhode Island, described the action taken by Hamilton's Battery when the Union army made contact with the Confederates:

> Our columns were at once deployed into line, and our advance was sharply engaged. Hamilton's battery was then ordered forward.

> Four pieces of the battery, including my section, were placed in position, within two hundred and fifty yards of the rebels line, under a severe fire of musketry.... In twenty minutes we lost forty-four men, forty horses, two pieces and four officers, when we managed to get off with what little there was left.

In a letter later published by the *Providence Journal*, Eddy recapped the casualties among the officers of Hamilton's Battery:

> Capt. Hamilton is wounded in the left arm severely, and in the hip; Lieutenant Myrick, wounded in the left foot, badly — probably will lose some of his toes. Lieut. Dodge, wounded in the left arm, not badly. I am wounded in the right leg about three inches above the ankle joint, not bad by any means. I have had the ball taken out, and think the wound will heal in a few weeks. All of us officers had our horses shot under us. Myrick and Dodge left theirs on the field dead. Captain and myself brought ours off ... Lieutenant Irwin, whose section was not quite so hotly engaged as the balance of us, is now in command of the battery, what there is left of it. He was struck on the little finger of his left hand, but so slightly hurt that he was capable of performing duty. Taking everything together, we have done pretty sharp work. In ninety hours we have marched 110 miles, fought a battle of three hours duration, got badly whipped.

In this letter, Eddy echoed the sentiment of many of his artillery comrades by saying: "It was our misfortune to have for support a negro regiment, who, by running, caused us to lose our pieces." The facts lend themselves to absolving the Eighth U.S.C.T. from any blame in the action, but the members of Hamilton's Battery would hold hard feelings against the black troops for the rest of their lives. They would contend to their final days that the battery could have held, if properly supported, but, under the circumstances, the men of the Eighth U.S.C.T. would have had to be more than human to hold out under the extreme pressure being exerted against them by Colquitt's regiments.[34]

According to accounts left by Confederates who were in the battle, it would seem that the Eighth U.S.C.T., for a period of time, occupied the complete attention of the Southern battle line. One Confederate soldier noted the lack of any supporting troops, saying,

> Not so much as a support to keep the poor beggars up to their work and in line. Do as they would, the niggers couldn't stand the fire, and small wonder too, for it was terrific, so they would huddle ten to twenty behind each of the few scattering pine trees. Word was passed down the line to cross the firing, that is, those at the right instead of firing at the enemy directly fronting, would fire at the negroes opposite the left of each command those at the left reversing; the result being that the negroes simply lay in piles around the bases of the pine trees.

Under such a severe and concentrated fire, it is little wonder that the Eighth U.S.C.T. was forced to withdraw from the fight. It is doubtful that any of the veteran regiments on the field could have done better, under the circumstances.[35]

The report of the battery commander, Captain Hamilton, places the blame for losing the cannon on their initial placement, and would seem to clear the Eighth U.S.C.T. from any wrongdoing.

> Upon the general engagement of the pickets along the line, Colonel Henry went forward on our left to reconnoiter the enemy's position. Coming back he informed me, in General Seymour's presence, that by planting, say two sections of artillery at a point he would designate, he thought I might enfilade their line, and that we might worst them in a short time. The sections were advanced, but received, on coming into battery, a fire from a more extended line of infantry than what had been first observed. My battery was under 250 yards from the enemy's right of infantry, while an oblique line of cavalry bore off to their right and nearly as far as I could see into the woods.

The battery had been placed in a position where it was already flanked, and too close to the Confederates, before it ever went into action. As for the Eighth U.S.C.T., Captain Hamilton acknowledged the fact that its "left wing filled all the intervals of my pieces and prevented their working to any advantage." He states that he immediately recognized the error in placing the guns there, but was afraid, with the Eighth U.S.C.T. being a new regiment, that he would cause a panic among the men if he withdrew his pieces. Hamilton felt that by staying where he was, he was keeping the Union left from folding. "By the sacrifice of five pieces of artillery I saved the whole of our left flank from breaking and its disastrous consequences." Of the Eighth U.S.C.T., he said, "They should not be condemned, for I saw nothing wrong that could not be accounted for by want of experience and ignorance of object, apparently."[36]

Captain Romanzo Bailey, now the ranking officer of the Eighth U.S.C.T., took command of what was left of the regiment and attempted to lead it off the field. Instead of moving straight back, he moved the regiment by the right flank, passing behind the Fifty-fourth Massachusetts, which was just coming on the field. Bailey described the action: "Seeing that a regiment at least of the enemy was moving down the railroad to attack our left, and knowing that our ammunition was exhausted, I took the responsibility to withdraw the regiment from the field, moving by the right flank, and in good order." It was during this retreat that the regiment lost its national colors. Once it reached a position of relative safety, the regiment remained in the rear for the remainder of the battle. The time was now approximately 4:30 P.M., and the Eighth U.S.C.T. had stood their first test of battle for almost 90 minutes.[37]

Of the 550 men that the Eighth U.S.C.T. took into the fight, 310 were listed as casualties. It was a commonly held belief at this time in the war that black troops could not, or would not, stand the rigors of the battlefield. Most whites doubted that they would stand and fight. The heroic stand of the Eighth U.S.C.T., despite all of their handicaps, went a long way toward changing that mindset. The regimental surgeon of the Eighth U.S.C.T. summed it up eloquently:

> Here they stood for two hours and a half, under one of the most terrible fires I ever witnessed, and here, on the field of Olustee, was decided whether the colored man had the courage to stand

without shelter, and risk the dangers of the battlefield, and when I tell you that they stood with a fire in front, on their flank, and in their rear, for two hours and a half, without flinching, and when I tell you the number of dead and wounded, I have no doubt as to the verdict of every man who has gratitude for the defenders of his country, white or black.[38]

Seymour would later be highly criticized for allowing the Eighth U.S.C.T. to take part in the battle. Major William E. Furness, a judge advocate in the army, would write in 1904 that it "was a mistake to take this regiment into battle unless the compulsion of necessity which did not exist when the advance left Barbours." Furness cited that "at Baldwin was the Third U.S. Colored Regiment quite as large in numbers, which had seen service on Morris Island and under fire since August, 1863, and I am quite sure there were other regiments in or near Jacksonville—in saying this no reflection upon the men of the 8th is intended, and their behavior was exceedingly good." It was felt by many that Seymour had made an error in judgment when he included this green regiment in his invading army and left other, more seasoned units to perform guard duty along the line of march.[39]

Surgeon Adolph Major, of General Seymour's staff, began looking for a likely spot to establish a field hospital as soon as the engagement was fairly joined. The only buildings in the vicinity were a couple of log houses near the right of the line, but Major discovered that they were far too exposed to allow their use. He then spied a cluster of trees, to the left and rear of the Union line, and directed that his 12 ambulances be parked in line there, and that the surgeons ready their operating kits for use. It was only a short time after he set up the hospital till patients began to arrive "first in single drops, then trickling, after a while in a steady stream, increasing from a single row to a double and treble, and finally into a mass." The Major and his surgeons were already operating at full capacity, less than an hour after the commencement of the battle, when they were forced to relocate the hospital due to Confederate artillery fire that was exploding in the tops of the trees they were concealed in. The hospital was moved one mile farther to the rear, as the mass of wounded men kept pouring in.[40]

The Battle of Olustee, 1864

General Seymour was described as

> almost recklessly brave, exposing himself at every point along his entire line of battle, but his troops could not successfully contend with such an enemy in such a place. Colonel Fribley was now dead on the field; Captain Hamilton, with a broken arm and a bullet in his thigh, was still the inspiring presence on the left. Lieutenant-colonel Reed, and his major, Archibald Bogle (of the Eighth U.S.C.T.), now stretched upon the field severely injured.

With only a third of his army on the field, Seymour was indeed hard pressed, and his decision to press forward, into the interior of Florida, was beginning to look like a rash and ill-advised move.[41]

On the Confederate side, the battle was going better than expected. Thus far, Colquitt had been the beneficiary of the Federals throwing their forces piecemeal into the fight, and he had had the advantage of superior numbers throughout the engagement. The firepower of the Seventh Connecticut had stunned the Sixty-fourth Georgia momentarily, but Colquitt had enough men on the field to overcome the rapid volleys of the Spencer repeaters. Gamble's Leon Light Artillery had been particularly hard hit in the opening phases of the battle, due to its exposed position opposite the center of the Union line. The battery suffered only seven casualties, but it also lost nine horses and had considerable damage done to its guns and equipment.

The wounding of some horses threw several teams into a panic, causing two of the limbers to be severely damaged. The trail of Gamble's 12-pounder howitzer was snapped off by the recoil of the gun but "firing was continued from the piece until the broken end of the trail was so deeply imbedded in the earth as to render the gun no longer serviceable, when it was carried off the field." Colquitt ordered the Chatham Artillery, already in battery on the right of the Confederate line, to limber and move to the center so that it could relieve Gamble's battered command. Captain John Wheaton, in command of the battery, responded immediately, and

> we opened with shell, firing 50 rounds, when [we] again advanced and directed our fire against the enemy's batteries, with good effect. As the enemy retired we were again ordered to the front, and took position in the rear of the marsh, directly in rear of the center of our lines, directing our fire on all parts of the enemy's lines and batteries until he was forced from his position and fled the field. The battery was constantly engaged from the commencement to the close of the action, and expended nearly all its ammunition, except its canister.

The Chatham Artillery suffered only slightly in the fighting, having no men killed and three only slightly wounded.[42]

Corporal Henry Shackelford, of the Nineteenth Georgia, described how his unit went into the fight. The regiment was resting, in line of battle, when

> a scout came in and reported the enemy advancing and were within four miles, tearing up the railroad track as they came. "Fall in" was the word and we moved on down the railroad, which was as straight as an arrow, though keeping in the edge of the woods until we got within about one mile of the Yankees advance skirmishers. We filed off to the right in the woods and formed a line, shucked off knapsacks and all heavy baggage, and threw out skirmishers about two hundred yards in advance. They were not out long before the enemy made their appearance, advancing slowly. We could see them a half mile, as the country is quite level, and no undergrowth. They soon drove in our skirmishers and firing commenced. One could plainly see the blue coats army in fine order. The order was given to up and at them, which was no quicker said than done, and then what an awful roar of cannon and musketry, men falling and groaning, officers giving commands, the balls flying as thick as sleet. Cheer after cheer went up, onward pushed the rebels firing and yelling.[43]

General Colquitt stated that the "ground was stubbornly contested" once the engagement became general, and that the Union artillery was playing havoc with his infantry. The stand of the Seventh

Connecticut was especially hard on the Sixty-fourth Georgia, with both the colonel and lieutenant colonel falling as casualties, and the men of the regiment on the verge of breaking before being steadied by the presence of the Twenty-eighth Georgia. After the initial contact between the two forces, Colquitt assigned Colonel Harrison to command of the left half of the Confederate line, and it was largely under his direction that the battle on that part of the field had been fought. Colonel Harrison, a native Georgian from the Savannah area, had been a student at the Georgia Military Academy when war broke out. He had served in several Georgia units before being elected as the colonel of the Thirty-second Georgia Infantry in May of 1862. Harrison was not the only member of his family to hold a command with Georgia troops. His father, George P. Harrison, Sr., had been commissioned by Governor Joseph Brown at the beginning of the war to serve as a brigadier general of state troops.[44]

General George Harrison. Along with General Colquitt, he was responsible for the tactical front-line fighting of the battle (courtesy United States Army Military History Institute).

"I had advanced about a mile to the front when I received a message from General Colquitt urging me to move up rapidly," Harrison would later write. "I had scarcely put my command into double-quick when the sound of artillery in my front indicated that the fight had opened. Quickening our pace, we moved on until within a few hundred yards of the place where the road we were on crossed the railroad. At this place the shells of the enemy's artillery were exploding over us. I halted for a moment to take in the situation and observed the enemy's position across the railroad, which was then sweeping the front of my command with a battery stationed near the cross-roads. I saw General Colquitt forming a line of battle, and then I moved my command in double-quick time across the railroad and formed a line of battle on the left of that just established by General Colquitt. In doing this my formation was delayed by our retreating cavalry, who at a rapid gait rode through and over my line, many of them shouting as they did so: 'Lie down; the Yankees are coming!' But my gallant men failed to obey the cavalry, kept on their feet and were soon facing the pursuing enemy, who armed with repeating Spencer rifles, had utterly demoralized our cavalry. On the first volley from our infantry, however, they stopped their chase and fell back to their main line. Our cavalry continued its retreat and, with the exception of one squadron of the 4th Georgia Cavalry, under command of Captain Brown, was not seen or heard of again during the battle. I well remember Captain Brown, at the head of his squadron, riding up to me in the midst of the fight and demanding that I assign him a place in the line of battle. I told him he had made a mistake, that I had nothing to do with the cavalry. To this he replied: 'I know that; but you are the ranking officer I find in the fight, and I demand that you assign me a place.' I then told him that if it was a fight he wanted here it was and directed him to deploy his squadron on my left and keep me posted of the movements of the enemy. This he gallantly did, and it was on account of information given by him and communicated by me to General Colquitt that the 6th and 32d Georgia Regiments were moved to the right flank of the enemy and caused them to fall back in confusion."[45]

Harrison continues:

> As soon as my line was well established I received a message from general Colquitt directing me to assume command of the left of our line. This I did, and the engagement soon became general.

I then reported to general Colquitt and asked for instructions. He replied that I was in proper position to fight my own line and that he would fight his. This we proceeded to do. Being now at long range (about three hundred yards), I advanced, in conjunction with the right of our line, to within about one hundred and fifty yards of the enemy, who stubbornly stood his ground. About this position the field was hotly contested by both sides for an hour, when the enemy gave way slowly before the close pressure of our gallant men. (It was during this encounter, while riding with my staff down the line from the left toward the center, that the results of the day seemed doubtful. It was whispered that my ordnance officer, Lieut. R.F. Dancy, was instantly killed, and my aide-de-camp, Lieut. Horace P. Clark, and one of my couriers had their horses shot from under them, and my own horse was badly wounded.)[46]

Not much time elapsed before the enemy was re-enforced by fresh troops, and our advance was checked. His resistance now seemed more stubborn than before for more than twenty minutes, when sullenly he gave back a little, apparently to seek a better position; but he still held us at bay. Now the results of the day seemed doubtful.[47]

James M. Dancy, an officer with Dickison's Confederate Cavalry, was near Colonel Harrison when the battle began.

My father, then in Lake City as C.S. Commissary Collector of the tax in kind, furnished the horse for him [Colonel Harrison] to ride to the battle field. The Gen. [Colonel Harrison] and his staff were assembled nearly a mile from the enemy's front line. The enemy opened fire with twelve-pound shell artillery, and almost at the first fire a shell exploded in their midst, and my brother, Robert Dancy, was struck in the left side by a piece of shell about the size of my fist, and was instantly killed, falling from his horse.

Robert Dancy was an officer in the First Georgia Regulars, then forming to go to Colquitt's assistance. Dancy states, "His Captain Cannon was later killed in action, and both bodies are in one grave in Lake City

Florida." When Dancy and the rest of the men with Harrison reached the front, the engagement became general. "The opening fire of the gallant 32nd Georgia Regiment, the finest body of men I ever saw in line, and the short distance between the forces, were so effective that very few escaped instant death," he would later write.[48]

Lieutenant Stinson Asbury Freeman, of the Thirty-second Georgia, wrote to his fiancée to tell her that he was safe.

> By a kind and merciful Providence I escape unhurt, it was a hard fought battle, the Yanks was stubborn to move, but when we did get them started, they left with rapid speed. The 32nd told that her troops were Georgians and bore her part, though suffered very much, some near two hundred killed and wounded. There was two killed from my company & 10 wounded.[49]

The First Georgia Regulars, though few in number, only about 150 men being in the ranks, took a conspicuous part in the battle on Harrison's portion of the line. Their commanding officer, Captain Henry Cannon, was killed, as was the regimental adjutant. The position of the First Georgia Regulars on the line was a depression that had been filled with logs to the front. While most of his men took cover behind these logs, Cannon remained standing, waving his sword and exhorting the men to stand firm. Lieutenant John Fort pleaded with Cannon to take cover, but that officer was hit before he could respond to the urgings. "He staggered backward saying, 'I am a dead man.' With my left arm under him I lowered him to the ground. He died at once." The regimental color bearer, Sergeant Bennett, displayed exceptional gallantry, when he advanced "some 50 yards in front of his regiment while waving his flag and calling on his comrades to keep up with him." Bennett was shot down and seriously wounded while thus exhorting the members of his regiment.

> There was five or six comrades with him when he fell. J.J. McMullen of Company M ... was by his side when he fell. As the colors struck the ground, they were quickly raised by one of the boys and again thrown to the breeze and advanced to the

front. The boys who were with the flag shot away all of their ammunition, and crowded around the one bearing the colors to get ammunition out of his cartridge box.

Private Sam Hunter had a portion of his foot shot off while defending the flag. Hunter had served until this battle in the hospital department, as a non-combatant. His first exposure to combat left him a cripple for life.[50]

Owing to the fact that the Union forces were coming on the field piecemeal, Colquitt's line of battle was able to overlap the Federals, particularly on the portion he had assumed direct command of. From left to right, the Confederate line consisted of the Twenty-third Georgia, the Thirty-second Georgia, the First Georgia Regulars, the Sixty-fourth Georgia, the Sixth Georgia, the Twenty-eighth Georgia, Gamble's (then Chatham's Artillery), the Nineteenth Georgia, and the Sixth Florida Battalion. The right of the Nineteenth Georgia overlapped the left flank of the Union forces, and the Sixth Florida Battalion was formed completely on the flank of the enemy. Hawley's three undersized regiments were no match for the troops arrayed against them, and the slaughter in the Eighth U.S.C.T. that caused the regiment to retire from the field was largely caused because it was caught between the flank and frontal fire coming from the Nineteenth Georgia and the Sixth Florida Battalion. Harrison was also overlapping the Union line, on his portion of the front, with the Sixth and Thirty-second Georgia regiments. Under this pressure from flank and front, from superior numbers, it is no wonder that the Seventh New Hampshire and Eighth U.S.C.T were driven from the field.[51]

The initial phase of the battle of Olustee had been a disaster for the Federals. Three Northern regiments had been mauled and five Union cannon were captured by the Confederates. Thus far, everything had gone in favor of Southern arms. Colonel William B. Barton's brigade was now on the field, however, and his three New York regiments were about to be thrown into the fray.

FOUR

A BRAVE AND BLOODY STAND

The brigade led by Colonel William Barton consisted of the Forty-seventh, Forty-eighth, and 115th New York regiments. "As the Eighth [U.S.C.T.] fell back, Barton Brought his brigade forward on the double-quick into action. Their position was at the center, where the fire of the enemy was terrific. To say that the whole brigade did its duty nobly is but faint praise. Under the most terrible fire it stood its ground with an unsurpassed courage." With Hawley's Brigade collapsing, it was now up to the New Yorkers to try to stem the tide of battle and prevent the day from being lost to the Confederates.[1]

Barton put his brigade into line just to the right of the position recently vacated by the Seventh New Hampshire and Eighth U.S.C.T., and it was at once engaged by the Confederates. The 115th New York held the right of the Union line. To its left was the Forty-eighth New York, and to the left of them stood the Forty-seventh New York. What remained in the field of the Seventh Connecticut and Eighth U.S.C.T. were placed on the extreme left, with the left flank of the Eighth U.S.C.T. resting on the railroad. Captain Loomis Langdon's Battery M, First U.S. Artillery, took up a position approximately 100 to 150 yards to the left and rear of the spot then held by Elder's Battery, on the extreme left of the Union line.

Lieutenant James Clark, Company B, 115th New York, described the anticipation with which the men in his regiment entered the fight:

The Battle of Olustee, 1864

Before we became engaged, some of our comrades were falling back, and many were dragging themselves to the rear covered with blood. Our men became frenzied at the sight, and begged to be hurried to the front that they might avenge the death of those already fallen, and hurl their patriotic columns against the foe. They did not wait long, for the command to move forward soon rang along the line: "Battalion, forward! guide center, double quick-march!" thundered the Colonel. We instantly swept forward in a beautiful line in the face of a galling fire, through reeds higher than our heads, and over logs and fences, until the hateful columns of southern gray were plainly visible. We halted and began to fire, and they greeted our appearance with a deadly volley of musketry.

It was now confusion and roar on both sides, and for three long hours the swift tide of battle surged with cruel fury. There was no lull in the rattle of musketry—no calm and serene moment of security. The leaden messengers of death hailed down in unceasing torrents. Grape and canister swept by with hideous music, and shell after shell tore through our ranks and burst amid heaps of our wounded heroes.[2]

The damage being done by the Confederate artillery was not the result of the field batteries that were in line with Colquitt's infantry. By all accounts, the fire of these batteries was very inaccurate and did but little harm to the opposing infantry, with most of their shells bursting high above the Yankees in the treetops. The exception to this was the "sixty-four pound swivel, fixed on a truck-car on the railroad." The huge railroad gun was performing deadly execution, with each discharge from its muzzle belching forth grape and canister that enfiladed the ranks of the Union infantry, tearing gaping holes with each shot.[3]

A trooper in the Second Florida Cavalry said that the cannon

> mouth looked to me to be as large as a flour barrel, and they moved and shot that big gun about every five minutes. They shot chain and pot shot both from that big gun. The chain shot would cut pine trees down like broomstraws, killing and wounding many each time it was fired. The pot shot blew up destroyed many of Seymour's casons [sic] and ammunition wagons.[4]

Four • A Brave and Bloody Stand

The 115th New York was facing the Sixth and Thirty-second Georgia regiments, from left to right, and was also taking some fire from the First Georgia Regulars, who occupied the space where the left flank of the 115th joined the right flank of the Forty-eighth New York. The ranks of the Union line were thinned in order to present a line of battle that was the same length as the Confederates, and the

> rebels observing our fearfully thin ranks, boldly advanced to drive us back. The 115th closed up and stood the shock like a mountain of adamant. Our men poured such a withering and destructive fire into their massed columns that they soon began to waver, and at last went reeling and staggering back with tremendous loss.... The balls were flying thicker and thicker, the 115th was growing smaller and smaller, and the boys were falling faster and faster, but they kept closing up to their battle flag, and sent cheers of defiance to the rebels. All the officers were dressed in full uniform, and with swords raised, cooly urged the men to be steady and fire low. Our fire now began to tell dreadfully in the ranks of the enemy, and their fire grew feebler.[5]

Lieutenant Nocholas DeGroff, of the 115th New York, later recalled his feelings during this part of the battle: "While dreading the onslaught, the excitement of the battle so engaged my attention that I did not realize my peril and now it seems like a hideous dream, rather then authorized warfare."[6]

True enough, the 115th was making a gallant stand, but the cause of the lessening fire from the Confederates in their front was not due to the marksmanship of the New Yorkers but rather from an inability of the Southerners to respond. The Confederates were running out of cartridges and had reached a crucial moment in the battle. If, while they were unable to fire back, the Union forces mounted a countercharge, the battle might yet go in favor of the North. Seymour could be proven right in invading the interior, and Finegan would have committed a grievous error in fighting outside his entrenched position.

Colonel Colquitt later recounted this period of the battle, when

The Battle of Olustee, 1864

The Forty-eighth New York Infantry. Part of Barton's New York brigade, they made a gallant stand before being forced to withdraw. This regimental picture was taken about a year prior to Olustee, when the regiment took part in the capture of Fort Pulaski, in Savannah, Georgia (*The History of the Forty-eighth New York Volunteers in the War for the Union 1861–1865*).

> the ammunition beginning to fail, I ordered the commanding officers to halt their regiments and hold their respective positions until a fresh supply could be brought up from the ordnance wagons which, after much delay, had arrived upon the field. Major Bonaud's battalion came upon the field, followed soon after by the Twenty-seventh Georgia and the First Florida Battalion. These troops were put in position near the center of the line and a little in advance to hold the enemy in check until the other commands could be supplied with cartridges. As soon as this was accomplished I ordered a general advance, at the same time sending instructions to Colonel Harrison to move the Sixth and Thirty-second regiments [Georgia] around on the right flank of the enemy.

According to one source, Colquitt, when apprised of the shortage of ammunition, simply said "Let the men hold their ground."[7]

Four • A Brave and Bloody Stand

It was just before the Confederate line started to run short on ammunition that a group of Union prisoners was being escorted to the rear, in close proximity to Colonel Colquitt. One of the Yanks, looking at Colquitt, asked, "Who is that man on the gray horse?" J.W. McCook, of the Sixth Georgia, replied, "That is General Alfred H. Colquitt, who commands this brigade." The Yankee looked a Colquitt again, then asserted "God Almighty must be taking care of him, for I shot at him twelve or thirteen times as he was riding up and down your lines when we were fighting in those woods yonder, and I could not hit him." It was afterward discovered that Colquitt had had two buttons shot off of his overcoat, and his horse had been slightly wounded in the neck.[8]

The Georgia regiments that Beauregard had sent to reinforce Finegan, had arrived at Olustee minus their ordnance trains. The ordnance office at Olustee had been instructed to send ammunition by train in the event of a battle, but the cars had not yet come down to the scene of the fighting. Colquitt sent forward a line of skirmishers supplied with cartridges from the pockets of dead Yankees, in order to present a bold front, while he waited for the ammunition to arrive. Guerard's Battery was moved to the left of the Chatham Artillery, and arrived just as the latter was expending its last rounds of shot and shell. By sharing the ammunition in the limbers of the Guerard Artillery, both batteries were able to stay in the fight.

Colonel Harrison took immediate action to remedy the situation. He dismounted and turned his horse over to a member of his staff with instructions to ride back one-half mile to a train of railway cars and personally bring cartridges forward. Harrison employed all of his mounted staff officers and couriers in like manner. The officers returned with cartridges carried in every possible manner, and by making several such desperate trips were able to ensure that the left of the Confederate line never ran completely out. The timely arrival of the First Florida Infantry Battalion, under the command of Lieutenant Colonel C.F. Hopkins, also helped to lessen the emergency. The First Florida was ordered to the support of the Sixty-fourth Georgia, whose ammunition was all but gone, thus making stable that portion of the line.

One of Colquitt's staff officers, Lieutenant Hugh H. Colquitt, displayed exceptional gallantry during the emergency. The lieutenant galloped up and down the Confederate battle line, brandishing a Confederate battle flag, and exhorting the men to stand fast, in full view of the Yankees, to bluff the enemy and keep them from discovering the precarious situation. The men heroically obeyed, and the line held where it was. The arrival on the field of the Twenty-seventh Georgia further served to bolster the line and alleviate the emergency. Colquitt had them go into to line near the center and a little in front of his main line, with orders to hold the Federals in check until the rest of the command could be re-supplied with ammunition. Captain John Keely, of the Nineteenth Georgia, recalled that by 3:00 P.M. his men were out of ammunition, and the Yankees were seen to be advancing in his front. The Confederates were ordered to fix bayonets and advance to meet the charging enemy. The gray-clad infantry responded and was in the process of moving forward "when to our joy, new supplies of cartridges came to us, we grabbed them more eagerly than hungry men ever grabbed loaves of bread, and now, in a minute, we were again masters of the field, for on our next volley the enemy fled precipitately."[9]

The crisis was over. Colquitt's entire line was being re-supplied, and the Confederates were once more preparing to press the fight and try to push the Union battle line off the field. The 115th New York was being hotly pressed on the Union right flank. Southern artillery was being used more effectively, as shell bursts among the trees brought limbs down upon the hapless Yankees. Confederate sharpshooters, hidden in trees or in patches of tall grass in front of and on the flank of the Union line, were proving particularly deadly. The wounded men of the regiment were falling back along the line of the railroad in a steady stream. One wounded soldier of the 115th described the scene upon reaching the place where a field hospital had been set up. All around him, the doctors were engaged in the work of amputating wounded limbs, when "just then a cruel shell burst in their midst, and sent the mangled remains of several of them flying in all directions. I turned away from the sickening sight with horror."[10]

Four • A Brave and Bloody Stand

Ammunition was running short in the Union ranks, as well. Almost all of the cartridges in the 115th New York had been expended, including those that had been gathered from the cartridge boxes of the dead and wounded. But the men of the regiment refused to vacate their place in the line. Though outnumbered and outgunned, and facing an enemy who was attacking from front and flank, they defiantly fixed bayonets and prepared to meet the foe with cold steel. A staff officer, with General Seymour, noted the firmness with which the regiment was holding, and pointing toward the 115th, he asked: "What stone wall is that standing there?"[11]

Stone wall indeed. A Union surgeon who had been captured by the Confederates "said that our command gave the Rebels such a smashing fight that they were in a panic." Lieutenant Nicholas DeGroff felt, "We would have given them more if our ammunition had held out longer." The regiment's commander, Colonel Simeon Sammons, was displaying unusual bravery in leading his men, remaining on his horse after being twice wounded. When the regiment was ordered to withdraw, they were told to do so "with face to the enemy." Colonel Sammon, displaying firm leadership, rode along his line to explain the meaning of the order to his men and to keep them from stampeding to the rear. Sammon's slow withdrawal prompted General Barton to send a message to him to hurry his men back. Sammon continued his slow and deliberate withdrawal, however, causing the message from Barton to be sent two more times. Finally, in exasperation, Sammon bellowed at the messenger, "Give my compliments to Genl Barton and tell him to go to Hell. I will fall back with my Regiment when I am ready to do so."[12]

Lieutenant James Clark, the historian of the 115th New York, later recalled his own experiences in the battle.

> For nearly three hours I escaped injury, and when I saw my comrades shot down around me and myself uninjured, I began to conclude that I was bullet proof. Suddenly a stinging sensation was felt in my right side, and I realized that I was wounded. I remained with the company a short time, but beginning to grow faint I informed my captain and started for the rear. In a short

time I came across a surgeon with about twenty wounded lying around him, and saw the he was engaged in the bloody work of amputation. I next approached the quarter of our own surgeon, and found him surrounded by fifty wounded, his sleeves rolled up, his arms crimsoned with blood, and himself engaged in cutting out balls. With the stream of wounded men from different regiments I hurried towards Sanderson.[13]

The Forty-eighth New York, in the center of Barton's line, was also hard pressed and running low on ammunition. The regimental historian stated, "The Forty-eighth was subjected that day to an ordeal — than which hardly anything is more trying to soldiers — that of holding their line under a terrible fire from the enemy after the exhaustion of their own ammunition." The writer believed that the stand made by the regiment on that field was the crowning achievement of its services in the war.

> Nothing more heroic in all its history will be recorded than the manner in which the Forty-eighth held its ground that day against a direct and double cross-fire from the enemy while its own ammunition was exhausted. From two till five that terrible afternoon it held its line unbroken. It went into the fight a second time after it had secured ammunition. Its terrible losses — only second to those it suffered at [Battery] Wagner — are the best indication of its valor.[14]

Sergeant Henry Lang of the Forty-eighth later related the battle as he remembered it, in the center of Barton's line. He recalled that he was moving

> amongst the guns, abandoned by Battery M; then again I am left alone, firing away from sixty rounds I had in my pockets. The rebels had a good mark at me, standing amongst the guns. They crept nearer and nearer, jumping from trunk to trunk. Everything about me was shot away — my canteen, my haversack, the skirts of my blouse; on the other hand, my cartridges were also ominously disappearing down to the fifty-sixth. I leveled to fire the fifty-seventh round at a cluster of heads behind

a pine trunk; we were at close quarters; I pulled, my ball sped on its way, a crash, and I fell to one side, propping myself up with my gun. At the moment my gun went off, another ball had hit at last its mark, and my leg was smashed; a friendly hand assisted me to a tree and fled for dear life because the enemy advanced, and in another moment all my adversaries came rushing to the tree where I was reclining; all shouted, "Are you the man that was among the guns?"

Having told them that that was so, they all exclaimed "Bully boy!" One of them began to question me concerning how many men we had in the battle; I told him about fifteen thousand [a gross exaggeration]. They spoke about our regiments who had made such a "devilish noise" with their sharp-shooters [the Spencer repeaters]. Flushed with victory as they were, they only went about three hundred yards beyond where I was, and ordered a halt. I grew faint and fainter, and yet with an iron determination raised myself from my faintness, cut open my trousers, and with only a handkerchief found about me, and the help of a stick, succeeding in stopping the bleeding of my wound. I took out my pipe, and finding just enough tobacco, I began to smoke to keep away faintness and kill the wretched thoughts ... and to divert my thoughts from listening to the groans of the dying and wounded, and from the blasphemous language of some marauding soldiers who were ill-treating wounded negroes.

Lang would himself be taken prisoner by the Confederates, but his treatment at their hands would prove to be kindly. Two rebels who hailed from Savannah stopped to talk to him. After a pleasant conversation, one of the Southerners built a small fire to keep Lang from freezing in the night, while his comrade unbuckled his blanket and covered the fallen enemy with it. Before leaving, the two good Samaritans made sure that Lang had water and left him a plug of tobacco. Lang could only say of these enemies, "May these Savannah boys be blessed."[15]

A complaint of the men in both the 115th and Forty-eighth regiments was that the Union artillery was posted too far forward to be of any real service in the engagement. Their proximity to the Confederate line had been the cause of the too numerous casualties sustained by the gunners and had thus prevented them from using the guns to their greatest advantage against the enemy. It is possible that this situation arose not from poor judgment in the placing of the guns, but rather from a lack of suitable options. While the battle ground was fairly free from underbrush, allowing for long range visibility to the infantry, the trees of the open forest presented a problem for the Union gunners. Though the gunners could see the Confederate infantry through the trees, they could not effectively fire against them at any great distance, because the shells were sure to strike those same trees instead of finding their marks. For this reason, it was felt that the guns needed to be moved closer to the action in order to avoid, as much as possible, the intervention of the woods in delivering their fire. It is also possible that this accounts for the acknowledged lack of accuracy by the Confederate gunners, as, by most reports, their fire struck in the trees, doing little damage to the Federal infantry. The Confederate batteries, as a rule, had positioned themselves further away from the opposing infantry than had the Union gunners, and their fire emphasized the difficulty in firing through the trees that the Union artillerists had noted. Under the circumstances, it is probable that the Union artillery did not have the opportunity to make a difference in the battle. Had their guns been placed further back, their fire would have been obstructed and ineffective. As it was, they were under too heavy a fire from Confederate musketry to bring their guns to bear in a manner that could have aided in resisting or breaking up the enemy assault.

In his report of the battle, Colonel Barton was very complimentary of both the 115th and Forty-eighth regiments, citing Colonel Simeon Sammon and Major W.B. Coan, their respective commanders, for their coolness and gallantry. For whatever reason, no reports of the battle were filled by any of the regimental commanders serving under Barton, and his account, as brigade commander, is the only one to be found in the Official Records. Barton stated that the

> enemy's fire was both of musketry and artillery, and was extremely intense and galling. It was soon apparent that we were greatly outnumbered, and were facing a foe well skilled in taking

Four • A Brave and Bloody Stand

> advantage of every cover, and disposed to turn to the best account his superior numbers and position. His fire was rapid, accurate, and well sustained, and for a long time we were sorely pressed, but the indomitable and unflinching courage of my men and officers at length prevailed.

Barton went on to state that

> the fire during a great portion of the time we were engaged was both direct on our front and oblique on our flanks. The enemy formed three distinct lines of battle against us, constantly bringing up fresh troops, and finally attacking in close column by division. All their efforts against us were, however, frustrated, and in their last attempt their loss must have been immense.

But the New Yorkers

> "notwithstanding our heavy losses" were clinging tenaciously to the field. By the time dusk was beginning to gather in the Florida sky, they were doing so "with not a single round of ammunition remaining."[16]

The Forty-seventh New York was bearing the brunt of the assault by Colquitt's portion of the Confederate line and was suffering equally with its fellow New Yorkers who were facing Harrison's troops. In their front, from left to right, were the Nineteenth, Twenty-eighth, and Sixty-fourth Georgia regiments. The Sixth Florida was on their extreme left, beyond their flank, and formed up in line facing that flank. Colonel Henry Moore, the commanding officer of the Forty-seventh, had been shot down and severely wounded, further adding to the high casualty rate among the Federal officer corps. The Southerners were pressing the Forty-seventh hard, and though the line wavered and trembled under each new volley delivered by the Confederates, it did not break. Casualties in the regiment would attest to both the fierceness of the combat and the resolve of the men in the ranks. The Forty-seventh would lose more men than any other regiment in Barton's Brigade, a total of 313. As with the other regiments in the brigade, a shortage of

The Battle of Olustee, 1864

ammunition became apparent as the struggle wore on. All of Barton's men were running low on cartridges, with some having none at all to fire. The cartridge boxes of the dead and wounded had been stripped, in order to keep the men in the fight, but the heroic stand of the New Yorkers was becoming desperate. Colonel James Montgomery's Brigade was now on the field and coming into line, and it was not a moment too soon.

The Union army was in dire need of Montgomery's men, even though he commanded only two regiments in his small brigade. The Fortieth Massachusetts Mounted Infantry and the Independent Massachusetts Cavalry Battalion were supposed to have been a part of Montgomery's force, but they had been detached to serve with Henry's Cavalry brigade. That left only the First North Carolina Infantry and the Fifty-fourth Massachusetts under his command. In the reorganization that had taken place at the Federal War Department, regarding black troops, the designation of the First North Carolina had already been changed to the Thirty-fifth United States Colored Troops, but the officers of the regiment chose to retain its original designation until after the conclusion of the current campaign. This would be the last action the regiment saw as the First North Carolina.

Colonel James Montgomery. His black brigade fought valiantly and held the field long enough to allow the rest of the army to disengage and retreat (courtesy United States Army Military History Institute).

The two black regiments came onto the field and formed a line of battle just in front of the one occupied by the New York brigade and in the shape of an open V. The disparity in numbers between the men in Montgomery's Brigade and the enemy meant that his troops could cover only a portion of the Confederate line of battle. Facing the black troops was a double line of rebels. In the first line, from left to right, as seen by the Federals, were Bonaud's Battalion, the First Florida Battalion, and the Twenty-seventh Georgia. Behind them were the Sixth Florida, the Nineteenth Georgia, the Twenty-eighth Georgia, the Sixty-fourth Georgia, and the Twenty-third Georgia. Extending beyond and on the right flank of the First North Carolina were the First Georgia Regulars, the Thirty-second Georgia, and the Sixth Georgia. Montgomery's Brigade found itself poised to receive the full brunt of the Confederate assault.

Both of Montgomery's regiments had undergone a trying ordeal in just reaching the battlefield. The brigade had been about six miles distant when the engagement was joined, and the sounds of artillery and musketry announced that a fight was in progress. Montgomery had sent his adjutant forward for orders, but without waiting to receive them, he had started to march his brigade toward the sound of the guns. The men had already marched some twelve miles that day and had just halted for a half-hour rest, due to the wagon train for Seymour's army being directly in its line of march. When the sounds of firing first reached the ears of the men in Montgomery's Brigade, they were taken to be nothing more than skirmish action. "Surely the enemy could not be in force ahead," wrote an officer of the Fifty-fourth Massachusetts. "We thought they were probably posted in the woods & were harassing our advance & our batteries were shelling them out."[17]

Upon hearing the report of a cannon, one man in the brigade remarked "That's home-made thunder," to which a comrade responded, "I don't mind the thunder if the lightening don't strike me!" Yet another soldier, apparently fearing a battle, said, "'I want to go home.' 'You'll stay forever, maybe!' was the reply."[18]

"Presently dispatches came for the Colonel, and we were immediately ordered forward," wrote Captain Robert Newell of the Fifty-fourth Massachusetts. "It was evident that we were in for a fight, and I at least did not suppose we should be fifteen minutes in dislodging the rebels and serving them as the cavalry had served the Militia Artillery, having conceived a great contempt for the Florida Militia from what I had seen of them at Jacksonville, where we had a number of prisoners."[19]

Sergeant George Stephens, of the Fifty-fourth Massachusetts, recalled that the men of the regiment were in "heavy marching order, with knapsacks, haversacks, canteens, and every other appurtenance of the soldier." As they marched forward, the men began to discard much of the baggage and equipment that was slowing down their progress.[20]

"The road was sandy," Private Joseph Wilson related, "and the men often found their feet beneath the sand, but with their wonted alacrity they sped on up the road, the 54th leading in almost a locked running step, followed closely by the 1st North Carolina."[21]

"From the time we were ordered forward," Captain Newell recalled, "the way we were managed was unlucky, to say the least. We found a moment to cap the guns and then hurried forward." One of Seymour's aides found the Fifty-fourth's commander, Colonel Edward Hallowell, and implored him forward with all possible haste. "For God's sake, colonel, double-quick, or the day is lost!" Hallowell immediately gave the order, and the last two miles that separated the regiment from the battlefield were covered on the run.

> Before we reached the battlefield, there was not a knapsack left, the men threw away everything to lighten themselves and I finally followed their example, trusting that they would be collected and [unknown word] after, not because I felt the weight at all, for sore feet & shoulders were cured by the prospect of a fight, and I did not feel the slightest bit of fatigue till we had left the field & were ten miles away on our way back. I thought however, that it might be troublesome in the battle, and so away went blankets, shirts and new shoes [?], never to appear again, unless I find them in the possession of some captured rebel, when we make our next advance.... As we approached the battlefield, the cannonading became positively terrific, and drowned out all

Four • A Brave and Bloody Stand

other noises. As I said, the men primed their pieces as we came to the scene of the engagement, and in their excited state, the sternest warning and threats did not prevent a number of accidental discharges. I heard a musket go off behind me and a cry of pain, but I did not stop to look around. I found out after the fight that this was one of our men, one of the worst in the company, who had wounded himself & killed a man near him by the careless discharge of his piece. One of our Sergeants wounded himself in the same way, and has since been reduced to the ranks in consequence. It is positively horrible to lose men in this way, & is more demoralizing to the men than the loss of ten times the number by the enemy.

Colonel Edward Hallowell, commander of the Fifty-fourth Massachusetts Infantry (courtesy United States Army Military History Institute).

Newell felt that the men were far too careless in handling their weapons, once loaded and primed, and believed that it would be good to have "one or two men shot for negligence in this respect — a severe remedy — but the only one that would be fully effectual."[22]

As the brigade neared the battlefield it was met by the scenes of an army in defeat. Hundreds of wounded stragglers streamed past, along with a disabled battery, making its way to the rear. The Fifty-fourth was greeted with discouraging statements made by the retiring troops, who announced, "We are badly whipped!" or "You'll all get killed!" The men pressed on, undaunted by the words. The men in Colonel Montgomery's bigade had heard the sounds of battle for some time now. "When it became evident that our men were having hot work in front, [Montgomery] sent his adjutant, Lt. Loveridge, forward for orders, but without waiting for his return, he moved forward with the 54th Massachusetts [leading]." As they came to the scene of conflict, Sergeant Garnet Cezar, a member of the Fifty-fourth, bellowed at the top of his lungs, "Three cheers for Massachusetts and seven dollars a month!" The reference to seven dollars a month concerned the fact that the Federal government had decided that black troops were to be paid less than white troops, a decision that caused a great deal of hard feelings and resentment in the ranks of black regiments. In the Fifty-fourth, it had become their battle cry, a sort of defiant gesture of pride that here we are, underpaid and Abe Lincoln's bargain troops, but watch what we can do![23]

Knowledge that their comrades in front of them were hotly engaged caused the men to speed forward. "In a few moments the regiment was moving at the double-quick, urged on by the heavier sound of battle," wrote one member.[24]

General Seymour met the regiment as it reached the battlefield. He galloped up to Colonel Hallowell and implored him to put his men into the fight. "Colonel we have lost everything, and it all now depends upon your regiment." He informed the colonel that the army would be annihilated unless the Fifty-fourth could hold the Confederates long enough for a new line of battle to be formed. It was a lot to expect from this veteran but undersized regiment. The bloody assault on Battery Wagner, the previous summer, had seriously thinned the ranks. Adding to that, two companies of the regiment had been left behind, at Barber's, to guard the line of march. There were now just over 500 officers and men remaining in the regiment. It seemed hardly enough to stem the tide of the victorious Confederates.[25]

Seymour was everywhere on the battlefield, deploying troops and issuing orders. Colonel Hawley thought that he was recklessly endangering himself to the extent that Hawley cautioned him about his

Four • A Brave and Bloody Stand

exposure, drawing a "sharp reply" from Seymour. The commanding general knew that a critical moment was at hand, and he was doing everything he could, personally, to try to salvage the situation and avoid a disaster. Captain Gustavus Dana, chief signal officer on Seymour's staff, was given an assignment that he considered to be "fun at the time. A number of officers were behind trees and I was told to order them into the front rank of the nearest regt., no matter whether their own or not." Seymour was trying to get everyone he could into the fight.[26]

As the Fifty-fourth Massachusetts went into line, the blacks let out what was described as a "hearty cheer." in response to Sergeant Cezar's battle cry. Their arrival on the field seemed to encourage the white troops in the New York regiments, and the pivotal timing helped to prevent the turning of the Forty-seventh New York's left flank by the Confederates. Their timely arrival also prevented the capture of a field hospital that was about to be overrun by the rebels. While the Massachusetts men were entering the fray, their regimental band took up a position along the side of the road, and their instruments "burst out on the sulphurous air" with patriotic tunes. One Union veteran remembered being able to hear the band's "soul-stirring strains" above the roar of the artillery and musketry. He recalled how the sound of the "Star Spangled Banner" seemed to give the men spirit. The nearby New Yorkers were heartened by the music, and some of the retreating New Hampshire soldiers even halted and went back to fight some more when they heard the strains of the song being played. "Its thrilling notes, soaring above the battle's gales, aroused to new life and renewed energy into the panting, routed troops."[27]

The regimental historian of the 115th New York recalled that at the time the Fifty-fourth Massachusetts came on the field there was not a single round of ammunition to be found among the New Yorkers. Still, the sight of the Union reinforcements so enthused them that the men of the 115th fixed bayonets and with a "soul-stirring cheer, rushed forward with the 54th." Whether or not this action took place in conjunction with the Fifty-fourth Massachusetts coming on the field may be questioned. The 115th New York occupied the extreme right of the Union line. The Fifty-fourth, when it came on the field, occupied the extreme left. There was a gap amounting to a regimental front between the two regiments, which was filled by the First North Carolina. It is possible that the historian of the 115th was referring to these troops, and not the Massachusetts men, when remembering the bayonet charge made by his regiment. Otherwise, the two regiments would have been advancing, each with their flanks completely exposed and in the air.[28]

It was now after 4:00 P.M., and there would be only about an hour of daylight remaining on this late February day. If Montgomery's Brigade could hold, Seymour would be able to extricate his army, and the Federal army would live to fight another day. If the black troops could not stem the Confederate advance, all would be lost, and Seymour's little army would likely be gobbled up and eliminated as a fighting force. Defeat was apparent. Disaster could yet be avoided.

Colonel Montgomery placed the battle lines of his two regiments at a 120 degree angle to one another, an open "V" facing the Confederates, with the Fifty-fourth Massachusetts on the left and the First North Carolina on the right. Montgomery took a position in the middle of the line and directed the action while sitting on the stump of a tree. Colonel Hallowell also "mounted the stump of a tree some fifty feet in rear of his center to oversee his men and the position." Both regiments were immediately engaged by the Confederates, who sought to brush them aside and rout the Federal army. The first volley of the Fifty-fourth stopped the Southern advance, and a vicious firefight ensued. Confederate sharpshooters and snipers, posted in trees, added their fire to that of the main battle line. On their second volley, many members of the regiment became so excited that they forgot to remove their ramrods from their muskets, shooting the three foot spears, along with the bullets, toward the rebel line. All of these men were thus left with no rammer with which to load their muskets, but the order was given to load the weapons, jam the butts hard against the ground to seat the cartridges, then cap and fire. The tactic worked, and the muskets fired. George Stephens, a soldier in the regiment, would later state that the men found this to be a faster way of loading than using a ramrod, and it was adopted by all of the men. The volleys were so rapidly delivered that a nearby unit of white troops, armed with breech-loaders, called out: "Ha! You fellows have breech-loaders too!"[29]

In a short time, half of the color guard had been shot down. Sergeant James Wilkins carried the Stars and Stripes and Corporal Peal carried the Massachusetts state flag, both men defiantly keeping their colors to the front of the line. Corporal James Goodling, a whaler from New Bedford, Massachusetts, and a member of the color guard, was shot down and reported killed to the folks back home. But Goodling had only been wounded in the thigh. He would survive the battle to become a Confederate prisoner, but he would not survive the war. Goodling was sent to Andersonville, where he died on July 19, 1864. One man was observed to be overcome with the zeal of battle. He would load his musket, then charge out well in advance of the main line to deliver his fire at the enemy. The soldier repeated the process several times before a shot through the head stopped his one-man counter-attack. Lieutenant Colonel Henry Hooper's groom was caught up in the struggle and gave up his non-combatant status when he seized a musket and shot down a rebel captain who was charging the position. Sergeant Stephen Swails was cited for conspicuous gallantry, despite receiving a severe wound in the fight. He would later become the first black to receive a commission as an officer in the Fifty-fourth.[30]

The rapid firing of the Fifty-fourth Massachusetts quickly expended their supply of ammunition, some 20,000 rounds. A newspaper correspondent from the *Boston Journal* thought that the men of the Fifty-fourth "fought like tigers." A correspondent for the *New Bedford Mercury* asserted, "The fifty-fourth did honor to themselves and our city. All concede that no regiment fought like it." Corporal Henry Shackelford, of the Nineteenth Georgia, also paid tribute to the fight being waged by the black troops, stating that the Yankees had "pitched three negro regiments against us, and all acknowledged that they fought well."[31]

Captain Luis Emilio said,

> Upon taking position the regiment received a steady but not severe musketry fire, with a flanking fire of shell from the artillery

on our left flank. The horses of the field and staff had been sent to the rear.... After a time Companies D and B on the left were thrown back to present a better front and guard that flank.

Hallowell was refusing his line, on the left, in an effort to try to keep from being flanked by the Confederate forces that were building up there. Emilio also stated,

> So open was the forest that the enemy's line and colors could be seen about four hundred yards distant, with two guns in front of our right well advanced, apparently without much support. On the extreme left front were guns covered by a railroad embankment.... Bonaud's battalion advanced, supported by the Nineteenth Georgia and Sixth Florida, all between the wagon road and the railroad, while beyond the railroad to their right were two guns of Guerard's battery and some cavalry. Only the Fifty-fourth in the latter part of the action was on our left of the wagon-road in the battle front.... In the center, where Captain Bridge was prominent, our companies were enduring an increased musketry fire from front and flank. Sharpshooters were observed perched in the trees, but a few volleys brought them down. We were sustaining casualties every moment, but most of the missiles passed overhead.[32]

Colonel Montgomery had left his place in the center of the brigade line and was, at this time, prominent in the ranks of the Fifty-fourth. He and his staff were up and down the regiment's line of battle, freely exposing themselves to the enemy fire and steadying the men to their purpose. Cognizant of the strong fire coming from the direction of the railroad and the rebel units that were trying to flank the Massachusetts men, Montgomery ordered the troops to concentrate their fire there, shouting "Fire to the left! Fire to the left!"[33]

On the extreme right of the Fifty-fourth's line, Lieutenant Homans noticed the exposed position of two guns of the Chatham Artillery, as had Captain Emilio, and sprang to the front of his line yelling, "Now is a good opportunity; we'll try and take those guns!" In an instant, the brash young lieutenant was leading his company toward the rebel guns. Hallowell observed the movement and quickly ordered Homans to call off the attack and return his men to their place in the line.[34]

Lieutenant Homans was not the only member of the Fifty-fourth chafing at the bit to get at the Confederates. Sergeant Wilkins, the bearer of the national colors, was seen advancing across the field, accompanied by all of the men who were nearby to him. The group had advanced some 150 yards before Colonel Hallowell noticed what they were doing. He immediately ordered them to return to the line, afraid that the rest of the regiment might follow the colors, without orders, into an unsupported position in which they might be cut off and surrounded.[35]

When a new supply of cartridges was hurried to the front the apprehension over the shortage was temporarily alleviated, but they were found to be of the wrong caliber and therefore useless to the troops. "Men, we are whipped!" cried Lt. Col. Henry Hooper of the regiment. Colonel Montgomery was with the Fifty-fourth at this moment in time and advised that the men be dispersed, with every man trying to make it back to the rear on his own. Colonel Hallowell had become separated from the main body, and Lt. Col. Hooper took responsibility for ignoring Montgomery's advice and ordering that the position be held. The men were ordered to fix bayonets and hold the line with cold steel. In order to calm the troops and hold them in position, the officers put the men through the manual of arms and continued to drill them as they slowly withdrew from the field.[36]

The intense horror of the carnage and the ear-splitting roar of the cannon and musketry proved to be too much for at least one member of the Fifty-fourth. Private Thomas Jackson, of Company A, was obviously a victim of battle fatigue because of his experience at Olustee. After the battle, it was reported that he began to act in a very strange manner, prompting his transfer to a mental asylum in Washington, D.C. Jackson would later die while still a patient at the asylum. His comrades in the ranks believed that Olustee had destroyed his sanity and was the cause of his untimely death, stating that "previous thereto he was perfectly sound and free from any defect."[37]

To the right of the Fifty-fourth, the First North Carolina had been facing extreme pressure from the Confederate attackers. Unlike the Fifty-fourth Massachusetts, the First North Carolina had been in light marching order when they were hastened toward the front, lacking the knapsacks and other gear that had hampered the march of the Bay Staters and sapped away precious strength. General Seymour had hoped that the First North Carolina could drive back the left flank of the Confederates when he brought them on the field. Lieutenant Colonel W.N. Reed led the regiment in, sword in hand, as the North Carolina boys formed in line and immediately charged against the advancing Confederates. A sergeant in the regiment described the scene of Barton's hard-used brigade that beheld the men as Colonel Reed was getting them into line: "What we saw made our blood run cold. Everywhere, men were staggering out of the forest, faces blackened, dripping with blood and sweat, dragging themselves and their wounded comrades to safety." The opposing lines charged to within 20 yards of one another before the Confederates broke and fell back. But the black troops were seriously outnumbered and unable to deliver anything more than a momentary check to the enemy. A second advance, by a reinforced rebel battle line, forced the First North Carolina to give ground, which they did in good order, pouring a destructive fire into the ranks of the gray line. Lieutenant Colonel Reed fell mortally wounded. Reed had been struck while imploring another of his officers to leave the field. Adjutant William Manning had been wounded, and Reed had gone to the spot where he lay, embraced him, and was trying to convince him to leave the field when Manning was struck a second time and the colonel received his own mortal wound. In the next moment, the two friends were lying side by side on the field. Major Archibald Bogle, the regiment's second in command, was also wounded and thought to be killed. In fact, reports of his death were printed back home in the Boston papers, but Bogle had been wounded and captured and would survive not only the battle, but the war.[38]

The gallantry of the color guard was without equal. Three of the color sergeants had been shot down, the last, Sergeant Samuel Waters, receiving three wounds before consenting to relinquish the colors. Sergeant Taylor carried the battle flag throughout the engagement, grasping it in his left hand after having his right hand all but shot off.[39]

One of the officers later recalled, "we went in, in double column, closed in mass and deployed under fire, eliciting from all observers the warmest praises, by the performance of the movement and then in line when formed." All who witnessed the fighting agreed that the First North Carolina was making a heroic stand. The effects of the enemy musketry were intensified by the almost constant crashing of tree limbs in the ranks caused by the Confederate artillery. Several members of the regiment were wounded by the falling branches. One enlisted man was seen "terribly wounded by a musket ball through both cheeks, and bleeding in torrents from his wounds, mouth and nose, but shouting aloud through swollen lips, dripping with blood, 'Shree Sheers for Union! Gimmum'll Gimmum'll' [He] went to the extreme rear yelling in his broken style the same old rallying cry of 'Gimmum'll.'" Private Joseph T. Wilson, watching the thinning of the ranks by enemy fire, noted, "Men fell like snowflakes."[40]

A newspaper correspondent left the following tribute to the conduct of the First North Carolina:

> No regiment went into action more gallantly, or did better execution than the First North Carolina [colored] troops. Their white commanders generally taking pleasure in awarding them this honor. Men were dropping constantly all along the line, but the living fought all the more bravely. These freedmen evidently preferred falling on the field of battle to falling into the hands of their barbarous foes. This regiment was not in action over two hours and a half and yet its loss in officers and enlisted men was nearly as heavy as that of any other regiment.

A reporter for the *New York Herald* declared,

> The men behaved most gallantly, and never wavered, but stood their ground manfully, and even drove the left of the line [the left of the Confederate line].[41]

When Major Archibald Bogle was wounded, one of his men exhibited the special attachment that black troops seemed to form for their

White officers. The soldier, seeing Bogle go down, sprang forward to rescue him, only to fall wounded himself, with a bullet to the shoulder. Undaunted in his purpose, the soldier continued toward Bogle and had picked the officer up into his arms when a second bullet struck him in the head, and his lifeless body slumped over his wounded commander.[42]

Captain Charles Jones had exhibited an attachment to the men in his command even by being on the battlefield. Jones had been a non-commissioned officer in the Twenty-first Massachusetts Infantry, and all-white regiment, and was so well thought of in his own regiment that he had been recommended by his commanding officers for a commission. Jones turned down this honor to accept a commission with the First North Carolina, preferring, for personal reasons, to lead black troops into battle. He would be killed leading those troops at Olustee.[43]

Colonel Harrison received instructions from Colonel Colquitt to move the Sixth and Thirty-second Georgia regiments so as to place them on the right flank of the First North Carolina. In the meantime, Colquitt placed the Sixth Florida Battalion on the left flank of the Fifty-fourth Massachusetts. The result was a galling fire delivered into the front and flank of Montgomery's battered command. The First North Carolina was being sorely pressed, and the men in the ranks were dropping with alarming rapidity. Some 230 officers and men would become casualties during the short time the regiment spent on the battlefield. When the Twenty-seventh Georgia, in the middle of the Confederate line, surged forward, it was the signal for a general assault all along the rebel line. The massed gray lines were sweeping everything before them, and the men of the First North Carolina could stand no more. At first, the line wavered, then it began falling back toward the rear. It was at this time that the First North Carolina lost its national colors. Confederate fire had decimated both the color guard and the color company, and Lieutenant Elijah Lewis noticed that the flag was lying on the ground, its bearers all shot down. He retrieved the banner and carried it to the battery of cannon the regiment was trying to support, in the hope of being able to rally the men to the guns. At the

Four • A Brave and Bloody Stand

recommendation of another officer, Lewis handed the flag to one of the gunners before attempting to form the men into a new battle line. In the heat of battle, and while trying to accomplish their task of getting the men in line, Lewis and the other officers of the First North Carolina lost track of the flag. When the regiment retreated from the field it was left behind. The gunner to whom it had been handed had either been shot down, or had dropped it, but either way, the banner became a battle prize for the Confederates. The right flank of the Fifty-fourth Massachusetts was uncovered when the First North Carolina left the field, and that regiment was now left to face the full onslaught of the Confederate charge alone.[44]

As the First North Carolina was retiring, its surgeon, Doctor Heichold, tried to evacuate as many of the black wounded as he possibly could. Heichold made sure that black troops were the first to be loaded on to the ambulances and gave orders that white soldiers were to be let aboard only if there was room. The doctor feared the consequences of leaving the black wounded behind, and though criticized that the "white troops should be brought away also, but Dr. H. said: 'I know what will become of the white troops who fall into the enemy's possession, but I am not certain as to the fate of the colored troops.'" Even before the regiment had been forced back, the doctor saw that defeat was inevitable and "went around among the wounded and told them, as many as could get away, to start for Barber['s]," in hopes of removing them from the field.[45]

With the departure of the First North Carolina, the men of the Fifty-fourth received the full attention of the Confederates. So exposed were the positions of the soldiers that an officer in the Fifty-fourth speculated that the regiment had either been forgotten or was to be sacrificed for the purpose of allowing the rest of the army to retreat. It was now 5:30 P.M., and darkness was falling over the landscape. Captain Gustavus Dana noted,

> Just at dusk (there is no twilight there, it is dark almost immediately after sundown) there was a lull that betokened a charge, and then General [Seymour] ordered us all to ride along the

The Battle of Olustee, 1864

front and set up a shout that would indicate we considered ourselves the victor. Just as I spurred my horse forward to do this, a poor fellow limping to the rear and near enough to Gen. Seymour to hear the order to his staff, shouted hurrah for gen. Seymour and with the last word a stream of blood spurted from his mouth and he fell on his face dead.[46]

Captain Robert Newell was perplexed by the order to withdraw. The regiment had been putting up a good fight, and Newell felt that the battle was going in their favor. Then came the order to retreat. "The sudden retreat of the whole line was however, completely astounding to me, not understanding the circumstances, as I was just congratulating myself that we were going on so well, and expecting an order for a charge presently."[47]

The men of the Fifty-fourth were instructed to raise nine hearty cheers, which they did with enthusiasm. It was hoped that the Confederates would think that the Federals were receiving reinforcements and would therefore halt their advance. Then, in an act of defiance, the men of the Fifty-fourth did an about-face and marched off the field with their backs to the foe. The regiment was ordered to stop, about-face, and fire a volley every two or three hundred yards. Captain Dana believed that the cheering "had its effect" and the battle of Olustee was ended. Indeed, the cheering probably gave the Confederates a moment to pause, but the darkness that had settled over the field was the major reason for the halting of the advance. The Confederates were becoming intermingled in the blackness of the pine woods, and men were exhausted from their victorious efforts. Night had become an ally of Seymour's army.[48]

Captain Newell was not nearly so confident during the retreat as he had been in the battle.

> "Now it was that the trying time came," he wrote. "The rebels, seeing us run, rushed forward with cheers and poured in a more accurate fire than they had done before. I got a considerable distance behind the regiment as they retreated, and looking toward the right saw that the rebels were coming along with very

unpleasant rapidity, and the bullets began to sing round my ears in such a way as to excite a disagreeable suspicion that they had caught sight of my sword. I had no shoulder straps, which I had not worn for a month, as they were on my dress coat I left behind at Hilton Head. There were a number of stragglers on my right and left, who had rushed forward & been fighting on their own account, several of these were hit, and I shall never forget the cry of agony of one poor fellow who was hurrying to catch up to the rest & fell forward on his hands & knees disabled, for the men expected no mercy if taken remembering Fort Wagner, & made desperate exertions to get away.... After retreating some distance, we got out of fire, & reformed the line & Col. Hooper made the men go through the manual to steady their nerves.... As generally happens, men got very much mixed up and a number of the 1st North Ca. were also among them. After retreating from the field we halted collected the scattered men & rearranged the companies."[49]

With darkness settling in the pine forest, General Seymour knew that his little army had done all that it could. The Confederates were threatening to turn both of his flanks, and it looked as if they might be able to gain the rear of his position. To avoid being completely overrun or surrounded, the general ordered a withdrawal of all his forces, including Montgomery's Brigade, which had done so much to stem the Confederate tide and save the army from annihilation.

Lieutenant Charles Duren, of the Fifty-fourth, vividly remembered receiving the orders to withdraw. His was a completely different remembrance from that of Captain Newell's. While the latter stated that he was ready and eager to charge forward, the former seemed more than ready for a retreat. "When we came out of the fight [I] had felt so much care and responsibility that when the order came to fall back — I was perfectly exhausted, faint, and entirely worn out," Duren would later remember.[50]

The Fifty-fourth Massachusetts had fared far better than had the First North Carolina in the fight. They had been able to hold their position, an act that allowed the rest of the Union army a chance to retire, and in doing so, they had somehow sustained a fraction of the

The Battle of Olustee, 1864

casualties suffered by the North Carolinians. Even so, their losses were high, prompting one of their officers to write:

> We have had a fight, a licking, and a foot-race.... We marched 110 miles in 108 hours, and in that time had a three hour's fight. Our regiment lost one man in every five — going in five hundred strong, and losing one hundred in killed, wounded and missing.... Gen. Seymour said to Colonel Hallowell, "The day is lost; you must go in and save the corps." We did go in and did save it, checked the enemy, held the field, and were the last to leave — and covered the retreat.[51]

In reality, the regiment had lost 84 men out of the 530 it had taken into the battle, an amazing statistic considering the casualty rates in the other regiments and the fact that the Fifty-fourth had faced the entire Confederate army by itself for a period of time. It was only little more than a third of the casualties suffered by the First North Carolina.

That the Fifty-fourth Massachusetts and First North Carolina were selected to hold the field while the rest of the army retired was probably a matter of good fortune for the Union army. It was well known that Confederates did not feel themselves bound by the laws of civilized warfare when it came to black troops, and blacks who fell into their hands were afforded no rights as soldiers. This knowledge caused blacks to be tenacious fighters when used as holding forces, or in rear guard actions, as most of the men in the ranks feared capture by the Confederates more than they did death on the battlefield. Capture could mean a return to slavery, and almost any fate was better than that.

The two black regiments would receive assistance in holding the rear guard from members of the Seventh New Hampshire Regiment. Captain James M. Chase was with a number of men from the regiment who had "got left" when it retired from the field. Captain Chase

> proposed that we gather up all the men we could and act as a rear guard, as none seemed to have been detailed to perform that duty before leaving the field, and we at once commenced

Four • A Brave and Bloody Stand

> collecting all the men we could find as we slowly retreated. Our defeat was so severe and unexpected, and our lack of transportation so meager, that we were compelled to leave our killed and most of our wounded in rebel hands. However, we soon succeeded in stopping and collecting nearly a hundred soldiers belonging to the different organizations.... The captain, as the ranking officer present, assumed command, dressed the line, and at once advanced towards the rebel line over a portion of the field which our defeated troops had just left, until we came upon a rebel skirmish line slowly but cautiously advancing, and whose fire we at once received, at which time a Minie ball struck the captain on the instep of the left foot, but not disabling him. Noticing a heavy line of battle following close in the rear of the rebel skirmishers, we had no alternative but to retreat, which we did, firing as we went, for nearly half a mile.

The writer, Lieutenant Henry Little, claims that this detachment of the Seventh New Hampshire was the last Union unit to leave the field, a distinction generally accorded to the Fifty-fourth Massachusetts.[52]

Lieutenant M.B. Grant, Finegan's engineering officer, derisively commented on the placement of the black troops on the battlefield. "As usual with the enemy, they posted their negro regiments on their left and in front, where they were slain by the hundreds, and upon retiring left their dead and wounded negroes uncared for, carrying off only their whites, which accounts for the fact that upon the first part of the battlefield nearly all the dead found were negroes." Grant's assessment seems flawed on a number of levels, not the least of which is his assertion that Union officers commonly placed black troops in the same position on a battlefield. At the time Olustee was fought, black troops had participated in a small number of engagements, and no such conclusion could possibly have been drawn from past experience. The Fifty-fourth Massachusetts had become famous in their first grand assault against Battery Wagner, only six months before, one of the first times that a black unit had taken a major part in an attack. As to the preponderance of black soldiers found dead upon the field, the lieutenant was assuming that they had all been killed in battle, an assumption that was incorrect in a most ghastly manner.[53]

The Battle of Olustee, 1864

Colonel Harrison, in commenting on the battle in later years, would state that the reinforced pressure his line was exerting against the Yankees

> served to embolden our men and intimidate the enemy; for the latter's retreat now became more hurried and his fire less rapid and effective. Under instructions from General Colquitt, I threw forward the 6th and 32nd Georgia Regiments, the extreme left of our line, to flank the enemy upon his right, which movement succeeded admirably, for soon his right was exposed to a cross-fire which told upon his ranks with fine effect. A general advance of our line now drove the enemy, who retreated sullenly at first, then precipitately, before our victorious arms.

Harrison described the battle as a "fair, square, stand-up fight," and stated that it had been, for the number of troops engaged, "one of the bloodiest encounters of the whole war." Lieutenant Winston Stephens, of the Second Florida Cavalry, in a letter written just after the battle, thought that he had experienced "one of the hottest contested battles of the war" and that "men never fought better then our men did, and God seemed to shield them in great measure from destruction as the loss on our side is comparatively light."[54]

Indeed, when one considers the numbers engaged, the short duration of the battle, and the resulting casualties, Olustee must be considered to be one of the most sanguinary engagements of the war. The Union army lost 1,861 men in killed, wounded and missing, or approximately 34 percent of those engaged. This percentage is much higher than is to be found in numerous battles renowned for their carnage, such as Gettysburg, Chickamauga, and Shiloh. On the Confederate side, casualties totaled some 946 men, or approximately 17 percent of Finegan's effective force. This breaks down to a rate of about 700 casualties per hour for the four-hour fight, an astounding number given the fact that there were only about 5,000 men in either army. Of the Union total, 503, or approximately one-third, were attributed to the three black regiments.[55]

Four • A Brave and Bloody Stand

One young Confederate, assigned to the staff and with an obvious knack for dramatic prose, left the following romantic reminiscences of the day. He probably captured, in his eloquent prose, the feelings of most of the Southerners who had taken part in the battle.

> There are the pine woods of Olustee. Night had come on and the ill clad army is suffering from the cold — cold most unusual for Florida. A young man and a boy are hovering over a camp fire, yet failing to keep warm. Thus they spend the night before the battle of Olustee, and they welcome the coming of daylight.
>
> There comes a scout galloping from the front.... His horse is ridden hard. The enemy is advancing in force. We rush off to saddle up. My bridle is gone, and Dick goes plunging away on his spirited mare, finds me another, and we go galloping off in the wake of General Finegan and his staff. There is the hurrying Infantry, regiment after regiment, marching under the proudly waving folds of our battle flag.... I hear the tramp of the Cavalry and the bugle calls. Over yonder under the tall whispering pines comes the blue line, with its glittering equipments. I hear the rumble of the Artillery as the plunging horses wheel the polished guns into position.
>
> There is the white smoke rushing along the ground as the bursting shells are hurled into the ranks of gray that are coming up so steadily. There are the wounded, some limping, some crawling, some sinking down to rise no more and slowly bleeding to death. There are the dead faces with wide open eyes turned up to the cold sky of winter. There is an ambulance with blood on the wheels and door.... There are the panting horses of the couriers, heads hanging low, rushing from place to place. There is Lieutenant Dancy lying by the rail fence on the road side. Here comes Colonel Clinch of the Georgia Cavalry. A man is leading his horse. The saddle is bloody, and blood is dripping down the stirrup leathers. I pass him running. I have been sent to hurry up the ordnance wagons.
>
> Our cannon are speaking slowly. Ammunition is nearly out.... Now the reserve is coming up in a run, their yell ringing through the pine woods. As they fall into line of battle, I hear the ring of the rifles. I see the blue line wavering.

The Battle of Olustee, 1864

Ah, I feel the exultation. The enemy is retreating — retreating before the brave fellows who wear the tattered gray; and I smile to see the bullet scarred flags of my country floating triumphantly in the pine scented air of my native land![56]

FIVE

THE TWILIGHT OF BATTLE

As night descended on the hard-fought field, the triumphant Confederates looked to complete their victory by turning the Union retreat into a rout. The Fifty-fourth Massachusetts continued its measured retreat until it came upon the main body of Seymour's army, where Colonel Hallowell rejoined the regiment and resumed command. At this place, Lt. Henry Metcalf's section of Company C, Third Rhode Island Artillery, Captain Elder's Horse Artillery, and the Seventh Connecticut Infantry were ordered to form a rear guard. Lt. Metcalf remembered that this was a time of chaos, with every man seemingly looking out for himself, and Sergeant Patrick Egan recalled, "By this time most of the army was in disorder." The battery "crossed the open field to the narrow road leading to the field," where one gun, "unlimbered and loaded with double shot of canister, waited for the rebel column coming across the open field." Metcalf stated that when the Confederate pursuit advanced to within 100 yards of the battery, the gun was fired, "mowing them down like grass, this checking their whole army." He went on to assert that this action "checked the advance of the rebel army and saved hundreds of men from being killed or captured," and Egan thought that the Southerners "probably thought the Yankees had formed another line of battle." While the firing of the artillery no doubt discouraged the Confederate pursuit, the action was hardly as significant as Metcalf describes. Most of the Confederate army was still back at Olustee, taking a breather and congratulating themselves on the victory they had just won. The pursuit that Metcalf talks about was a half-hearted effort that was more shadowing than pursuing. Colquitt's infantry had driven the Yankees off the field and probably would have continued to pitch into their retreating ranks, but that was supposed to be a job for the cavalry. Indeed, General Finegan had ordered Colonel Carroway Smith's cavalry to "press the enemy on his flanks and continue the pursuit," but Smith did not respond. In fact, the Confederate cavalry was conspicuous by its absence. With the Union army defeated and in retreat, it was the perfect target for the harassing tactics of the cavalry, and if pressed, the retreat might have been turned into a rout, but the Confederate horse were no where to be found.[1]

When the cavalry pursuit failed to materialize, General Finegan ordered Colonel Colquitt to leave one regiment behind, as a forward guard, and return to Olustee with the rest of his army. The battle was now officially over. Colonel Smith would undergo severe criticism after the battle for his failure to press the advantage, and he would offer numerous reasons, in his own defense, why such a pursuit had been impracticable. According to Smith, the onset of darkness made it impossible for him to distinguish the location of his own lines. He also stated that the terrain lent itself to ambush, and he had received reports of a large concentration of Union cavalry nearby that he wanted to verify before taking action. One handicap to the Confederate troopers seems to have been legitimate. Telegraph wire had been stretched between the trees by the Union army, on both sides of the road, hampering the troopers' movements and proving a hazard in the dark.[2]

All of what Smith stated was true, but the colonel's activity, or rather lack thereof, during the battle created the impression, rightly or wrongly, that Caroway Smith was not inclined to fight on this day. Had his cavalry brigade taken a greater role in the battle, his explanations for its lack of pursuit would doubtless have been given more credit. As it was, many in the army saw it as simply another instance of his shying away from a fight.

A portion of the Second Florida Cavalry did continue the pursuit of the Federals. Lawrence Jackson, a trooper in Company C of that regiment, left an account of the pursuit:

Five • The Twilight of Battle

We reached Baldwin next morning about sunrise [Feb. 21]; found that little town burned — every little shanty was a pile of smoking ashes. A.J. Decosta had an old warehouse full of bales of Sea Island cotton. Every bale had been cut open and set afire. We found that a large number of wagons and teams had just left Baldwin for Jacksonville only about thirty minutes before our arrival at Baldwin. As we had nothing there to eat, we started for those wagons that were ahead, I saw a chunk of meat — it was raw pickled pork — on the side of the road. I stuck my sword in it, picked it up, cut off a small piece; passed it back down the line. Just a little ways ahead we came to a large pile of boxes of hardtack which were broken open, and almost every cracker was bloody or had signs of blood on them, as wounded soldiers had been riding in the wagon on the boxes, as we had passed numbers of bleeding, dying soldiers all the way from Olustee down. Every one of our men that passed near enough to those crackers grabbed a hand full. They would scrape the blood off of those crackers and eat them, and that raw pickled pork was good. Our officers would cheer us to come. We would catch them soon. We overtook the last of Seamore's [sic] fleeing Army at the Hart place, seven miles from Jacksonville. They stopped and surrendered without any trouble. There we captured a very large number of the finest teams of mules and horses that I ever saw, and the wagons were all loaded with all kinds of Army supplies, provisions of every kind, also shoes, clothing and everything that an Army could use. Then and there we had breakfast on February 21st, 1864. Thus ended the Fight at Olustee.[3]

Sergeant A.J. Clement, along with the rest of his company of the First Massachusetts Cavalry Volunteers, was positioned at the rear of the Union army, charged with the mission of keeping the troops moving forward and reducing straggling, in an effort to prevent the sort of captures made by Trooper Jackson and his comrades. Clement recalled, "It was fearful work to keep the men attentive. They didn't 'care a damn' for anything. They believed we were sure to be gobbled anyway. But not a shot did they [the Confederates] fire, nor did we discover that they followed us that night."[4]

An officer in the Fifty-fourth Massachusetts recorded an incident that shows that the Confederate cavalry was at least making its presence known during the retreat.

> One of our men a Serg't — on the retreat — was helping along a wounded man — when he was overtaken by reb cavalry — and ordered to surrender, he dropped his comrade [and] brought his gun to his shoulder — but the officer in charge of the reb cavalry aimed his revolver at his heart — both fired as one — the Sgt. shot dead — the officer wounded.[5]

Sergeant Clement recalled how hard it was to keep many of the white troops organized and attentive. Reports would seem to indicate that there was no such difficulty among the men in the black regiments. A sergeant in the Eighth U.S.C.T. commented, "It looked sad to see men wounded ... with their arms and equipments on," and observed that "so great was their endurance and so determined were they to defend themselves till the death. I saw white troops that were not badly wounded, that had thrown away everything."[6]

Finegan's victorious army held the field, and to them went the spoils of the battle. They had inflicted a large number of casualties on the Union army, but the reduction in Yankee manpower was only one of the things they gained that day. Five cannon, sixteen hundred small arms, four hundred sets of accoutrements, 130,000 rounds of ammunition, and a regimental flag had been captured from Seymour's army. More importantly, the Confederates had also gained absolute supremacy in the campaign. Seymour's gamble had proved to be a bust, and the defeat of his army at Olustee signaled the end of the Florida campaign and of the Administration's designs to reconstruct a Union government in the state. Florida would not be forcibly led back into the Union by an invading army, and the vast resources of the state would continue to aide the Confederate armies in resisting the North in other theaters of the war.

Seymour's army continued its retreat west toward its base in Jacksonville. Montgomery's Brigade was relieved, as the rear guard, with the Seventh Connecticut and Henry's Mounted Brigade assuming that role. The Union troops marched all the way back to Barber's that night,

Five • The Twilight of Battle

Picture of a portion of the Fortieth Massachusetts in skirmish drill. The regiment was mounted immediately prior to the Olustee Campaign and took a conspicuous part in the fighting, including covering the army's withdrawal toward Jacksonville (courtesy United States Army Military History Institute).

not stopping as they passed through Sanderson, where "wounded men lined the railroad station, and the roads were filled with artillery, caissons, ammunition and baggage wagons, infantry, cavalry and ambulances." But at Sanderson, Seymour's men came across a Union line of battle, formed and ready to resist the enemy. Major Appleton, of the Fifty-fourth Massachusetts, had been with the detached companies of the regiment, at Barber's, while the battle was being fought. Just before dusk, he was relieved of this duty and immediately started his small command forward, in the direction of Olustee. As they neared Sanderson, Appleton's men started to encounter the retreating remnants of the Union army. Appleton would later write that "my command was small but all the time there streamed by on the road groups of retreating soldiers.... I drew my pistol, ordered the non-commissioned officers to assist, and drove into my line every man that had cartridges in his cartridge box.... I soon had a motley regiment, white and black, that swore and growled but marched." Appleton's made-up force was not used to establish a new line at Sanderson, however. It instead accompanied the main body in the retreat toward Barber's.[7]

Back at Olustee, the smoke-shrouded field was witness not only to the darkness of the night, but also to the darkness that existed in the hearts of some of the Confederates who now walked over the

The Battle of Olustee, 1864

ground. William Penniman, a member of the Fourth Georgia Cavalry, was riding over the field after the Union retreat, noting, "It was niggers dead, niggers wounded in all directions, some severely, others not so much so, groans and prayers heard from them in all directions." He was confused, however, by the sound of firing "going on in every direction" which "sounded almost frequent enough to resemble the bark of skirmishers." Penniman observed a Confederate officer in the darkness and inquired as to the meaning of the firing. "Shooting niggers, Sir," was the answer he received. "I have tried to make the boys desist but I can't control them." Penniman protested that it was "horrible to kill the wounded devils" and the officer replied "That's so, Sir, but one young fellow over yonder told me the niggers killed his brother after being wounded at Fort Pillow, and he was twenty three years old, that he already killed nineteen and needed only four more to make the matter even, so I told him to go ahead and finish the job." Penniman went out to the field first thing next morning, "when the results of the shooting of the previous night became quite apparent. Negroes, and plenty of them, whom I had seen lying all over the field wounded, and as far as I could see, many of them moving around from place to place, now without motion, all were dead. If a negro had a shot in the shin another was sure to be in the head." Penniman did not conclude his recitation of the atrocities there. He went on to recount how "one ugly big buck was interrogated as to how it happened that he had come back to fight his old master, and upon his giving some very insolent reply, his interrogator drew back his musket, and with the butt gave him a blow that killed him instantly." He also speculated about cruelty among those black captives who had not been murdered. "A very few wounded were placed on the surgeons' operating table — their legs fairly flew off, but whether they were at all seriously wounded I have always had my doubt."[8]

It is estimated that some fifty wounded black soldiers were murdered on the field of Olustee that night. Considering the fact that the Confederates captured some two hundred prisoners, approximately 25 percent were killed after they became prisoners of war. There are several existing accounts of the atrocity, mentioned in letters and

Five • The Twilight of Battle

reminiscences, with the sentiments of the writer easily recognizable in each. Lieutenant Winston Stephens, in a letter to his wife written just after the battle, stated, "I wish I could never see a sight as I witnessed after the battle." Corporal Henry Shackelford, of the Nineteenth Georgia, wrote a letter to his mother, in which he bragged about how the Confederates had "walked over many a wooly head" and how "Our boys did walk into the niggers, they would beg and pray but it did no good." Another Georgian, Joab Roach, remembered that "after the battle the boys went over the battlefield and knoct [sic] the most of the wounded negroes in the head with lightwood knots." A wounded New Yorker, from Barton's Brigade, watched in horror as a wounded black soldier from the Eighth U.S.C.T. was attacked. "A rebel officer happened to see him, and saying 'Ah, you black rascal, you will not remain here long!' and dismounting from his horse, placed his revolver close to the negro's head and blew his brains out."[9]

Private James Jordan, of the Twenty-seventh Georgia, was another Confederate who related the barbarous acts. In a letter written the following day, he stated that the "negroes were badly cut up and killed. Our men killed some of them after they had fell into our hands wounded." Jordan also stated that the Northern prisoners expressed surprise to have run in to a Confederate army at Olustee. "They said they did not expect to meet nothing but cavalry here."[10]

Another Confederate, J.C. Rice, did not mention the killings in his remembrances, but he graphically described "the wounded filling the night air with lamentations, the crippled horses neighing in pain, and a full moon kissing the cold, clammy lips of the dying."[11]

To be sure, it was a minority of the Confederate army that participated in the atrocity that took place against the wounded black troops on the field that night. There was also a minority who actively tried to stop the killing and prevent the atrocity. Most of those who were aware of what was going on seemed to fall into the category of the "silent majority," those who neither participated nor tried to intercede on behalf of the wounded blacks. Dr. Heichold, of the First North Carolina, had been right in trying to remove every black soldier he could from the field before the army retreated. His anxiety over their

The Battle of Olustee, 1864

safety at the hands of the Confederates had proven to be correct in a most horrible fashion.

Lieutenant Oliver Norton, of the Eighth U.S.C.T., in a letter to his sister, displayed deep concern for his missing and wounded men. "A flag of truce from the enemy brought the news that prisoners, black and white, were treated alike," he wrote. "I hope it is so, for I have sworn never to take a prisoner if my men left there were murdered." Norton could not have known it, but many of his wounded men had already been the targets for acts of murder.[12]

In an effort to save his black soldiers who had been captured from becoming the objects of such retribution, General Seymour sent a message to General Finegan, a few days after the battle.

> To the general commanding the Confederate Forces, Florida:
>
> SIR: In view of the inconveniences to which the wounded prisoners in your hands since the action of the 20th, near Olustee, Fla., may be unavoidably subjected, I have the honor to propose that they may be paroled and delivered within my lines as soon as possible, and Capt. G.S. Dana, of my staff, the bearer of this communication, is authorized to make such arrangement therefore as may be convenient, and a horse-car or ambulance will be sent for the wounded at such times as may be designated, should this proposal be acceded to.
>
> The body of Col. C.W. Fribley was left upon the field at Olustee. If there have been any means of identifying his person, I request that his grave may be so marked that at some future day his family may be able to remove his remains.
> And I am, very respectfully, your obedient servant.
> T. Seymour
>
> Brigadier-General, U.S. Army

General Finegan responded to Seymour's request the very next day:

> Brig. Gen. T. Seymour,
>
> Commanding U.S. Forces, Jacksonville:

Five • The Twilight of Battle

> GENERAL: I have the honor to acknowledge the receipt of your communication of the 23d instant, proposing that the wounded prisoners left by you on the field of battle at Ocean Pond, on the 20th instant, be paroled and sent within your lines, and requesting that if the body of Col. C.W. Fribley, left on the ground, could be identified, his grave might be so marked that his family at some future day may be able to remove his remains.
>
> In reply, I have to state that the wounded prisoners have been sent forward and properly taken care of, to await the future action of my Government with reference to an exchange of prisoners.
>
> I regret to say that the body of Colonel Fribley has not been identified.
>
> Very respectfully, your obedient servant.
> Joseph Finegan,
> Brigadier — General, Commanding.[13]

In truth, General Finegan was not interested in cooperating with any search for either Fribley's body or his personal effects. He would later turn down another entreaty for information about the colonel, which included a request to allow Fribley's wife to pass through the lines. General William Gardner would later forward several of the colonel's personal items through the lines, to be given to his widow, but he made clear the fact that the act had not been done as a result of military courtesy. Gardner informed Seymour that he had no sympathy for the fate of any officer who commanded Negro troops in battle. His action was based solely on "compassion for a widow in grief," which had "induced these efforts to recover her relics which she must naturally value."[14]

A letter published in the Savannah Daily Morning News showed even less sympathy than had either Gardner or Finegan:

> Such was the case with the redoubtable Col. Frieble [sic], of a negro regiment, in whose pocket was found a letter from his wife (query black or white?) asking him to "confiscate" for her "a nice saddle when he reached Tallahassee."

The Battle of Olustee, 1864

> Yes! The black-hearted Frieble had a dog's burial. A leader of a horde of infuriated negroes, on a mission of murder, robbery and rape, ought he not have been left to rot on the plain, to the obscene birds to fatten on his vitals, and the great wolves to gnaw on his bones?[15]

Southern sentiments against the black troops and their white commanders were definitely at a fevered pitch following the close of the battle, as evidenced by the atrocious acts committed upon the wounded black soldiers on the field of Olustee following the battle. As this was still one of the early uses of black troops in combat, neither side was exactly sure what to expect as an outcome. True, black troops had previously seen action at Battery Wagner, Port Hudson, and Fort Pillow, but their use at Olustee was still considered by both sides to be a novel occurrence. As 1864 wore on, black troops would play an ever-increasing role in the battles that took place in all theaters of the war, but in February, they were just starting to make their presence known. Many Confederate soldiers held a strong prejudice against blacks serving in the Northern army, and the Southern government and military had inflamed this bias by proclaiming that the result of uniformed blacks would be servile insurrection throughout the South. Black troops had been portrayed as the harbingers of murder, plunder, and rape, and the average Southerner was led to believe that their wives and families would be the targets of black troops who would endeavor to punish every white person in the South for the institution of slavery. It was in this atmosphere of prejudice and fear that the despicable acts of a minority of Confederate soldiers took place. To be sure, many in the army entertained hatred for black soldiers, but the vast majority refrained from succumbing to acts of barbarity.

But there were also acts of heroic kindness that took place the night of the battle. When he heard of the battle, A.B. Day, an agent of the Sanitary Commission in Jacksonville,

> rushed to the very front, and [was] most assiduous in his attention to the wounded, regardless of danger or toil. In company with Mr. Taylor, the head of the Christian Commission here,

Five • The Twilight of Battle

> and Chaplain Haskell, of the 40th Mass. Regiment, who also deserves much credit, he remained behind, looking after the wounded, at the imminent danger of being captured, and they did not leave till every wounded man was started ahead of them.

With super-human effort, Day and his companions saved every wounded soldier they could get to, but that was limited to those who were in front of the Confederate lines only. Still, the humanitarian efforts of these brave men prevented a large number of wounded Federals from suffering the same fate as those who were unlucky enough to find themselves trapped behind the Rebel lines.[16]

By all accounts, those black troops who were lucky enough to survive the night of the battle were well treated once they were sent away for detainment. As well treated as were their white counterparts, that is. The Confederate government did not make good on its threat to place all such prisoners back into slavery, or to summarily execute them as insurrectionists. They were instead placed in the general population of the Confederate prisoner of war camps, with many of the blacks captured at Olustee being sent to Andersonville. Though the black troops fared well after being removed from Olustee, their white officers received the full ire of their Confederate captors and were roundly denounced for the part they played in leading black soldiers in battle.

Private James Flynn, of the Seventh New Hampshire, was among the wounded prisoners who had been captured following the battle. He had entered the army in the hope of finding his son, Thomas, who had run away to enlist at the age of fifteen. In fact, this was his third enlistment for that purpose, having previously served in the Lincoln Cavalry and in the Union Medical Department. In a letter written to his wife from Tallahassee shortly after the battle, Flynn said "If you were to see the wounded men you would pity them." He went on to assure her that they were "treated very kindly by the enemy as much so as the Circumstances care to admit." Flynn was never heard from again after sending this letter, and it is presumed that he died in a Confederate prison camp. His son had enlisted in the Sixty-second New York, and though he was never found by his father, he survived the war.[17]

Other Confederates scoured the field in search of valuables. Lieutenant Winston Stephens was one of these. "I am now writing this with a Yankee pen, Yankee ink, and Yankee paper captured on the battlefield," he would write to his wife. "I got several things of value, a blanket, tent, 2 oil cloth haversacks full of provisions and 2 flannel shirts, 1 pr. drawers, 1 pr. gamulletts, 3 canteens and I have got a fine sword from one of my men that got it on the field." Stephens went on to state that he was "so tired and dirty, I can hardly keep my eyes open to write." In canvassing the field for plunder he had also gotten a close-up look at the carnage of the battle, and related with horror that "never in all my life have I seen such a distressing sight, some men with their legs carried off others with their brains out and mangled in every conceivable way and then our men commenced stripping them of their clothing and left their bodies naked."[18]

By all accounts, the Confederates were celebrating their victory and were occupied in gathering up the spoils from the field. Though the pursuit had been called off by the infantry, due to darkness, precious hours were spent gleaning the field for trophies, time that could have been better spent in pressing the already defeated Union army. In all fairness, Finegan undoubtedly felt that his infantry deserved a rest. His cavalry had practically not been engaged in the battle, losing a total of three men in the entire brigade, and he probably assumed that his mounted force would press the enemy until he was ready to follow with the foot soldiers.

Corporal Henry Shackelford, of the Nineteenth Georgia, was another soldier who wrote of the spoils he gathered from the field at Olustee. Shackelford noted that he had been among those "detailed to bear the wounded from the field and we did a good deal of it too.... Our regiment supplied themselves with an outfit of oil cloth blankets, knapsacks, haversacks, and a number of gold and silver watches. I have donned a new Yankee suit." He also talked of the huge amount of rations that had been left upon the field. "How we did enjoy captured coffee, hams, bread, and everything else."[19]

Captain Wheaton's Battery was detailed to take charge of the Union artillery pieces, ammunition, and equipment that had been left on the field. Three of the five captured pieces were taken back to Wheaton's bivouac at Olustee Station, and the members of the battery spent all night and most of the following day gathering ammunition and artillery stores.[20]

But the spoils of victory were not the only thing the Confederates had to take from the countryside. Many soldiers were employed in removing the human cost of the battle from the smoke-covered field. General Finegan, in his report, listed that the Federals had left behind 418 wounded, nearly 400 dead, and some 200 prisoners. All of these would need to be tended to, particularly the wounded and the prisoners, most of whom were forwarded to Tallahassee, pending shipment to some other prisoner of war camp. The Tallahassee Floridian reported,

> Some 200 Yankee wounded have been brought to this city since the battle of Olustee, mostly foreigners and negroes, the foreigners were miserable looking fellows, not a bit too good to be put on an equity with the negroes; and in the hospital in every case, whites and negroes were laid side by side, in order to give the whites a taste of the equality they are fighting for.[21]

February 21 was a Sunday, and the people of the surrounding countryside availed themselves of the opportunity to give thanks for the Confederate triumph. Local ministers canvassed their congregations for bandages, lint, and any hospital supplies that could be gathered and forwarded to the army at Olustee. A number of wounded Southerners had already been taken to some of the small towns near Ocean Pond, and the residents quickly turned churches, public halls, and private homes into hospitals to care for the fallen soldiers. There were a number of wounded Yankees who found themselves among those being sent to local towns, and not to Tallahassee. For them, this first period of captivity was surprisingly kind. Several Union officers noted how well they were treated by the residents of the towns, and they especially noticed how the few black troops among their number received tender treatment at the hands of these benefactors. Possibly it was because their "mutilated bodies awakened no feeling but that of pity." Whatever the cause, those wounded Union troops who were held in the towns around Olustee and Ocean Pond certainly received better treatment than those who were forwarded to Tallahassee.[22]

But whether they were first sent to one of the small towns and hamlets around Olustee or to Tallahassee, most of the Union prisoners were eventually forwarded to the Confederate prison camp in Andersonville, Georgia. Major Archibald Bogle, of the Eighth United States Colored Troops, was among this number. Though Andersonville was intended to hold only enlisted men, Bogle's affiliation with black troops caused his captors to refuse to recognize his status as an officer. It also caused them to refuse to recognize his status as a soldier, or a human being. The Confederate medical staff would not attend to him, "perhaps hoping that he would die of his wounds." But Bogle survived. When he had regained his strength enough to be able to move about on crutches, he went to the hospital, where a steward, a fellow prisoner, started to apply a bandage to his leg. Confederate guards recognized his shoulder straps of rank and ordered the steward to stop ministering to his wounds and to send him back out "with his niggers." To his credit, Major Henry Wirz, the commandant of Andersonville, attempted to arrange a prisoner exchange for Bogle, or, at the very least, to have him sent to an officer's prison camp, but his efforts were in vain. Bogle would remain at Andersonville with his men until the camp was evacuated, many months later, to keep the prisoners from being released by Sherman's advancing army. Bogle would eventually be paroled at Wilmington, North Carolina, in March of 1865. He continued to serve in the army until 1871, when he was dismissed over an altercation with another officer.[23]

For his part, Finegan seemed content to gather up the Union plunder from the field and to collect and forward wounded Union prisoners. He and the main body of his army were still engaged in this activity on February 22, two days after the battle. General Beauregard, in Charleston, was chafing over what he saw to be a missed opportunity to finish off the Yankee army, and he was questioning the slowness of Finegan's pursuit. Finegan, in his own defense, cited the large number of wounded prisoners as a source of the delay. He also informed his superior that the number of his own wounded far exceeded that which he had originally reported. "The list will reach between 600 and 700, 300 or 400 of whom will be fit for duty in a few weeks, being but flesh wounds." Lastly, he stated that the Federals had damaged the railroad, which cost him a day to repair.[24]

Finegan made reference to the wounded, who occupied his time, and delayed his advance, but he made no mention of the many dead, both Union and Confederate, who also needed to be attended to. The Confederates, by and large, were buried on the south side of the railroad and were carefully interred. The bodies of the Union soldiers were handled with less care. They were buried on the north side of the railroad in shallow graves, "in such a careless manner that the remains were disinterred by the hogs within a few weeks after the battle, in consequence of which the bones and skulls were scattered broadcast over the battlefield." Lieutenant Frederick E. Grossman visited the battlefield in 1866, two years after the battle, with orders to gather the bones of the Federal dead and give them a proper burial. Grossman reported,

> I proceeded to collect those remains, to accomplish which I deployed a detachment of Company B, 7th Infantry, on the battlefield. The men carried an empty bag each, into which they gathered all the human bones found over the ground as they advanced.
>
> In many instances where portions of bones protruded, we removed the earth and disinterred all the bones that had not been disturbed by the hogs. In this manner and by carefully searching over an area of about two square miles, I collected two wagon loads and a half of bones. I then had a large grave dug eighteen feet by twelve feet, in which all the bones collected were deposited. I counted one hundred and twenty-five human skulls among the remains....
>
> Around the above ground I erected a fence twenty-seven feet long and eighteen feet wide, around which a ditch has been dug. I caused to be erected, by direction of Col. J.T. Sprague, a wooden monument twelve feet high with the following inscription:
>
> South side—"To the memory of the officers and soldiers of the United States army who fell in the Battle of Olustee, Feb. 20, 1864."

The Battle of Olustee, 1864

West side — "Our Country"

North side — "May the living profit by the example of the dead."

East side — "Unity and peace."[25]

SIX

FLIGHT TO THE COAST

Most of the soldiers in the defeated Union army were little concerned with the spoils they had left for the Confederates, or the fate of their comrades who had been captured. Jacksonville, and comparative safety, lay before them, and they plodded toward that city with a steady gait. No, they were not a fleeing mob. They were still soldiers in an organized army, but the men in Seymour's command were wasting little time in reaching their goal of the friendly confines of Jacksonville. Lieutenant James Clark, of the 115th New York, was streaming along with the wounded of the army.

> Some lay down along the road and declared that they could go no further. Others were fast bleeding to death, and some fell down exhausted to die. At last I reached Sanderson, nine miles distant. Several of us who concluded that we could go no further went into a hotel and lay down on the floor. A surgeon soon came in and said that unless we made all possible haste towards Barber's we would all be captured, and the rebels were close by. We all concluded that it would be better to die walking or even crawling towards freedom than to starve to death in rebel dungeons; so we moved off towards Barber's. A company of the 40th Massachusetts Mounted Infantry, came along and generally dismounted, helping thirty of our boys on their horses. This saved almost all of the party from capture. The animal which I rode carried me a mile with great difficulty, and then lay down in the mud to die. I started on again, when pretty shortly a mounted officer approached, and after inquiring my name, rank, and regiment, assisted me in mounting his horse which I rode two miles,

The Battle of Olustee, 1864

when I was again forced to try the virtue of "shanks horses." I reached Barber's at 3 o'clock in the morning, nearly dead, and found the remnant of the regiment asleep. I sat down on a cracker box to warm myself by a camp fire, when I fainted away and pitched into it headlong. There were four cars at Barber's to carry the many hundreds of wounded, but I was fortunate enough to get on one.[1]

When the army marched into Barber's, it was retracing its way back toward Baldwin. Barber's had been reached at 2:00 A.M., the morning after the battle. "You may imagine in what condition," wrote one footsore and weary soldier in the ranks. It had been an eighteen-mile march from Olustee for men who had marched all the day before, and fought a battle, before starting this retreat for the coast. Many had not eaten since early the previous day, and fatigue and hunger were beginning to show in their faces.[2]

At Barber's, General Seymour made arrangements for the burning of all the stores that had been stockpiled for the use of the army that could not be taken along with them. In all, some $60,000 worth of military stores and confiscated property were put to the torch. A train that had recently arrived, loaded with additional stores, was unloaded, and the contents were consigned to the fire. It was then filled with wounded troops, Lieutenant Clark among them, and sent back to Jacksonville. This train would later become the focus of an extraordinary act of heroism by the men of the Fifty-fourth Massachusetts. While in Barber's General Seymour also caused the destruction of personal property belonging to a local resident by the name of Derby. It seems that Derby had sought and obtained protection for his house from the Union army. He was afterward found to be providing the Confederates with information concerning the size and intentions of the Yankees. Seymour personally directed that his property be destroyed before the army, after its brief halt, marched out of the town. Orders were given to the officers to push the men forward. Jacksonville was to be reached by nightfall. At Barber's, Seymour received his first reinforcements, as he made contact at that place with elements of the Fifty-fifth Massachusetts that had been in bivouac there.[3]

154

Six • *Flight to the Coast*

The scene of destruction continued when the army reached Baldwin. Captain Gustavus Dana reported,

> We found 183,000 rounds Enfield & 2 boxes Spencer ammunition on the depot platform which I was ordered to destroy. One wing of a colored regt was reported to me to open the boxes and empty the cartridges into a deep ditch beside the track. Several of the darkeys couldn't wait to unscrew the box covers but used axes to chop them off & got the flat of a sword over their backs to pay for it. A few hundred yards from the station a large warehouse with an immense pile of bbls of crude turpentine was fired and the dense smoke so obscured everything that it seemed night had fallen.[4]

Lieutenant Henry Little, of the Seventh New Hampshire, recalled the scene in detail:

> Here we stopped to rest a few moments, and during our halt at this place a large quantity of cotton and five hundred barrels of resin which had been captured were ordered to be burned, together with such of our own stores and government property as it was found impossible to remove. As we got into line to resume the march, I think the comrades of our regiment will remember what a dense, black smoke-cloud the resin and cotton made, so black, even, that we could not see the sun, although the day was clear and fine. Each man was here given ninety rounds of ammunition and as much more as he chose to carry, in order to save it from being destroyed.[5]

Dana's efforts to keep the ammunition from falling into Confederate hands were in vain, however. Flames spread through the little town, engulfing the depot, as well as a nearby hotel, and the heat was so intense that it dried up the water in the ditch where the cartridges had been dumped. The Confederates were later able to retrieve the ammunition and make use of it. The damaged cartridges were sent to the ordnance bureau, in Savannah, where they were salvaged and later used against the Yankees.[6]

Seymour had good reason for wanting to abandon Baldwin and

push on for Jacksonville. He was governed by the belief that the Confederates greatly outnumbered his own army, and his actions were those of a commander who was trying to save his command from being gobbled up by a superior force. Before leaving Baldwin, Seymour had sent a dispatch to General J.W. Turner, Department of the South, stating that he had received "authentic information" regarding the size of the army he had faced at Olustee, and this intelligence placed the number of men in the Confederate force to be as high as 15,000, or roughly triple that of Seymour's command. Though a defensive position had previously been constructed at Baldwin, Seymour did not believe it to be strong enough to withstand the number of troops he believed to be in the Confederate army. Jacksonville, he felt, offered a much better defensive position against these overwhelming odds. In reality, the Union army did not need to be in a rush to leave Baldwin, as the Confederate force was the same size as Seymour's. The Federals should have easily been able to defend the prepared position, especially since reinforcements from the coast were already being hurried to their assistance.[7]

Colonel J.L. Otis's Tenth Connecticut, stationed in St. Augustine, was ordered to march for Jacksonville without delay. Otis replied that his regiment would assist "with everything possible with the means at my disposal," but the addition of the Tenth Connecticut would not materially strengthen Seymour's force. Otis had but 180 men in his command, and of these, 16 were musicians and 30 were staff clerks. The Ninety-seventh Pennsylvania, stationed at Fernandina, was also instructed to move to Jacksonville, without delay. More substantial aid was coming from Charleston, in the form of the brigades of General Adelbert Ames and General Robert Foster. Ames was instructed to embark some 1,300 troops "with all possible dispatch, sending them to report at Jacksonville as soon as the vessels can cross the bar after receiving troops." The remainder of his brigade, as well as that of Foster's, was to follow as soon as possible. Ames' initial reinforcements set sail on February 23, from Folly Island, followed the next day by Foster with the main body.[8]

Help was on its way, but Seymour still had to get his own fatigued army back to the Jacksonville area to effect a rendezvous with these forces. The men of the Fifty-fourth Massachusetts plodded through the night, many of them throwing away anything that might slow them down in their march. One soldier wryly commented that they had been in "a fight, a licking, and a foot race." When they marched out of Baldwin, at 9 A.M. on the 21st, there were still 22 miles that stood between them and Jacksonville. It was a weary and footsore group of soldiers who trudged into the environs of the city later that day, and one can imagine that every enlisted man and officer was looking forward to a well deserved respite. But the men of the Fifty-fourth were not to be given a rest period; not quite yet. They would be called upon to perform one more service to the army before being allowed to rest. Back at Olustee, the regiment had materially aided in allowing General Seymour the opportunity to extricate his army from the field. Now, they were called on to save a portion of that army from being captured by the Confederates. The train that had been unloaded, at Baldwin, and filled with wounded soldiers had broken down at Ten Mile Station, ten miles west of Jacksonville. The engine had been overtaxed and rendered useless, and the men in the cars were stranded on the track. "Through eagerness to escape the supposed pursuing enemy, too great pressure of steam was employed, and the flue collapsed," one man stated. Over 300 wounded Union soldiers lay on the flatcars, unable to escape any pursuit that the Confederates might mount. The Union commanders did not yet know that Finegan's entire army was not in their rear. Instead, it was merely a couple companies of the Second Florida Cavalry, but that was all that would have been necessary to bag this lot of defenseless wounded men. The Fifty-fourth was ordered to march to Ten Mile Station, with all possible haste, and to bring back the wounded men who were trapped there.[9]

The men "faced about cheerfully," when informed of the nature of their mission by their officers. They marched back to Ten Mile Station despite the fact that most of the men were thoroughly exhausted and hadn't eaten since before the battle had been fought. The event was chronicled by a correspondent, who wrote: "And here the immortal Fifty-fourth [colored] did what ought to ensure it higher praise than to hold the field in the face of a victorious foe — with ropes it seized the engine [now useless] and dragged it with its doomed freight for many miles.... They knew their fate if captured; their humanity triumphed. Does history record a nobler deed?" The men of the Fifty-fourth didn't just bring back the helpless men who were stranded on the flatcars. They scoured the local countryside, gathering up any wounded stragglers they could find, and added them to the train as well. "The cars were terribly crowded; as many as seventy being on a small platform," and in many cases, the wounded had to "hang together to keep from falling off.... They had nothing to eat or drink, were so crowded that they could not sleep, and no chance to change their cramped and painful positions." Through brute strength, the men of the Fifty-fourth propelled the train along the tracks, some using ropes, some using vines they had found nearby, and some merely placing a shoulder to the load and pushing with all the strength they had left. There are reports that some mules that were found nearby were also pressed into service. In the end, the train was man-handled back to Jacksonville, and none of the wounded were left to be captured by the Confederates. Once safely back in Jacksonville, many of the wounded were loaded on to hospital boats and sent to Hilton Head and Beaufort, some 160 miles away.[10]

When the wounded from Olustee arrived in Beaufort aboard the *Cosmopolitan*, many of the officers at that place were engaged in the merriment of a ball. The arrival of the wounded did not suspend the festivities, but one Union soldier remarked, "Although war has hardened our hearts, and rendered us callous to its horrors in a great degree, yet few could look upon such a scene of festivity without being struck with its incongruity, when within a few hundred yards of it lay groaning and dying men."[11]

The Fifty-fourth Massachusetts had marched 120 miles in 102 hours. It had taken a conspicuous part in a battle and had saved a large number of men from capture, and amazingly, "the roll-call showed no stragglers." By the time the Fifty-fourth Massachusetts arrived back in Jacksonville, nearly half the men were barefoot, having worn out their shoes during the march, "their blankets and knapsacks were sacrificed to get speedily into action; they had no rations or shelter, so with crippled feet and weary limbs they cast themselves on the bare ground for rest...." Captain Robert Newell described the march as "the hardest day of all." Abolitionist leaders in Massachusetts had determined to raise the regiment, in an effort to prove to the world that the black man was capable of being the equal of whites in the army and that blacks were ready, willing, and able to fight for their own freedom. It had been something of an experiment, designed to increase awareness and lessen prejudice among the white population of the North. The experiment was a great success. The conduct of the men of the regiment, at Battery Wagner and at Olustee, served to convince large numbers of whites, both inside the army and out, that black troops could assume an important role in putting down the rebellion and ending the war.[12]

Though not called upon to rescue stranded wounded comrades, the other regiments of Seymour's army were experiencing hardships similar to those of the Fifty-fourth during the retreat. A member of the Third Rhode Island Battery wrote, "In ninety hours we have marched 110 miles."[13] Men in most of the regiments underwent difficulties such as those related by the historian of the Seventh New Hampshire. At approximately noon of the 21st, the army stopped briefly at Camp Finegan, the permanent camp used by the Confederates prior to the expedition. It had been used as a garrison post for the Southern troops stationed there, and was "provided with log houses ... instead of tents." One soldier in the Seventh New Hampshire related,

> Here the stores which our troops had captured at the time of our advance, consisting of bacon or smoked sides, tobacco, sugar, and clothing, were dealt out promiscuously to all the troops, the men of the Seventh managing to get a goodly share of the bacon and tobacco. What was not used or taken by the men was destroyed. We rested here only a few moments, and again started on our march, reaching a place on King's Road about six miles out from Jacksonville that night, where we went into camp temporarily, and were at once ordered on picket duty.

As the weary Union soldiers of Seymour's army tramped into Jacksonville, they were not allowed to rest as most "at once commenced work on the yet unfinished earthworks around that city" Captain Newell recalled, "For two or three days after getting here, the men had hardly anything to eat, as it was impossible to get rations. We have been particularly unfortunate, having lost all our hardtack by the wreck of the Burnside, as well as our clothes on the march & partly to the horrible bread which is baked for the men." The Union army was hungry and almost tired out. but help was already arriving from other parts of the Department of the South, in the form of manpower, as well as rations and supplies. Though they may not have been aware of it then, the men of Seymour's command would be able to hold their positions around Jacksonville against anything the Confederates might throw against them.[14]

Thus far, Confederate pursuit existed only in the imagination of the Federal troops. Only a small harassing force of cavalry was nipping at the heels of the tired Northern men, but that was soon to change. General Finegan, with his army well rested and largely re-equipped, was now ready to march out of his position at Ocean Pond and Olustee and press the Yankees. General Beauregard, at Charleston, was showing signs of exasperation in his messages to Finegan, fearing that each passing minute lessened the chance that Seymour's army could be destroyed. Finegan related,

> On the 23d instant, having repaired the railroad so as to secure my supplies, I advanced the command to Sanderson, pushing the cavalry rapidly in the direction of the enemy, and from Sanderson to Barber's, and thence to Baldwin, and to this place, twelve miles from Jacksonville, where my further progress was arrested by orders from Brigadier-General Gardner, who had been directed to assume command, by whom I was here, for the first time, officially notified, that the command had been transferred.[15]

Finegan's leading role in the campaign had come to a close. He had not been Beauregard's choice for army command, and had assumed that position only because General Gardner was not immediately on hand when the army was being collected together at Ocean Pond. When

Gardner did arrive, it was determined that Finegan be allowed to continue in command, as it was felt that a change on the eve of battle would negatively impact the army and upset the plans that were then in place. Now, with the battle over, Beauregard took the opportunity to place the ranking officer in the district in his proper position, at the head of the army, but even this was a temporary solution. General Patton Anderson was on his way to Florida, with orders from Beauregard to replace Gardner upon his arrival.

Beauregard's first choice for the Florida command was General Alexander Taliaferro, but he was not readily available for transfer to that theater, so Patton Anderson got the nod. General Gardner, for his part, was somewhat uncomfortable about replacing Finegan, as can be seen by his official response to that officer upon taking command.

> General, I have sent you by telegraph a message from department headquarters, handed to me after leaving Lake City for this place, directing me to assume command of the forces now operating in East Florida until the arrival of General Taliaferro [Gardner had not yet learned that the assignment was going to Anderson] who has been ordered to that command. I feel extreme delicacy in assuming command over an officer whose forces have gained so recently such signal success over the enemy, but the receipt of the telegram from the general commanding the department necessarily imposes upon me some responsibility for the future movement of our forces. I cannot think but that the moment for reaping the full benefit of your success has passed. The enemy has doubtless taken full advantage of the interval since the battle of the 20th instant to reorganize his defeated forces, and he may not only have strongly entrenched himself, but may be receiving reinforcements. In view of the fact that heavy reinforcements, both of infantry and cavalry, are now en route and may soon be expected to arrive, it appears more prudent to act on the defensive for the present; but if, through Maj. G.W. Scott, appointed chief of the vendettas, or any other reliable information, you are convinced that no considerable body of the enemy are occupying a strong position between the Saint

Mary's and Jacksonville, you will be authorized to cross that river with the main body of your forces, provided measures are taken to secure your safe retreat across the river if it should be found necessary to do so. Keep me advised by telegram of what is transpiring. Should General Taliaferro not arrive in a few days I will return to the front.

Very respectfully, your obedient servant,
W.M. Gardner,
Brigadier-General, Commanding"[16]

Gardner was following orders and assuming command of the army, but he would direct its activities from a distance until his replacement arrived. He did not hurry to the front to personally supervise the immediate situation, instead choosing to remain right where he was, in Tallahassee, showing General Finegan the professional courtesy of allowing him to continue in field command of his forces. He did, however, change the focus of the army from offensive to defensive operations, acknowledging that the time to achieve a crushing blow over Seymour's defeated army was gone. The Confederate army would content itself, from this point onward, to guarding against any further Federal incursions and defending the territory it now held in the state.

Seymour was aware that the Confederates were on the move, but he was not quite sure how close the rebel army was, in what numbers, or the nature of its intentions. On February 24, he sent Captain Gustavus Dana to make contact with the main body, ostensibly for the purpose of proposing an exchange of the wounded. In reality, Seymour merely wanted Dana to scout the Southern position and ascertain its location and strength. Dana later wrote,

> It was supposed the rebels were certainly as near as 10 mile station where their cavalry had appeared, so on nearing that point I moved in cautiously.
>
> The rebels were a primitive set down there. Capt. Chambers' guerrillas had so far had full swing, shooting and hanging all suspected of Unionism and Gen. Seymour had assured me if they did not respect my flag of truce and harmed me he would hang

every white resident in Jacksonville but I couldn't see how that would affect my status after I was done for. Col. Henry advised me to let them know as soon as possible that I was in the regular army as their special spite was against volunteers & for me to conceal the fact that I was not a West Pointer. I had arrived within sight of the earthworks we had erected at Baldwin 21 miles from J(acksonville) before I saw a sign of life, then three vendettas threw their legs over their horses and skipped. I kept on up to where their post had been, sent my escort in the edge of the timber bordering the road and stood in the middle of the road with my flag. Soon sixteen mounted & fully armed officers came galloping towards me and apparently intended to run me down. When they halted I asked for the senior officer and handed him my dispatches for Gen. (Joseph) Finegan, asking how long I must wait for an answer; after some study over that, he named the time that showed me at once (Knowing the route so well) that the general was at Barber's, and I already had all the information I needed.

They were green enough to ask me to come with them to Baldwin but I declined and said I would stay with my escort. Shortly after while seated on a log by the side of the road and slyly making notes of the information gained I heard a stealthy step behind me and I had just time to pocket my memorandum and turn to greet a sorry looking specimen; he proved to be a lieut. of Chambers Guerrillas and had been sent to keep me company. He sat on the log handling his pistol as if he wanted to accidentally use it; noticed how well-equipped my escort was. We were rigged up in our best and I had borrowed a quartermaster's full rig for my mare. He remarked "We are pore, we know we are pore, but our cause is just." After a while he said if he had anything to eat he would offer me some so I took the hint and shared my hardtack, raisins & whiskey with him. Some of the other rebel officers came out from Baldwin and the senior, a Colonel, apologized for having first appeared with arms; said they noticed I had none and learned since that it was not proper but said it was the first flag of truce he had met and next time would know how. They were friendly and cordial but didn't bring me any lunch; perhaps had none.

When the response to Seymour's message finally was delivered, Dana and his escort took their leave of the Confederates, and made haste to get back to Jacksonville and deliver the news that the Confederate main body was between Baldwin and Barber's.[17]

The Confederates continued to press in toward Jacksonville, and their position was being entrenched and protected by earthworks, called Camp Milton. The fortified camp was started immediately upon the arrival in the vicinity of Finegan's army, and it was completed by March 3, at which time there were some 8,000 Southern soldiers occupying the line in front of Seymour's army.[18]

Beauregard was correct in his assessment of the situation in Florida. The Union army was being strengthened, and any possibility for delivering a knock-out blow was gone. While at Jacksonville, most of the furloughed veterans returned to their regiments, following their re-enlistment leaves, and these units were brought up to full strength. More than that, these additions were tried and true troops, not the substitutes and replacements who had largely fought in the battle. In the case of Battery C, Third Rhode Island Light Artillery, the portion of the battery that was still at Hilton Head was immediately forwarded to Jacksonville. Of more consequence than the returning veterans were the additional regiments that General Gillmore was releasing from his own army to augment Seymour's force. The brigades of General Adelbert Ames and Robert Foster had set sail from Folly Island on February 24 and were arriving in Jacksonville later that night and into the following morning. Colonel Louis Bell's Fourth New Hampshire Infantry had also been added to Seymour's army, and with the additional manpower and the work on his entrenchments, Seymour was able to report on the 25th that his position was "sufficiently advanced to insure, I believe, a successful defense."[19]

The addition of Ames's and Foster's brigades led to a reorganization of Seymour's army, and his force was split into two divisions, as follows:

First Division — Brigadier General Israel Vogdes
    First Brigade — Brigadier General Robert Foster

Six • Flight to the Coast

  Thirteenth Indiana Infantry
  112th New York Infantry
  169th New York Infantry
  Fourth New Hampshire Infantry
  Twenty-fourth Massachusetts Infantry
 Second Brigade — Colonel Lloyd Tilghman
  First North Carolina Infantry (Colored)
  Third United States Colored Troops
 Third Brigade — Colonel James Montgomery
  Second South Carolina Infantry (Colored)
  Third South Carolina Infantry (Colored)
  Langdon's Battery, 1st United States Light Artillery

Second Division — Brigadier General Adelbert Ames
 First Brigade — Colonel John Noble
  Seventeenth Connecticut Infantry
  Fortieth Massachusetts Infantry
  147th New York Infantry
  157th New York Infantry
  Twenty-fifth Ohio Infantry
  Seventy-fifth Ohio Infantry
 Second Brigade — Colonel Joseph Hawley
  Seventh Connecticut Infantry
  Seventh New Hampshire Infantry
 Third Brigade — Colonel M.S. Littlefield
  Fifty-fourth Massachusetts Infantry (Colored)
  Fifty-fifth Massachusetts Infantry
  James's Battery C, 3rd Rhode Island Light Artillery

Unassigned
 Barton's Brigade — Colonel William Barton
  Forty-seventh New York Infantry
  Forty-eighth New York Infantry
  115th New York Infantry
 Henry's Brigade — Colonel Guy Henry
  Fortieth Massachusetts Mounted Infantry

The Battle of Olustee, 1864

Independent Battalion Massachusetts Cavalry
Elder's Battery B, First United States Horse Artillery[20]

These troops were not part of an effort to resume the offensive in Florida. They had been sent there to insure that Seymour's army was not gobbled up by the Confederates and to consolidate the hold the Union had on the area in and around Jacksonville. As such, their time spent in Florida would be brief. On February 28, General Gillmore was already informing Seymour that his forces in Florida would be reduced as soon as the situation was stable there. The previous day, he had been instructed to send Vogdes's Brigade back to South Carolina and to retain only three of the transports that had been used to carry the reinforcements to him. The Ninety-seventh Pennsylvania was also released from duty at Jacksonville and ordered to return to Fernandina.[21]

Seymour's defensive strategy involved the construction of "an extensive line of earthworks ... encircling the town." Jacksonville was to become and entrenched city, capable of being held by a relatively small force.

General Beauregard had responded to the Union build-up in Florida by stripping his defenses in Charleston and Savannah and sending every available man to General Gardner's command. Though Beauregard felt his own position at Charleston to be tenuous, and Brigadier General H.W. Mercer, at Savannah, believed his position to have been left vulnerable, the following reinforcements were sent:

First Georgia Regulars (remainder of the regiment)
Fifth Georgia Cavalry
Eleventh South Carolina Infantry
Eighteenth South Carolina Infantry
Twenty-sixth Virginia Infantry
Fifty-ninth Virginia Infantry
Holcombe Legion
South Carolina Siege Train (one company)
Villepigue's Battery, Light Artillery
Wheaton's Battery, Light Artillery

Six • *Flight to the Coast*

These additions placed the number of men in, or en route to, Florida at approximately 17,000 Confederacy was being sorely pressed on all fronts, and this collection of manpower was more than its armies could reasonably sustain for any period of time. The Army of Tennessee, under General Joseph E. Johnston, was in dire need of reinforcements, and Beauregard had promised to help with everything he could spare. The concentration in Florida temporarily upset those plans, but Beauregard informed Richmond that he was confident the situation in Florida would soon be in hand and that he would be able to send Johnston about 8,000 men in the very near future. At this time, the Southern commander was not aware that his Union counterparts were also scrambling to down-size their commitment to the Sunshine State. Both sides seemed content to assume a status quo posture and return to the military conditions that had been in place before the Union expeditionary force had landed in the state.[22]

The arrival of General Patton Anderson witnessed a reorganization of the Confederate army in Florida. Anderson divided his regiments into three brigades, commanded respectively by Generals Finegan, Colquitt, and Harrison. Colonel Charles Jones was given command of the artillery, (four batteries of light artillery) and two batteries of siege guns were put under the command of Major George L. Buist. The cavalry was organized into a brigade under the command of Colonel Robert H. Anderson. General Anderson's objective in Florida was clear. He was to guard the state from further penetrations by the Union army and safeguard the valuable supplies that Florida provided to the Confederate armies. In addition, he was to protect the railroad leading to Cedar Key. His mission was to be defensive in nature, blocking the Federals from making excursions into the interior of the state. He was not to pursue offensive operations against Jacksonville, St. Augustine, Fernandina, or any other point along the coast where the Union had established a stronghold. In essence, he was to hold the Federals to the sections of the state that they had held prior to the Olustee campaign, with the only notable addition being another occupation of Jacksonville. By adopting this strategy, the number of Confederate troops in Florida could be greatly reduced, and manpower could be sent to other theaters of conflict, where it was more sorely needed.[23]

Skirmishes and brushes with raiding parties and Confederate guerrillas became the order of the day, as both sides focused their attention on the major campaigns that were shaping up in Virginia and in Georgia. Aside from the occasional small disturbances, the troops in Florida, on both sides, settled back into a garrison existence and the constant effort to supplement a soldier's rations with additional fare. James Dancy was a member of the Fifth Florida Cavalry. He noted that when the excitement of the campaign had died down, the men

> were moved west on the outskirts of Lake City to camp in Ross's field. In this enclosure were all species of farm and domestic animals — cattle, sheep, hogs, etc. I had a colored boy as body servant and cook. One morning he came to tell me that our mess chest was too full of meat for the cover to shut down. I went to see what the trouble was. There was at least one-half of a large hog. I was told by one of my mess to be quiet. He explained that a raiding party had been out that night and had killed and cleaned one of Ross's fattening hogs. Several days after, it appeared that the Confederate Commissary supply department was located in an old storage warehouse near the railroad depot. The train would bring in cars loaded with government supplies. The commissary captain would ask for a detachment of the men in camp to unload these cars. Part of this detachment was of our company. They found while they were storing supplies in this warehouse that the only fastening to the back door was a bar from one casing across to the other, placed behind loops, leaving a crack between the doors wide enough to insert a chisel and lift the bar out of the loops. As the door was wide open, they could easily load a wagon with just such supplies as they wished. One of my messmates assisted in doing this. One morning my servant came to me with the same complaint about the mess chest. I went to it and found it was full of sides of bacon, hams, etc., as it had been before. Very soon the commissary captain discovered the thefts and put bolts above the bar at each end to keep it from being lifted.[24]

Six • Flight to the Coast

Union soldiers were not against using the same techniques to add to their normal larder of hardtack and salt pork. Sergeant Patrick Egan, of the Third Rhode Island Light Artillery, recalled when the battery was detailed to garrison Palatka, a few days after it arrived in Jacksonville, following the battle.

> When we occupied Palatka the only white person in the village was an old lady who had a very nice residence, and Colonel Barton, the commander of the brigade, made his headquarters there. This woman had a very nice cow, the only one in the village, and Barton was dependent on her for milk.
> During the day the cow would feed in the door yards and on the lawns, and sometimes she would come around to where Battery C was camped. One day some of the boys thought what a nice steak and liver they could get from the cow, and at the same time get square with Barton, he not being a favorite with the boys. They thought they might kill two birds with one stone by getting the steak and liver and at the same time cutting off Barton's milk supply. So the next day when the cow came along one of the boys drove her into a back yard near the camp, and in a short time that cow was a thing of the past. Steaks and liver were cut out for those who had done the work and for their friends, and the rest of the meat was sent to the cookhouse, where all had nice beef stew. Everything was all right until milking time, when the cow failed to show up. Then the fun began. Men were sent out from headquarters and also from the provost marshal's office trying to find the cow and making inquiries. Of course the men of Battery C knew nothing about her. But they were eventually suspected, for the next morning the provost marshal came to our quarters asking all kinds of questions. Some of the boys, including your humble servant, knew nothing about it and were sorry for the colonel. The following morning Colonel Barton sent for the non-commissioned officers and told us that he was satisfied that the last seen of the cow was near Battery C's camp. He also said that all he wanted was the name of the man who killed the cow, and that some of the non-commissioned officers must know something about it. He then asked each one the name of the man who killed the cow, but each denied all knowledge about it. Well, someone must have given

the whole thing away, for the next day Captain James had the "Assembly" blown and the company fell in. He then called the names of nine men, comprising one sergeant, one corporal, and seven privates. The sergeant and corporal were reduced to the ranks, and with the other seven were confined in the guard house, put on a diet of bread and water, and made a "spread eagle" of until some one would tell who killed the cow. Morning and evening they were asked who killed the cow, but they denied they knew who did it. This was carried on for three days, when some one put up a job with the pickets, and on the afternoon of the third day they began firing, and the long roll was beat and the prisoners were released to man the guns. No "Johnnies" appeared, it being a bluff to get them released. They could not be punished again for the same offense, so thus ended the "cow incident," but Colonel Barton never found out who killed the cow.[25]

A return to garrison life may have provided the soldiers an opportunity for more of the comforts of life, but many in the army were ready to trade in those comforts for active campaigning. The defeat at Olustee was a sore spot with the Union army, and most of the troops who had been involved in the fighting wished the chance to avenge the loss. Now, with the return of the veterans, many clamored for action. Captain James, W. Grace, of the Fifty-fourth Massachusetts, wrote, "All we want now is more troops; with them we would go forward again and drive the rebels from the State."[26]

Captain Grace may have been presenting a fair assessment of the morale of the men, but it was far from a fair assessment of the military situation in Florida. The men who had fought there would have to avenge the loss and redeem the reputations of their regiments on some other field of battle. Union high command had already decided that enough time and effort had been expended in the state, and it was to be left in the hands of the victorious Confederates.

SEVEN

FINAL OPERATIONS

When news of the failed Florida campaign started to become known to the people of the North, the press led the charge in condemning the Lincoln administration for the calamity. The New York World offered an assessment that was typical of the sentiments of most of the people of the North: "Of course, no military purpose took an army into Florida, as the conquest of Florida would do no more to put down the rebellion than would the occupation of Yucatan or Coney Island. The object is political. Florida has been marked as one of the rotten borough states which are to help make Mr. Lincoln President." Gideon Welles, Lincoln's Secretary of the Navy, stated that he felt "the President has been trying a game himself." By March 1, John Hay admitted defeat and advised the president that after the battle of Olustee the prospect of inducing ten percent of the population to take the oath of allegiance was gone. "I am sure that we can not get the President's 10th," he wrote, and the project of bringing a reconstructed Florida back into the Union in time to affect the fall election was abandoned.[1]

Albert Stickney, who had stood to benefit greatly from a reconstructed Florida, was still full of schemes and unwilling to admit that the project was dead. He called for further military action, while denouncing Seymour as the sole cause of the reversal of fortunes the expedition had thus far sustained. He also took the opportunity to assail Seymour's political beliefs, laying the foundation for suspicions that Seymour's efforts were not what they should have been due to his lack of conviction in the purpose of the expedition. Stickney stated that the defeat was the result of incaution if not rashness akin to his assault on Ft. Wagner. I accord to him many high qualities of the soldier, but he is without the just balance of a military commander. The Florida campaign opened so well, I hoped, as it might have been and by proper direction reverse would not befall us. Gen. Seymour too is not in accord with us politically but if he will do the fighting in good style, his copperhead ablations might be pardoned.[2]

General Seymour also came under fire from the abolitionists for the part that his black regiments had played in the battle. Many in the North felt that the general had made poor use of these black troops and had sacrificed their lives in the battle in ways that he would not have done had they been white soldiers. A newspaper correspondent from the New York Times was quick to come to Seymour's defense, but in doing so he showed his own prejudices. He stated that Seymour was not an officer to "over-indulge any of his troops, either colored or white," and he told the supporters of the black troops in the North that they had no grounds to accuse Seymour of any misconduct pertaining to the usage of those troops. He went on to say,

> The value of the colored soldiers has been thoroughly tested, and as far as my experience goes, it is equal to that of white troops, when the latter are within supporting distance. They must have an example to go by. In my opinion, it would be a fearful mistake to send a body of colored troops into a fight without having nearby a force of white soldiers. I do not believe in placing him above the white one, for it is the latter after all that we must depend on to achieve our signal victories.[3]

Major William Furness, a judge advocate in the army, did not concern himself with whether Seymour handled his black troops improperly. To him, the entire army was the victim of the sub-standard performance of its commander. While not openly condemning Seymour, Major Furness was highly critical of his handling of the army at Olustee. He asserted that

Seven • Final Operations

> it hardly seems as if he [Seymour] observed due caution in going into action, since he did not begin to develop the plan until close to the hostile lines and already under fire. When aware of his advance being in contact with the enemy he ought with common prudence to have formed a line of battle, brought up his second and third brigades to within proper supporting distance and then his plan might have been successful. As it was, it was shattered before it was begun.

Furness's statement absolutely pointed to his mismanagement of the battle and forwarded the opinion that the battle could have resulted in a Union victory, if it had been conducted properly.[4]

One critic of the campaign thought,

> Had the advance been conducted with the same cautious, soldierly calculations which characterized the retreat the conflict would have ended in a victory for the Union. However, when he reached Baldwin and Jacksonville, Seymour again lost his head; for having lost about 250 killed and 1,200 wounded, he now destroyed over one million dollars' worth of Government stores.[5]

General Seymour, for his part, was not finding fault or placing blame for the defeat. Instead, he took the opportunity, once the army was safely positioned in the entrenchments around Jacksonville, to issue a congratulatory order to his men:

> Headquarters, District of Florida,
> Department of the South.
>
> General Orders No. 13.
>   The Brigadier General commanding, recurs with great satisfaction to the conduct of his troops in their late battle, and desires to convey to them in the most public manner, his full appreciation of their steadfast courage on that well contested field.
>   Against superior numbers, holding a position chosen by themselves, you were all but successful.
>   For four hours you stood face to face with the enemy, and

when the battle ended, and it ceased only with night, you sent him three cheers of defiance.

In your repulse there was perhaps misfortune; but neither disaster or disgrace; and every officer and soldier may forever remember with just pride that he fought at Olustee.

By order of Brig. Gen. T. Seymour.[6]

Although public opinion was largely against Seymour and his management of the campaign, the general did have his supporters, in and out of the army. A correspondent of the *Boston Herald* tried to put a spin on the situation when he wrote:

> The troops were held exceedingly well in hand, and perfect control of them was generally maintained. General Seymour, always brave, cool, quick in his perceptions and in forming his judgment, stands higher than ever with his troops. Through the fight he was in its midst, never excited while his officers and men were falling. That he got out of a very bad scrape exceedingly well, is admitted by everyone. Gen. Seymour never shirks responsibility, and I believe that he does not divide them in this case at all. At any rate General Gillmore is not responsible for the disaster, I understand that he disapproved of the advance, and I know that when he learned it was contemplated, he sent his Chief of Staff down with instructions forbidding it, but he arrived the evening of the battle.
>
> That Gen. Seymour did what he considered to be his duty, no one who knows him and appreciates him will question, or that he is an officer of great ability. Whether this move was a fault or misfortune, it is not my province to decide, but I know all intelligent and patriotic people will sympathize with him in either case, in whatever light the affair is viewed Gen. Gillmore's superior ability is more than ever apparent. I judged that this reverse will soon be redeemed, for I know we have the Generals and the troops to do it if there is the least opening.

The writer was obviously attempting to garner support for Seymour and his actions, as he extolled that officer's soldierly bearing and command ability.[7]

Seven • *Final Operations*

This same correspondent submitted another article a few days later in which he tried to further minimize the outcome of the campaign. In this submission, he stopped referring to the battle as a "scrape" or a "reversal" as he tried to paint as positive a picture of the proceedings as he could.

> We have had no casualties since Olustee, and our withdrawal towards Jacksonville is not a retreat, but only a common-sense result of the failure to proceed beyond that point.
>
> The list of casualties give rather an exaggerated idea of the damage done us in that fight, since a great proportion of our wounded were not permanently disabled, the wounds being principally from bullets. The enemy fired very low, and there are a great many lame shins, I assure you. Had the wounds been all of this character, it would have been almost ludicrous to see men catching up with their feet, all along the lines, when they were struck, as if they were walking on coals; but many an unerring rebel bullet reached a brave man's heart, and there were too many arms thrown up, as they toppled over, for any body on our side to feel other wise than sad.

It is hard to believe that even the most casual reader could have been duped by these words when they appeared in print. Seymour's advance had been checked and his army forced to not only retreat, but retreat hastily toward its base at Jacksonville and the protection of Union Naval gunboats The correspondent's attempts to downplay the casualties was an even weaker argument, citing that most of the wounded were not permanently disabled, and that their wounds were the result of bullets. Most of the wounded in any Civil War battle fell into these categories. Their wounds usually came from bullets, as infantry was generally the dominant force on any field, and most who were wounded were not permanently disabled.[8]

Though General Seymour received a great deal of criticism within the army, there were those who still supported the general and his actions. Lieutenant Colonel James Hall, First New York Volunteers, spoke for many of Seymour's supporters when he wrote to his wife:

"A good many noble spirits are gone. Seymour did gallantly and all together it was a gallant though unsuccessful fight."⁹

For the members of Seymour's command, the following weeks would be spent in strengthening fortifications and assuming the role of garrison troops. In addition to strengthening the works, General Seymour directed that a 110-foot signal tower be built near a block house situated at Yellow River, so as to better communicate with both his own forces and the navy. This was in addition to an 83-foot tower that had already been constructed on the steeple of a church on the west side of town. The general was going to make sure that he was not surprised by any Confederate activity, but his efforts proved unnecessary as the Confederates planned no activity against his position.¹⁰

To be sure, there were some scrapes with Confederate cavalry, mostly with the company of the Second Florida, under the command of Captain "Dixie" Dickison, but they were all minor affairs of a harassing nature. Seymour's chief signal officer, Captain Dana, recalled an expedition against these marauders while the army was in Jacksonville. "The rebels were acting nasty up the river and had a cavalry camp so located as to appear easy to capture so on the 7th of March we went up the river south about 100 miles with some gunboats, but found everything deserted and saw nothing worse than alligators which abound in that river." Small-scale sniping and hit-and-run raids were to become the norm in Florida, as neither side was willing to commit to another stand-up fight.¹¹

General Gillmore withdrew the many reinforcements he had sent to Florida as soon as he was sure that there was no danger of a Confederate offensive against Jacksonville, leaving Seymour and his command to consolidate its hold on the area in and around Jacksonville, including the construction of an armed camp at Palatka. The Forty-eighth New York took part in this latter operation, and its unit historian left an account to the regiment's days in Palatka:

> The town was entirely deserted, with the exception of one or two families, at the time of its occupation by the regiment, but fearing an attack from the enemy, they threw up earthworks and

constructed batteries in the rear of the town, details for fatigue duty in the trenches being regularly made for some days. The orange trees were loaded with large yellow fruit; but the oranges were rather sour for eating, although they made admirable orangeade. The gnats troubled the pickets more than the enemy during the month and more that the regiment remained at Palatka. The diaries which have been examined, and which were written while in camp there, contain few items of more importance than the following: "Killed a pig to-day and brought him into camp."[12]

Sergeant Patrick Egan, of the Third Rhode Island Heavy Artillery, was also at Palatka and stated,

> One of the objects of the Palatka expedition was the capture of a notorious rebel named Thigpen, who was furnishing supplies of beef and bacon to the Confederacy. Shortly after our arrival at Palatka the commanding officer sent for Captain James and asked him to mount a part of his battery as cavalry and attempt the capture of Thigpen. We started out the next morning, about four o'clock, with two Florida "Crackers" as guides. When a short distance from the home of Thigpen Captain James selected a dozen men and we made a dash for the house and surprised Thigpen as he sat on his porch with a rebel tax collector, who had his saddlebags spread out before them. We found large supplies of bacon on the place, and, after supplying ourselves with all we could carry, we set fire to the buildings and destroyed them. We returned to Palatka in the evening with thirteen prisoners, but the only one of importance was Thigpen. He was sent to Hilton Head, and was afterwards tried by the government and sentenced to three years in Fort Lafayette.[13]

The Seventh Connecticut Infantry experienced garrison life similar to that of the Forty-eighth New York, as the regiment made its camp on the west bank of the St. John's River. The furloughed veterans reported for duty while the unit was there, eventually increasing the number of men in the ranks to 720 enlisted men and officers, or approximately double the size the regiment had been when it fought at Olustee.[14]

The Battle of Olustee, 1864

For the Fifty-fourth Massachusetts, and the rest of the black troops in Seymour's command, the stay in Jacksonville gave time to reap the fruits of their recent accomplishments. The men of the Fifty-fourth had once again covered themselves with glory and were serving as a prime example of what black troops did as soldiers. The performance of the First North Carolina had done credit to themselves, and even the inexperienced Eighth U.S.C.T., through their heroic stand, had earned the plaudits of the army. Black supporters in the military and in the government were able to point to their performance as they lobbied for equality, starting with pay. Their arguments prevailed, and the pay to black troops was increased to parity with that of the white soldiers. Secretary of War Edwin Stanton finally urged Congress to pass the bill establishing equal pay, but even then, there were strings attached. Congress declared that only blacks who had been free men on April 19, 1861, were eligible for the additional pay. Those who had still been slaves as of that date would continue to receive the lower pay. Colonel Hallowell of the Fifty-fourth, a Quaker, decided to circumvent the law by devising what became widely known as the "Quaker Oath." Hallowell would ask for the statement: "You do solemnly swear that you owed no man unrequited labor on or before the 19th day of April, 1861. So help you God." Ex-slaves could honestly answer that they did not, as they had been in a state of forced servitude, and did not "owe" their labors to any man, and thus Hallowell got around the law and made sure his men were all equally paid. His ruse quickly spread through the army, causing all blacks to assert that they could be considered free as of that date. This action would go a long way toward allowing those black troops already in the army to remain there, and to induce huge numbers of blacks to enlist.[15]

Of the three black regiments that took part in the battle, the Fifty-fourth Massachusetts had the shortest stay in Florida. On April 17, the men of the regiment were loaded aboard the steamer *Cosmopolitan* and on the 18th they were back at Morris Island, in Charleston Harbor. On the day that the men of the Fifty-fourth were embarking on the ship, the Eighth U.S.C.T. was moved from Jacksonville down the St. Mary's River to Yellow Bluff, and "set to fortifying that point, and guarding

Seven • *Final Operations*

Monument to the Confederate victory erected on the field of Olustee (courtesy United States Army Military History Institute).

the stream to prevent the enemy from planting torpedoes." At Yellow Bluff, the regiment "participated in numerous raids into the surrounding country, destroying a portion of the railroad, and taking some of the enemy's ammunition." The regiment's mascot, the white dog named Lion, accompanied the troops "a little the worse for wear, having been slightly wounded in the foreleg at Olustee." One of the men said that Lion was a "soldier, and has no respect for citizens who may visit the camp and does not hesitate to bite. He attends the dress parade, has musical taste, and shows that he has not been brought up a savage."[16]

The 115th New York was stationed at Palatka, along with the Eighth U.S.C.T., and experienced similar raids into the countryside. They reported having several small skirmishes with the Confederates. "They also hunted down rebel conscription agents, captured rebel mails, picked up stray rebel soldiers, and kept the rebel camp in constant commotion." But the New Yorkers' stay in Florida was fast coming to an end. Like the Fifty-fourth Massachusetts and most of Seymour's expeditionary force, the middle of April found them boarding transports to sail via South Carolina to points farther North. Both sides were rushing for a concentration of troops in Virginia, just as they had rushed to get men into Florida.[17]

The Eighth U.S.C.T. would be among the very last to leave Florida, not doing so until August 4, when it was assigned to a brigade under the command of General William Birney and sent north to participate in the engagements around Petersburg and Richmond. Most of the regiments that had taken part in the Olustee campaign had already joined the eastern army in time for General Ulysses S. Grant's campaign that spring, including General Seymour, who arrived in Virginia in time to be captured at the battle of the Wilderness.

The Confederates mirrored the actions of the Federals, siphoning off most of the troops in Florida to be sent to reinforce General Robert E. Lee's Army of Northern Virginia to resist Grant's thrust. General Finegan, like Seymour, would also find himself in Virginia, leading his brigade, which had won its laurels at Olustee, to further glory. In the end, Florida was left to small Union garrison forces, small bands of Confederate irregulars, the alligators, and the gnats. The expedition had done little or nothing to affect the outcome of the war or the coming presidential election. It had only served to further drain the national treasury and add to the ever growing lists of casualties.

Epilogue

The Olustee campaign was filled with might-have-beans and missed opportunities on both sides and, in the end, was little more than a bloody stalemate, with each side occupying pretty much the same portions of the state at the end of the campaign as they had before it began. One Union veteran of the campaign was not impressed with the generalship that had been displayed by the commanding officers of either side. Jerome Tourtellotte, of the Seventh Connecticut Infantry, rather comically mused,

> In the eyes of intelligent privates the leadership on either side did not ring true. Parboiled down to a fine point it would, in concise treatment average up about as follows: Reckless galore, gallantry mere more, disgrace in store, Seymour; Union General Commanding. Feeble in vim, bluffing to win, shiftless as sin, Finnigan [sic]; Confederate General Commanding.[1]

Abraham Lincoln's plan to bring a reconstructed Florida back into the Union in time to take part in the 1864 presidential election was thwarted, and the Union missed an opportunity to occupy a large portion of the state and deny to the Confederacy the sorely needed food and materials the region was providing to the Southern cause. For the North, it was a disappointing and disastrous campaign that provided almost no results, politically or militarily, to justify the expenditure of men or material it had cost. To be sure, there had been a number of runaway slaves who had enlisted in the army, but not many more than could have slipped into St. Augustine or Fernandina for that same

Epilogue

purpose, even if Seymour's expeditionary army had never landed in Florida. Seymour had captured large quantities of contraband and war materials in his march through the interior, but most of these had been destroyed when his army retraced its steps back to Jacksonville following the defeat at Olustee, as well as a huge quantity of Federal arms, munitions, and supplies.

Both Lincoln and Seymour came under severe criticism for their roles in the Florida campaign. Lincoln's political motivations were roundly denounced in the press, and the whole affair was pronounced to be nothing more or less than a political manipulation, designed to pave the way for his re-election by adding the three electoral votes Florida could have cast, had the operation been a success. For Lincoln, the clamor, while intense, was short-lived. Salmon Chase, his chief political opponent, removed himself from consideration for the Republican nomination shortly after the battle of Olustee, and the public was quick to forget. The effects of the Florida expedition would be more far reaching for General Seymour, however. His failure in the campaign served to dredge up memories of his failure in the assault against Battery Wagner, the previous year, and his detractors, both political and military, denounced his leadership and ability for independent command. Olustee would be Seymour's last opportunity for such a command. Following the conclusion of the campaign, he was transferred to the Army of the Potomac, just in time to be captured at the Wilderness. He was exchanged a few months later and assigned to command a division in the Sixth Corps, serving in the Valley in 1864, the siege of Petersburg, and at Appomattox. Seymour remained in the army at the end of the war, being assigned to the Fifth U.S. Artillery with the rank of major. He would serve in this position until his resignation in 1876.[2]

General Finegan also became a focal point of criticism after the battle. True, his army had been victorious and had given the Federals a serious check in their attempt to wrest Florida away from the Confederacy, but many felt that Finegan was receiving too much credit for the accomplishment and wanted to set the record straight. To most of the men in the Confederate army, Colonels Colquitt and Harrison

Epilogue

deserved all of the credit for the victory. It was they who had been at the front, conducting the fight, while Finegan was still in the rear, in his works at Ocean Pond. One rebel soldier, in the Sixth Georgia, stated that they "did not see General Finegan at all that day." After the war, when veterans of the battle returned to Olustee, they were astounded to read the inscription placed on the monument to the battle, which paid tribute to Finegan for his victory. Most felt that that honor was reserved for the officers who had actually fought the battle: Colquitt and Harrison.[3]

Though Finegan did not maintain direct control over the fighting of the battle, he was still in overall command and responsible for its outcome. The Confederate battle plan was of his design, including the improvisation of fighting in front of his prepared works. Finegan devised the overall strategy, then allowed his subordinate commanders to carry out the plan. Colquitt and Harrison did an exemplary job of handling their troops, thus eliminating the need for Finegan to assume a direct part in the fighting. He was left to oversee the operation. The criticism concerning his personal attention to the battle may be unfair, owing to the fact that all things were progressing according to plan under the direction of his lieutenants, making it unnecessary for him to micro-manage the battle.

When one considers the fact that Finegan was a civilian, with no previous military training or experience, his accomplishments in the Olustee campaign are quite impressive. Seymour was a graduate of West Point, had served in the army for years, and had already commanded troops in battle. He enjoyed the confidence of his superiors and had been entrusted to carry out a mission that had been ordered by President Lincoln himself. Finegan had never seen an infantry battle prior to Olustee. He did not have the confidence of his superiors; General Beauregard was urgently trying to find another officer to lead the army in Florida from the time the Union expeditionary force first arrived in Jacksonville. But Finegan prevailed. He did so because he conducted a campaign that was fundamentally sound, and he utilized the resources he had at hand, including the battle experience of Colonels Colquitt and Harrison. He adopted an overall plan, then left the

Epilogue

implementation of that plan to his more experienced subordinates. Though his detractors pointed to his failure to follow up his victory and finish off the Union army, the fact is that Finegan accomplished his mission: he prevented the Union army accomplishing its designs in central Florida. He is deserving of praise, not only for his direct control over the campaign, but also for recognizing his own deficiencies and deferring to his subordinates, particularly Colquitt, and allowing them to take charge of the battle line. All things considered, the novice Finegan out-generaled the more experienced Seymour at Olustee. His actions saved Florida for the Confederacy, and he is deserving of recognition as the officer who was victorious in the largest land battle to take place in the state.

Following the campaign, General Finegan was sent east, along with his brigade, to reinforce General Robert E. Lee's Army of Northern Virginia. In the campaigns of that army, Finegan displayed firm leadership, and his Florida brigade fought heroically, adding to the glory that it had already won on the field of Olustee.

During the war, both Seymour and Finegan were convinced that they had each faced an enemy force many times larger than their own, and both pointed to this imagined disparity in numbers when discussing the battle. On Seymour's part, the contention that he faced an army more than double the size of his own served to underscore the contention that his conduct of the battle was not in error. He had been ambushed by a much larger force and had been fortunate to be able to extricate his own army without allowing it to be destroyed by superior numbers. As for Finegan, the exaggeration of enemy numbers served to heighten the glory that was to be attached to the Confederate success. To defeat a Union army was one thing, but to defeat one that was several times the size of your own carried with it additional accolades, and undying glory. It was not till after the war that both sides finally realized the truth of the numbers that had been engaged at Olustee. General Gillmore summed up the true picture of the conflict with the comment,

> We know since the close of the war that there was no disparity in numbers and we knew at the time that the results were a

Epilogue

decisive defeat upon the field of battle and the frustration — as well by the loss of men as by the loss of prestige — of a carefully-digested plan of campaign. General Finegan had only about 5,000 men in that battle. General Seymour, 5,500. Our losses were 1,800 men in killed, wounded, and missing.... Indeed our forces appear to have been surprised into fighting or attempting to fight an offensive battle in which the component parts of the command were beaten in detail. The enemy did not fight behind entrenchments or any kind of defenses.[4]

The campaign, on the surface, did little or nothing to advance the cause of either side and would appear to be only a waste of lives, time, and resources. Among the main reasons for the campaign was the effort to bring Florida back into the Union and to give Lincoln the state's delegates in the national convention, to be held later that year in Baltimore. Though Union sympathizers in the state did end up sending a delegation to the Republican Convention, they were there merely as observers, since Lincoln's bid to occupy and reconstruct the state ended with the defeat at Olustee. The greater part of Florida would remain Confederate territory until the close of the war. In fact, when hostilities were ended, that portion of Florida still in Confederate hands, was the largest single territory in the South still under Confederate authority, and Tallahassee was the only Southern state capitol that had not been captured by the North. The attempt to coerce Florida back into the Union and reconstruct the state for political reasons had been a complete failure.

From a military standpoint, the campaign was to occupy the resource-rich area of central Florida and deprive the Confederate army of the much needed provisions that it produced. The South was running short on everything in the year 1864, and cutting off this remaining source of supplies was deemed to be as important in the overall persecution of the war as winning a major battle. The Confederacy was in dire need of the food and materials that Florida supplied to the cause, and denying them to the southern and western armies would have had the same effect as the closing of the Port of Wilmington had on General Robert E. Lee's Army of Northern Virginia. Finegan's victory

Epilogue

at Olustee guaranteed that the Confederacy would be able to depend on these provisions and averted what might have been a severe supply problem for the South.

A second military goal of the expedition was the enlistment of blacks in Florida to swell the ranks of the Union army. In this, the North was sorely disappointed, as relatively few blacks came forward to offer their services to the cause. In fact, the numbers were not much more than what had already been coming in to places like Fernandina and St. Augustine.

But the campaign did have a subtle yet tremendous effect on the outcome of the war. In what was still one of the very early incidents where black troops were committed to battle, those black troops made a generally good showing of themselves. The Fifty-fourth Massachusetts, in particular, gained glory and honor on the field of Olustee, adding to the laurels it had already won at Battery Wagner, and in so doing, helped to set aside many of the notions and prejudices about the inability of black troops to perform in battle. What followed was increased usage and recruitment of black regiments, until some 180,000 colored soldiers filled the ranks of the Union army by the end of the war. By 1864, many in the North had become weary of the war, and enlistments were considerably short of the numbers needed to carry the fight through to victory. The draft had been instituted to make up for this shortfall, but it was so unpopular that armed resistance had been seen throughout the North, and New York City had been the scene of one of the most violent riots ever to take place in America. Union draft officers lived in constant fear for their lives, as many were murdered by citizens who were outraged over the government trying to force them to go and fight in a war they had lost faith in. The Northern military had always been hesitant to use black troops in combat, feeling that they made inferior soldiers and that white troops must be relied upon for accomplishing any success on the battlefield. Olustee was another of the very early usages of black troops that seemed to refute that idea and helped to change the opinion of those in command in the Union army. The fact that blacks would stand and fight and seemed to perform at a level equal to white troops meant that the North could now

Epilogue

tap into another resource of manpower to make up for the dwindling enlistments among whites. It also meant that the ranks of the army could be filled without forcing the confrontations that resulted from having to draft the needed men. Olustee served to propel black troops into prominence in the Union army. It served to prove the reliability of blacks as soldiers and paved the way for black enlistments in the tens of thousands. In that way, the Olustee campaign was a triumphant success for the Northern cause, as well as being a beginning point for the cause of equality in the minds of many Northerners.

The murders and other atrocities conducted by the Confederates against the captured black troops at Olustee showed that there was still a long way to go to establish equality for blacks in the army. Even so, Olustee helped to promote this mindset in the South as well. The many references made by Confederate soldiers in the battle admit that the black regiments did their duty and, for the most part, fought well. In the months after Olustee, Southerners would have many more opportunities to evaluate the performance of black troops in combat and would be forced to admit that they were worthy adversaries on the field of battle. By the end of 1864, there would even be some Confederate leaders who were advocating the enlistment of black regiments into the Southern army, and by the end of the war, the South would actively pursue the policy, with the backing of no less a figure than Robert E. Lee.

History has relegated Olustee almost to the status of a footnote in the Civil War. Statements from many of the soldiers who fought there contend that it was the fiercest fought battle that they had been involved in during the war, but that alone was not sufficient to elevate it to a position of importance in the history of the war. The fact that it was the largest land battle of the war to be fought in the state also did little to garner it fame. Simply speaking, the war had gotten too big, by 1864, for a battle involving only 10,000 men to capture the imagination of the military, or the public. By that time, both were accustomed to battles where the casualty lists were greater than the total number of men involved at Olustee, and the carnage of this Florida battle did not have the ability to shock a country numbed by

Epilogue

the ever soaring cost of the conflict. The battle was also void of any real strategic value, as none of the objectives of the expedition had been realized, and, at its conclusion, the situation in Florida remained pretty much as it had been before its commencement. Lastly, the large involvement of black troops in the battle also served to decrease its importance. The folks back home, the ones buying and reading the newspapers, were little concerned with the performance of, or casualties sustained by, black regiments. To be sure, black soldiers had their supporters among the Northern citizenry, but the commonly held opinion of the masses was that white troops would have to be depended upon to win this war. Olustee may have been a crucial step in establishing parity in the Union army for black soldiers, but, at the time of the battle, acceptance of black soldiers in the North was still only an argument and not a reality.

This book has been an attempt to pay tribute to the heroic sacrifices made in the Florida campaign by North and South, black and white. It is hoped that the reader will gain an appreciation for a battle that has long been overlooked by modern day historians and will not only understand what happened, but also the might-have-beens and missed opportunities that make up such a large part of history.

Today's visitors to Olustee will find only a small portion of the battlefield preserved. In fact, only about three acres of the original battlefield are owned by the state of Florida. A visitor's center is the focal point of the park, along with several monuments. The ground is relatively pristine and will give the visitor a good impression of what the landscape looked like in 1864, when the largest land battle ever to be fought in Florida took place there. The park also enjoys the support of an active organization called The Friends of Olustee, who, among other things, sponsor a well staged re-enactment of the battle each year, as close to the anniversary as possible.

Though Olustee will never be listed among the great and decisive battles of the war, it is deserving of an honored place in history. The ferocity of this sanguinary conflict, and the bravery of the men who fought in it, should earn it its proper place in the history of that war. As with many of the battles that took place in the last two years of the

Epilogue

war, Olustee is the victim of timing. The war had simply gotten too big for an engagement such as Olustee to garner the attention of the masses by 1864. Had the fight for Florida taken place in 1861, or 1862, Olustee would have undoubtedly enjoyed a stature similar to First Manassas or Wilson's Creek in the chronicles of the war. The old saying, "Timing is everything" holds true, however, relegating Olustee to a position of one of the sidelights and little known events to take place in the Civil War. To the men who fought there, it would always be remembered as one of the hottest fights they had ever been in.

APPENDIX I

The Opposing Armies

The Union Army
Brigadier General Truman Seymour, Commanding

Colonel William B. Barton's Brigade:
    47th New York Infantry: Colonel Henry Moore
    48th New York Infantry: Major W.B. Coan
    115th New York Infantry: Colonel Simeon Sammon

Colonel Joseph Hawley's Brigade:
    7th Connecticut Infantry: Captain Benjamin F. Skinner
    7th New Hampshire Infantry: Colonel Joseph C. Abbott
    8th United States Colored Troops: Colonel Charles Fribley

Colonel James Montgomery's Brigade:
    1st North Carolina Infantry (35th USCT): Lieutenant Colonel W.N. Reed
    54th Massachusetts Infantry: Colonel Edward N. Hallowell
    40th Massachusetts Mounted Infantry: Colonel G.V. Henry
    Independent Massachusetts Battalion: Major Stevens

Artillery: Captain John Hamilton
    Battery E, 3rd U.S. Artillery: Captain John Hamilton
    Battery M, 1st U.S. Artillery: Captain Loomis L. Langdon
    Sections C and B, 3rd Rhode Island Artillery: Lieutenant Henry H. Metcalf
    Companies A and E, 1st New York Engineers

Appendix I

The Confederate Army

Brigadier General Joseph Finegan, Commanding

   Brigadier General Alfred H. Colquitt's Brigade:
      6th Florida Infantry Battalion: Major Pickens Bird
      6th Georgia Infantry: Lieutenant Colonel John T. Lofton
      19th Georgia Infantry: Colonel James H. Neal
      23rd Georgia Infantry: Lieutenant Colonel James H. Huggins
      27th Georgia Infantry: Colonel Charles T. Zachry
      28th Georgia Infantry: Colonel Tully Graybill
      Chatham Georgia Artillery: Captain John F. Wheaton
      Gamble's Florida Artillery: Captain Robert H. Gamble

   Colonel George P. Harrison's Brigade:
      1st Florida Infantry Battalion: Lieutenant Colonel C.F. Hopkins
      32nd Georgia Infantry: Major W.T. Holland
      64th Georgia Infantry: Captain C.S. Jenkins
      1st Georgia Regular Infantry: Captain H.A. Cannon
      28th Georgia Artillery Battalion
      Abell's Florida Artillery
      Guerard's Georgia Battery: Captain John M. Guerard

   Colonel Caraway Smith's Cavalry Brigade:
      4th Georgia Cavalry: Colonel Duncan L. Clinch
      2nd Florida Cavalry: Lieutenant Colonel A.H. McCormick
      5th Florida Cavalry Battalion: Major G.W. Scott

APPENDIX II

CASUALTIES

The Union Army

Colonel William Barton's Brigade:

115th New York Infantry
  killed: 29, wounded: 208, missing: 59
47th New York Infantry
  killed: 30, wounded: 197, missing: 86
48th New York Infantry
  killed: 17, wounded: 154, missing: 44
Brigade total: 824

Colonel Joseph Hawley's Brigade:
7th Connecticut Infantry
  killed: 5, wounded: 42, missing: 22
7th New Hampshire Infantry
  killed: 17, wounded: 71, missing: 120
8th United States Colored Troops
  killed: 49, wounded: 188, missing: 73
Brigade total: 587

Colonel James Montgomery's Brigade:
1st North Carolina Infantry (Colored)
  killed: 22, wounded: 131, missing: 77
54th Massachusetts Infantry (Colored)
  killed: 13, wounded: 65, missing: 8
Brigade total: 316

Appendix II

Colonel Guy Henry's Brigade:
  40th Massachusetts Mounted Infantry
    killed: 2, wounded: 29, missing: 5
  Battery B, 1st U.S. Horse Artillery (Elder's)
    killed: 3, wounded: 13
  Independent Battalion, Massachusetts Cavalry
    wounded: 5
  Brigade total: 57

Captain John Hamilton's Artillery Command:
  Battery E, 3rd U.S. Artillery
    killed: 11, wounded: 22, missing: 6
  Battery M, 1st U.S. Artillery
    killed: 4, wounded: 22, missing: 6
  Battery C, 3rd Rhode Island Artillery
    killed: 1, wounded: 5
  Artillery total: 77[1]

The Confederate Army

Brigadier General Alfred Colquitt's Brigade:
  6th Florida Infantry Battalion
    killed: 22, wounded: 60, deserted: 2
  6th Georgia Infantry
    killed: 5, wounded: 56
  19th Georgia Infantry
    killed: 6, wounded: 88
  23rd Georgia Infantry
    killed: 2, wounded: 66, missing: 2
  27th Georgia Infantry
    killed: 7, wounded: 67
  28th Georgia Infantry
    killed: 10, wounded: 85
  Chatham Artillery
    wounded: 3
  Gamble's Artillery

Casualties

    killed: 2, wounded: 5
    Brigade total: 488

Colonel George P. Harrison's Brigade
  1st Florida Infantry Battalion
    killed: 3, wounded: 47
  32nd Georgia Infantry
    killed: 15, wounded: 149
  64th Georgia Infantry
    killed: 17, wounded: 88, missing: 2
  1st Georgia Regulars
    killed: 3, wounded: 25
  28th Georgia Artillery Battalion
    killed: 6, wounded: 9
  Abell's Artillery
    killed: 2, wounded: 4
  Guerard's Georgia Battery
    wounded: 2
    Brigade total: 372

Colonel Carroway Smith's Cavalry Brigade
  4th Georgia Cavalry
    wounded: 4
  2nd Florida Cavalry
    no losses
  5th Florida Cavalry Battalion
    no losses
    Brigade total: 4

APPENDIX III

ENLISTMENT OF BLACK TROOPS BY STATE

Black troops were prominent in the battle of Olustee, and they played an increasingly important role in the Union Army as the war dragged on, with some 180,000 black men serving in the ranks. The following is a statistical breakdown of black enlistments, by state.

Alabama: 2,969
Arkansas: 5,526
Connecticut: 1,764
Delaware: 954
District of Columbia: 3,269
Florida: 1,044
Georgia: 3,486
Illinois: 1,811
Indiana: 1,537
Iowa: 440
Kansas: 2,080
Kentucky: 23,703
Louisiana: 24,052
Maine: 104
Maryland: 8,718
Massachusetts: 3.966
Michigan: 1,387
Minnesota: 104
Mississippi: 17,869
Missouri: 8,344
New Hampshire: 125
New Jersey: 1,185
New York: 4,125
North Carolina: 5,035
Ohio: 5,092
Pennsylvania: 9,612
Rhode Island: 1,937
South Carolina: 5,462
Tennessee: 20,133
Texas: 47
Vermont: 120
Virginia: 5,723
West Virginia: 196
Wisconsin: 165

APPENDIX IV

THE FLAG OF THE 2ND FLORIDA CAVALRY (POETRY)

Unfurl thy bright folds to the breezes of war,
Thou banner of freedom! Thou flag of our corps!
While we swear by thy starry cross, gleaming on high,
In the cause of our country to conquer or die.
For thine be our motto, thou flag of the free;
"Where liberty dwells, there our country shall be."

By woman's hands wrought with a wonderful thrift;
By woman's heart brought unto us a gift;
With magical charms by her blessing endowed,
We hail thee our talisman "_pl_ar* and aloud."

And thine be our motto thou flag of the free
"Where liberty dwells, there our country shall be."

The women — God bless them! — like angels of light,
They cheer on our soldiers defending the right,
And we'll owe our glad triumph, whene're it shall come,
To the labors and prayers of the women at home.

Then ours be the motto that women gave thee;
"Where liberty dwells, there our country shall be."

With thee waving o'er us we'll rush to the fray,
To make, like bold Arnold to Switzer, a way
For freedom and joy, though we lose all in the strife;
For who, without freedom, would care for his life?

The poem was transcribed from an original in which some letters were missing or illegible. It appeared as shown in the southern newspaper that published it.

Appendix IV

Henceforth be our motto, thou flag of the free;
"Where liberty dwells, there our country shall be."

North's tyrants are trampling on liberty's laws;
We hear but of "war, and rumors of war;"
But we know by thy example, O thou banner of light!
That our God will yet favor and prosper the right!

So thine be our motto, thou flag of the free;
"Where liberty dwells, there our country shall be."

The base Northern tyrant is subtle and strong;
His myrmidons swarm all our borders along;
But we know, by the stars gleaming proudly and still,
That he'd ne'er bend the South to his insolent will.

For thine is our motto, thou flag of the free;
"Where liberty dwells, there our country shall be."

Yet while we oppose — by the robe ermine white
We would yearn to be just in the thick of the fight
And when wounded foemen are set in our path
Be _dial _f____ and well deserved wrath.

But aye be our motto, thou flag of the free;
"Where liberty dwells. there our country shall be."

Ne'er flaunted a flag _ere defiant __ foe,
Nor waved more triumphant o'er foeman laid low,
Than wilt thou when we meet them in battle array,
And a Heaven blest valor shall win us the day.

We'll fight by thy motto, thou flag of the free;
"Where liberty dwells, there our country shall be."

Nor e're floated flag on the zephyrs of peace
With more of a a__try like bounty and grace,
Than will thou when our liberty's sun shall arise,
Bringing joy to our hearts and glad light to our eyes.

We'll live by thy motto, thou flag of the free;
"Where liberty dwells, there our country shall be."

The Flag of the 2nd Florida Cavalry (Poetry)

The North, like Goliath, came forth in its pride,
And thought to appall by its gigantic stride;
But in many a stream of the South hath been found
A pebble to bring our proud foe to the ground.

Then triumph thy motto, thou flag of the free;
"Where liberty dwells there our country shall be."

The plains of Manassas and Shiloh shall prove
How Southerners fighting for freedom can move,
While Richmond and Charleston forever shall stand,
To point the heroic defense of our land.

All hail to thy motto, thou flag of the free;
"Where liberty dwells there our country shall be."

They boast of their navy — as though we had none —
Ignoring what Semmes and Moffit have done;
But we fling back the taunt — let them search o'er the main
For their lost steamers Hatteras and Harriet Lane.

Than show them thy motto, thou flag of the free;
"Where liberty dwells there our country shall be."

Then fling out thy folds to the breezes of war.
Thou banner of freedom! thou flag of our corps!
While we swear by the starry cross gleaming on high,
In the cause of our country to conquer or die.

For thine be our motto, thou flag of the free,
"Where liberty dwells, there our country shall be."

Chapter Notes

Introduction

1. William Watson Davis, *The Civil War and Reconstruction in Florida* (New York, N.Y., Columbia University, 1913), 269.
2. Ibid., 270.
3. Reminiscences of William Frederick Penniman (Tallahassee Fl., University of Florida, William Frederick Penniman Papers).

Chapter One

1. Davis, 269–270.
2. William H. Nulty, *Confederate Florida: The Road to Olustee* (Tuscaloosa, Al., The University of Alabama Press, 1990), 63–64.
3. Ibid., 64–65.
4. Colonel Thomas Wentworth Higginson, *The Reoccupation of Jacksonville in 1863, Civil War Papers Read before the Commandery of the State of Massachusetts, Military Order of the Loyal Legion of the United States* (Wilmington, N.C., Broadfoot Publishing Company, 1993), 467.
5. Nulty, 58.
6. Ibid., 57.
7. Ezra J. Warner, *Generals in Blue: Lives of the Union Commanders* (Baton Rouge, La., University of Louisiana Press, 1989), 176 and Major Eliot William Furness, *The Battle of Olustee, Florida February 20, 1864, Papers of the Military Historical Society of Massachusetts, Volume 9* (Wilmington, N.C., Broadfoot Publishing Company, 1989), 237.
8. Davis, 274.
9. Nulty, 70.
10. *Eastern Fields of Battle, Publications of the Florida Historical Society, Number Four* (Deland, Fl., Printed by the Society, 1925), 32.
11. Nulty, 70.
12. Ibid., 59–60.
13. Davis, 275.
14. Robert N. Scott, *The War of the Rebellion: A Compilation of the Official Records of the Union and Confederate Armies, Series 1, Volume 35, Part 1* (Washington, D.C., Government Printing Office, 1891), 278.
15. Tyler Dennett, *John Hay: From Poetry to Politics* (New York, N.Y., Dodd, Mead & Company), 43.
16. Scott, 278.
17. Ibid.
18. Ibid., 279.
19. Ibid.
20. Furness, 240.
21. Donald Yacovone, *A Voice of Thunder: The Civil War Letters of George E. Stephens* (Urbana, Il., University of Illinois Press, 1997), 65, Warner, *Generals in Blue*, 432–433, and Clint Johnson, *Bull's Eyes and Misfires: 50 People Whose Obscure Efforts Shaped the American Civil War* (Nashville, Tn., Rutledge Hill Press, 2002), 97–98.

Chapter Notes

22. Abraham J. Palmer, *The History of the Forty-Eighth Regiment New York State Volunteers in the War for the Union 1861–1865* (New York, N.Y., published by the Association of the Regiment, 1885), 8.

23. John David Smith, *Black Soldiers in Blue: African American Troops in the Civil War Era* (Chapel Hill, N.C., University of North Carolina Press, 2002), 137.

24. Letter from Lieutenant Tully McCrea dated February 5, 1864 (Tallahassee, Fl., University of Florida, Letters of Olustee Collection).

25. Jerome Tourtellotte, *A History of Company K of the Seventh Connecticut Volunteer Infantry in the Civil War* (Putnam, N.H., published by the author, 1910), 124.

26. Palmer, 130, Tourtelotte, 123, Patrick Egan, *The Florida Campaign with Light Battery C, Third Rhode Island Heavy Artillery, Personal Narratives of Events in the War of the Rebellion Being Papers Read Before the Rhode Island Soldiers and Sailors Historical Society* (Wilmington, N.C., Broadfoot Publishing, 1993), 482, and Scott, 303.

27. Nulty, 113.

28. Furness, 240, and Nulty, 76.

29. Luis F. Emilio, *A Brave Black Regiment: History of the Fifty-Fourth Regiment of Massachusetts Volunteer Infantry 1863–1865* (New York, N.Y., Arno Press, 1969), 150–151, and Nulty, 78.

30. Letter dated March 26, 1864 from an unidentified Union officer (Tallahassee, Fl., University of Florida, Letters of Olustee Collection).

31. Emilio, 151–152 and James H. Clark, *The Iron Hearted Regiment: Being an Account of the Battles, Marches and Gallant Deeds Performed by the 115th Regiment N.Y. Volunteers* (Albany, N.Y., published by the Regimental Association, 1865), 70–71.

32. Nulty, 85–86

33. Emilio, 152, Clark, 70, and Benjamin W. Crowninshield, *A History of the First Regiment of Massachusetts Cavalry Volunteers* (Cambridge, Ma., Houghton, Mifflin Company, 1891), 258.

34. In June of 1864, Congress finally passed legislation granting equal pay for black troops, but even then the law excluded most of the black soldiers in the ranks. According to the law, only those soldiers who had been free men on April 19, 1861, were eligible for the equal pay. All others were to remain at their current pay scale. Colonel Hallowell, of the Fifty-fourth Massachusetts, devised a plan to circumvent the injustice of the law. Hallowell, a Quaker, made up what came to be known as the "Quaker's Oath," and it was widely used in the Colored regiments. "You do solemnly swear that you owed no man unrequited labor on or before the 19th day of April, 1861. So help you God." Thousands of black troops took this oath, with clear conscience that they owed no debt of labor to their former masters. Clinton Cox, *Undying Glory: The Story of the Massachusetts 54th Regiment* (New York, N.Y., Scholastic Inc., 1991), 126–127.

35. The theater group was named the Barton Dramatic Association, in honor of their commander, and was immensely popular with the local residents as well as with the soldiers. Palmer, 128–129, and Tourtellotte, 124.

36. Nulty, 78.

37. Nulty, 78, 84–85.

38. William J. Jones, *Southern Historical Society Papers, Vol. IX* (Wilmington, N.C., Broadfoot Publishing Company, 1998), 12–13.

39. Ibid., 12

40. Cox, 121.

41. Scott, 325.

42. Ezra J. Warner, *Generals in Gray: Lives of the Confederate Commanders* (Baton Rouge, La., Louisiana State University Press, 1959), 88.

43. Scott, 322–323, and Warner, *Generals in Gray*, 97–98.

44. Scott, 322.

Chapter Two

1. Nulty, 87.
2. Nulty, 87, and Davis, 278.
3. Jones, 16.
4. Letter to the editor from an unknown observer, *Chelsea Telegraph and Pioneer*, March 12, 1864, pg. 2, col. 4.
5. Crowninshield, 258, and Clark, 72.
6. William H. Trimmer, *Olustee and How I Was Captured* (Nashville, Tn., *Confederate Veteran Magazine*, Volume 20, No. 6), 472.
7. Scott, 324.
8. Trimmer, 472.
9. Davis, 278-279.
10. Trimmer, 472.
11. Lester L. Swift, *Captain Dana in Florida: A Narrative of the Seymour Expedition, Civil War History* (Des Moines, The University of Iowa, September 1965, Vol. 11, No. 3), 247.
12. Clark, 72, and Nulty, 90.
13. Clark, 73.
14. Ibid., 74.
15. Ibid., 74-75.
16. Nulty, 92.
17. Galusha Pennypacker would go on to become the youngest man to be commissioned a brigadier general on either side and would win the Congressional Medal of Honor for conspicuous gallantry in the second expedition against Fort Fisher, North Carolina. Ibid., 92-93.
18. Ibid., 93.
19. Andrews was a bit of a free-spirited jokester, as can be seen by his statement about the soldiers killing any man's pig that tried to bite them and by his participation in taunting his commanding officer, Major Bonaud, in the lyrics of a song around the campfire. 1st Sergeant W.H. Andrews, *Footprints of a Regiment: A Recollection of the 1st Georgia Regulars 1861-1865* (Atlanta, Ga., Longstreet Press, 1992), 123.
20. Nulty, 93-94.
21. Swift, 247-248.
22. *Boston Herald*, February 22, 1864.
23. Thorndike D. Hodges, *Scattering Fire, 1863, Personal Recollections of the War of the Rebellion: Addresses Delivered Before the New York Commandery of the Loyal Legion of the United States, 1883-1891* (Wilmington, N.C., Broadfoot Publishing Company, 1992), 73-74, and *The Boston Herald*, March 2, 1864.
24. Nulty, 94.
25. Of the three men of the scouting party who were shot when they approached the rebel lines, one was killed and two were wounded. The trooper who was killed carried in his pocket a furlough for a 10-day leave, which he was expecting to take in a few days. The Fortieth Massachusetts Mounted Infantry in Florida, unknown correspondent, *The Boston Herald*, February 22, 1864, pg. 1, col. 6, and Clark, 77.
26. Nulty, 97.
27. Scott, 241-242.
28. Davis, 279-280, Clark, 77-78, and Nulty, 98-99.
29. Jones, 17, Clement A. Evans, *Confederate Military History vol. 16* (Wilmington, N.C., Broadfoot Publishing Company, 1989), 57-58, and Andrews, 123-124.
30. Egan, 484, and Nulty, 97.
31. Egan, 484-485.
32. Unknown author, *Florida in the War* (Nashville, Tn., *Confederate Veteran Magazine*, Vol. 22), 153.
33. Noah Andre Trudeau, *Like Men of War: Black Troops in the Civil War, 1862-1865* (Boston, Ma., Little, Brown and Company), 136-137.
34. Clark, 78.
35. Henry F.W. Little, *The Seventh New Hampshire Volunteers in the War of the Rebellion* (Concord, N.H. Ira C. Evans, 1896), 216-218.
36. Emilio, 155-156.
37. Emilio, 157, Andrews, 124.
38. Nulty, 105-106.

39. Ibid., 106.
40. Ibid., 107.
41. Ibid., 107–110.
42. Andrews, 123.
43. Ibid., 124–125.
44. Reminiscences of William Frederick Penniman (Tallahassee, Fl., University of Florida, Letters of Olustee Collection), 2
45. Nulty, 121–122.
46. Davis, 285.
47. Robert Underwood Johnson, and Clarence Clough Buel, *Battles and Leaders of the Civil War, Vol. 4* (New York, N.Y., Castle Books, 1956), 77.
48. Scott, 338–341.
49. Nulty, 122–123.
50. Scott, 277.
51. *The Boston Journal*, March 2, 1864.
52. *The Boston Herald*, February 22, 1864.
53. Trudeau, 136–137.

Chapter Three

1. Trudeau, 137–38, Palmer, 133, and Yacovone, 67.
2. Smith, 139.
3. Clark, 80–81.
4. Andrews, 126–127.
5. Nulty, 125.
6. *The Boston Herald*, March 2, 1864.
7. Reminiscences of William Frederick Penniman, 3.
8. Lawrence Jackson, *As I Saw and Remember the Battle of Olustee, Which Was Fought February 20, 1863* (Tallahassee, Fl., University of Florida, Letters of Olustee).
9. Nulty, 129–130.
10. Stephen Walkley, *History of the Seventh Connecticut Volunteers, Hawley's Brigade, Terry's Division, Tenth Army Corps 1861–1865* (published by the author, 1905), 120–121, and Nulty, 133.
11. Reminiscences of William Frederick Penniman, 3.
12. Tourtellotte, 125–126.
13. *The Boston Herald*, March 2, 1864, and Trudeau, 141.
14. Ibid.
15. Scott, 307.
16. Walkley, 121
17. Ibid., 122.
18. Scott, 308.
19. Walkley, 123–124.
20. Scott, 307.
21. Reminiscences of William Frederick Penniman, 3.
22. *Athens Southern Banner*, March 9, 1864.
23. Letter from Lt. Winston Stephens to wife, dated February 27, 1864 (Tallahassee, Fl., University of Florida, Letters of Olustee Collection).
24. *The Seventh New Hampshire Volunteers*, 221–222.
25. Little, 137–139.
26. Ibid., 139.
27. Scott, 311.
28. *The Boston Journal*, March 4, 1864.
29. William Welles Brown, *The Negro in the American Rebellion: His Heroism and His Fidelity* (Miami, Fl., Mnemosyne Publishing, Inc., 1969), 218.
30. Letter from Lt. Oliver Norton to "Sister L" dated February 1864 (Tallahassee, Fl., University of Florida, Letters of Olustee Collection).
31. Ibid.
32. Scott, 25.
33. Nulty, 142.
34. *Boston Herald*, March 1, 1864.
35. Reminiscences of William Frederick Penniman, 4.
36. Scott, 24–25.
37. Nulty, 152, and Trudeau, 144.
38. Ibid., 143.
39. Furness, 259–260.
40. Nulty, 144.
41. George Washington Williams, *A History of the Negro Troops in the War of the Rebellion 1861–1865* (New York, N.Y., Bergman Publishers, 1968), 208.
42. Scott, 345–346.
43. Letter from Corporal Henry Shackleford to his mother dated February

20, 1864 (Tallahassee, Fl., University of Florida, Letters of Olustee Collection).

44. Bruce S. Allardice, *More Confederate Generals in Gray* (Baton Rouge, La., Louisiana State University Press, 1995).

45. General George P. Harrison, *The Battle of Olustee* (Nashville, TN., Confederate Veteran Magazine, vol. 24), 346–347.

46. Ibid., 347.

47. Ibid.

48. James M. Dancy's Memoirs of the War in Florida (Tallahassee, Fl., University of Florida, Letters of Olustee Collection).

49. Letter from Stinson Freeman to Netti, dated February 21, 1864 (Tallahassee, Fl., University of Florida, Letters of Olustee Collection).

50. Andrews, 127–128.

51. Scott, 343–344.

Chapter Four

1. Palmer, 132.
2. Clark, 83–84.
3. Brown, 219.
4. Jackson, Lawrence, *As I Saw and Remember the Battle of Olustee* (Tallahassee, Fl., University of Florida, Letters of Olustee Collection).
5. Clark, 84–85.
6. Memoir of Lieutenant Nicholas DeGroff (Carlisle, Pa., United States Army Military History Institute, manuscript collection).
7. Scott, 66, and *Eastern Fields of Battle*, 37.
8. James A. Harley, *The Battle of Olustee* (Nashville, TN., *Confederate Veteran Magazine*, Vol. 22), 457.
9. Nulty, 162–163.
10. Ibid., 151.
11. Clark, 85–87.
12. Reminiscences of Lieutenant Nicholas DeGroff (Carlisle Barricks, Pa., United States Army Military History Institute), 1–2.
13. Clark, 88.
14. Palmer, 132–134.
15. Ibid., 135–136.
16. Scott, 302.
17. Letter from Captain Robert R. Newell to Will, dated March 9, 1864 (Tallahassee, Fl., University of Florida, Letters of Olustee Collection).
18. Nulty, 156, and Trudeau, 145.
19. Letter from Captain Robert R. Newell to Will, dated March 9, 1864.
20. Smith, 142.
21. Trudeau, 145.
22. Letter from Captain Newell to Will, dated March 9, 1864, and Smith, 142.
23. Emilio, 162–163, and Trudeau, 145.
24. Trudeau, 145.
25. Cox, 123, Yacovone, 68, and Nulty, 158.
26. Swift, 250.
27. Smith, 142, and Cox, 123.
28. Clark, 85.
29. Nulty, 158, Yacovone, and Trudeau, 147.
30. Cox, 123, and Yacovone, 68, *New Bedford Mercury*, March 9, 1864, and Dudley Taylor Cornish, *The Sable Arm: Negro Troops in the Union Army, 1861–1865* (New York, N.Y., W.W. Norton & Company, Inc.,1966), 268.
31. Yacovone, 68, *The Boston Journal*, March 2, 1864, Virginia Matzke Adams, *On the Altar of Freedom: A Black Soldier's Civil War Letters from the Front* (Amherst, Ma., University of Massachusetts Press, 1991), 115, Letter from Corporal Henry Shackelford to Mother, dated February 20, 1864, and Nulty, 166.
32. Emilio, 165.
33. Ibid., 166
34. Ibid., 165.
35. Ibid., 166.
36. Nulty, 165.
37. Trudeau, 147.
38. Smith, 142, Brown, 220–221, Trudeau, 147–148, and *The Boston Journal*, March 2, 1864.

Chapter Notes

39. Brown, 221.
40. Trudeau, 148.
41. Nulty, 159, and Trudeau, 148.
42. Brown, 222.
43. *Boston Journal*, March 4, 1864.
44. Nulty, 165, and Smith, 144.
45. Trudeau, 150.
46. Cox, 123–124, and Swift, 250.
47. Letter from Captain Robert R. Newell to Will, dated March 9, 1864.
48. Swift, 250.
49. Letter from Captain Robert Newell to Will.
50. Trudeau, 150.
51. *Chicago Tribune*, March 9, 1864.
52. Little, 225.
53. Cornish, 269.
54. Harrison, Gen. George P., 347, and Letter from Lt. Winston Stephens to his wife dated Feb. 21, 1864 (Tallahassee, Fl., University of Florida, Letters of Olustee Collection).
55. Cornish, 269.
56. *Eastern Fields of Battle*, 105.

Chapter Five

1. Nulty, 167, 170, and Egan, 492.
2. Nulty, 171–172.
3. Jackson, 2–3.
4. Crowninshield, 260.
5. Trudeau, 151.
6. Ibid.
7. Ibid., 150.
8. Reminiscences of William Penniman, 4, 6, and Trudeau, 151.
9. Letter from Lt. Winston Stephens to his wife, dated Feb. 27, 1864, Letter from Corporal Henry Shackelford to his mother dated Feb. 20, 1864, and Trudeau, 151.
10. Letter from James Jordan to Louisa dated Feb. 21, 1864 (Tallahassee, Fl., University of Florida, Letters of Olustee Collection).
11. J.C. Rice, *The Battle of Olustee* (Nashville, Tn., Confederate Veteran Magazine, vol. 22), 245.
12. Letter from Lieutenant Oliver Norton to Sister L., February 1864 (Tallahassee, Fl., University of Florida, Letters of Olustee Collection).
13. Scott, 329–330.
14. *American Annual Cyclopedia and Register of Important Events for the Year 1864* (New York, N.Y., D. Appleton & Company, 1872), 51.
15. *Savannah Daily Morning News*, March 30, 1864.
16. *The Boston Herald*, March 2, 1864.
17. Letter from James Flynn to wife dated March 30, 1864 (Tallahassee, Fl., University of Florida, Letters of Olustee Collection).
18. Letter from Lt. Winston Stephens to wife dated Feb. 21, 1864.
19. Letter from Cpl. Henry Shackelford to mother dated Feb. 20, 1864, and Nulty, 182.
20. Nulty, 182.
21. Ibid.
22. *Eastern Fields of Battle*, 105.
23. William Marvel, *Andersonville: The Last Depot* (Chapel Hill, N.C., University of North Carolina Press, 1994), 41–42.
24. Scott, 333, 328.
25. Report of Lieutenant Frederick E. Grossman Seventh United States Infantry, on the reburial of Union troops at Olustee, Florida (Tallahassee, Fl., University of Florida, Letters of Olustee Collection).

Chapter Six

1. Clark, 88–89.
2. Letter from Captain Robert Newell to Will, dated March 9, 1864.
3. *The Boston Journal*, March 2, 1864, and Swift, 251
4. Swift, 251.
5. Little, 229.
6. Little, 253, and Davis, 293.
7. Scott, 488.
8. Ibid., 488–489.
9. Cox, 124–135.
10. Cox, 125, and Clark, 90.

Chapter Notes

11. Clark, 93–94.
12. Cox, 125, and Letter from Captain Robert Newell to Will, dated March 9, 1864, Emilio, 175, and Clark, 90.
13. Egan, 496.
14. Little, 129, and Letter from Captain Robert Newell.
15. Jones, 20.
16. Scott, 335.
17. Swift, 252–253.
18. Emilio, 175.
19. Egan, 496, and Nulty, 189.
20. Scott, 491–492, and Johnson, vol. III, 75.
21. Nulty, 191.
22. Ibid., 196.
23. *Eastern Fields of Battle*, 46.
24. James M. Dancy's Memoirs of the War in Florida (Tallahassee, Fl., University of Florida, Letters of Olustee Collection).
25. Egan, 498–499.
26. Virginia M. Adams, *On the Altar of Freedom: A Black Soldier's Civil War Letters from the Front—Corporal James Henry Goodling* (New York, N.Y., Warner Books, 1991), 114.

Chapter Seven

1. Trudeau, 153.
2. Ibid.
3. Smith, 145.
4. Furness, 260–261.
5. Williams, 208.
6. Clark, 94–95.
7. *The Boston Herald*, March 2, 1864.
8. *The Boston Herald*, March 9, 1864.
9. Letter from Lt. Col. James Hall to his wife, dated February 23, 1864 (Tallahassee, Fl., University of Florida, Letters of Olustee Collection).
10. Swift, 253.
11. Ibid., 254.
12. Palmer, 136–137.
13. Egan, 499–500.
14. Tourtelotte, 126–127.
15. Cox, 127.
16. Trudeau, 145.
17. Clark, 101.

Epilogue

1. Tourtelotte, 125.
2. Warner, *Generals in Blue*, 433.
3. James A. Harley, *The Battle of Olustee* (Nashville, Tn., *Confederate Veteran Magazine*, Vol. 22), 457.
4. Furness, 292.

Appendix II

1. Scott, 298.

Appendix IV

1. *Ubi libertas, ibi patria*, Presentation of the flag of the 2nd Florida Cavalry by Miss Gilchrist, of Lake City, *Memphis Daily Appeal*, January 9, 1864.

BIBLIOGRAPHY

Primary Sources, Manuscripts

University of Florida
   James Dancy Papers
   Nicholas DeGroff Papers
   James Flynn Papers
   Stinson Freeman Papers
   James Hall Papers
   Lawrence Jackson Papers
   Loomis Langdon Papers
   Tully McCrea Papers
   Robert Newell Papers
   Oliver Norton Papers
   Winston Stephens Papers
   Daniel Stringer Papers
   William Trimmer Papers

University of North Carolina, Chapel Hill
   William Penniman Papers

Primary Sources, Books

American Annual Cyclopedia and Register of Important Events for the Year 1864. New York: D. Appleton, 1872.

Andrews, W.H. *Footprints of a Regiment: A Recollection of the 1st Georgia Regulars 1861–1865.* Atlanta, Ga.: Longstreet, 1992.

Briggs, Walter De Bois. *Civil War Surgeon in a Colored Regiment.* Berkeley: University of California Press, 1960.

Caren, Eric C. *Civil War Extra: A Newspaper History of the Civil War from 1863 to 1865.* New York: Castle Books, 1999.

Civil War Papers Read Before the Commandery of the State of Massachusetts Military Order of the Loyal legion of the United States, Volume II. Wilmington, N.C.: Broadfoot, 1993.

Clark, James H., *The Iron Hearted Regiment: An Account of the Battles, Marches and Gallant Deeds Performed by the 115th Regiment N.Y. Vols.* Albany, N.Y.: J. Munsell, 1865.

Croom, Wendell D. *The War History of Company C (Beauregard Volunteers), Sixth Georgia Regiment (Infantry), with a Graphic Account of Each Member.* Fort Valley, Ga.: Advertiser, 1879.

Bibliography

Crowinshield, Benjamin W. *A History of the First Regiment of Massachusetts Cavalry Volunteers.* Cambridge, Ma.: Houghton, Mifflin, 1891.

Dennison, Frederic. *Shot and Shell: The Third Rhode Island Heavy Artillery in the Rebellion 1861-1865.* Providence, R.I.: J.A. & R.A. Reid, 1879.

Emilio, Luis, F. *A Brave Black Regiment: History of the Fifty-Fourth Regiment of Massachusetts Volunteer Infantry 1863-1865.* New York: Arno, 1969.

Evans, Clement A. *Confederate Military History, Volume 16.* Wilmington, N.C.: Broodfoot: 1989.

Fox, Charles Barnard. *Record of the Services of the Fifty-fifth Regiment of Massachusetts Volunteer Infantry.* Cambridge, Ma.: Wilson & Sons, 1868.

Goodling, Corporal James Henry. *On the Altar of Freedom: A Black Soldier's Civil War Letters from the Front.* Amherst: University of Massachusetts Press, 1991.

Headley, J.T. *The Great Rebellion.* Washington, D.C.: The National Tribune, 1898.

Higgonson, Thomas Wentworth. *Army Life in a Black Regiment.* Williamston, Ma.: Corner House, 1971.

Ingersoll, C.M. *Catalogue of Connecticut Volunteer Organizations, Infantry, Cavalry and Artillery in the Service of the United States, 1861-1865, With Additional Enlistments, Casualties, &ct. and Brief Summaries Showing the Operations and Service of the Several Regiments and Batteries.* Hartford, Ct.: Brown & Gross, 1869.

Johnson, Robert Underwood, and Clarence C. Buel. *Battles and Leaders of the Civil War.* New York: Century, 1888.

Keylin, Arleen, and Douglas John Bowen. *The New York Times Book of the Civil War.* New York: Arno, 1980.

Lanier, Robert S. *The Photographic History of the Civil War.* Secaucus, N.Y.: Blue & Grey, 1987.

Little, Henry F.W. *The Seventh Regiment New Hampshire Volunteers in the War of the Rebellion.* Concord, N.H.: Ira C. Evans, 1896.

Moody, William H. *Official Records of the Union and Confederate Navies in the War of the Rebellion.* Washington, D.C.: Government Printing Office, 1894-1922.

Moore, Frank. *The Rebellion Record: A Diary of American Events.* New York: G.P. Putnam, 1861-1868.

Nichols, James M. *Perry's Saints or The Fighting Parsons Regiment in the War of the Rebellion.* Boston, Ma.: D. Lothrop, 1886.

Palladino, Anita. *Diary of a Yankee Engineer: The Civil War Story of John H. Westervelt, Engineer, 1st New York Volunteer Engineer Corps.* New York: Fordham University Press, 1997.

Palmer, Abraham J. *The History of the Forty-Eighth Regiment New York State Volunteers in the War for the Union 1861-1865.* Brooklyn, N.Y.: Veteran Association of the Regiment, 1885.

Papers of the Military Historical Society of Massachusetts, Volume IX. Wilmington, N.C.: Broadfoot, 1989.

Personal Narratives of Events in the War of the Rebellion, being Papers Read Before

Bibliography

the Rhode Island Soldiers and Sailors Historical Society, Volume IX. Providence, R.I.: Published by the Society, 1903–05.
Tourtelotte, Jerome. *A History of Company K of the Seventh Connecticut Volunteer Infantry in the Civil War.* Putnam, N.H.: Published by the author, 1910.
Walkley, Stephen. *History of the Seventh Connecticut Volunteer Infantry: Hawley's Brigade, Terry's Division Tenth Army Corps 1861–1865.* Published by the author, 1905.
The War of the Rebellion: A Compilation of the Official Records of the Union and Confederate Armies. Washington, D.C.: Government Printing Office, 1891.
War Papers Read Before the Commandery of the State of Maine, Military Order of the Loyal Legion of the United States, Volume III. Portland, Me.: Lefavor-Tower, 1908.
Welles, Gideon. *The Diary of Gideon Welles, 3 vols.* Boston, Ma.: Houghton, Mifflin, 1864.
Williams, George F. *The Memorial War Book.* New York: Lovell Brothers, 1894.
Yacovone, Donald. *A Voice of Thunder: The Civil War Letters of George E. Stephens.* Urbana: University of Illinois Press, 1997.

Primary Sources, Newspapers, Magazines and Periodicals

Athens Southern Banner, March 9, 1864.
Atlanta Intelligencer
Boston Herald, March 9, 1864.
Boston Journal, March 2, 4, 1864.
Carolina Spartan, March 31, 1864.
Chelsea Telegraph and Pioneer, March 12, 1864.
Chicago Times, March 9, 1864.
Chicago Tribune, March 9, 1864.
Confederate Veteran Magazine
   Vol. 19
   Vol. 20: Harley, James, "The Battle of Olustee," November 1912
   Vol. 22
   Vol. 24
   Vol. 25
Memphis Daily Appeal
New Bedford Mercury, March 9, 1864.
Providence Journal
Savannah Daily Morning News, March 30, 1864.
The Southern Bivouac
Worcester Aegis

Secondary Sources, Books

Abbott, John S.C. *The History of the Civil War in America.* New York: Henry Bill, 1865.
Alexander, Russell A., and David J. Coles. *The Confederate Roll of Honor: South-*

Bibliography

ern Casualties at the Battle of Olustee. Olustee, Fl.: Olustee Battlefield Citizens Support Group, 1997

Allardice, Bruce S. *More Generals in Gray*. Baton Rouge: Louisiana State University Press, 1995.

Amann, William F. *Personnel of the Civil War*. New York: Thomas Yoselof, 1961.

Anderson, Bern. *By Sea and by River: The Naval History of the Civil War*. New York: Alfred Knopf, 1962.

Blatt, Martin H., Thomas J. Brown, and Donald Yacovone. *Hope & Glory: Essays on the Legacy of the Fifty-Fourth Massachusetts Regiment*. Amherst: University of Massachusetts Press, 2001.

Bowman, John S. *The Civil War Almanac*. New York: Gallery Books, 1983.

Brevard, Caroline May. *A History of Florida*. New York: American Book, 1919.

Brown, William Wells. *The Negro in the American Rebellion: His Heroism and his Fidelity*. Miami, Fl.: Mnemosyne, 1969.

Buchard, Peter. *One Gallant Rush: Robert Gould Shaw and his Brave Black Regiment*. New York: St. Martin's, 1965.

_____. *We'll Stand by the Union: Robert Gould Shaw and the Black 54th Massachusetts Regiment*. New York: Facts on File, 1993.

Catton Bruce. *The American Heritage Short History of the Civil War*. New York: Laurel, 1960.

Chaitin, Peter M. *The Coastal War: Chesapeake Bay to Rio Grande*. Alexandria, Va.: Time Life, 1984.

Coles, David J. *Men and Arms: Sketches of the Commanders and Units of the Olustee Campaign*. Olustee, Fl.: Renaissance, 1995.

Commager, Henry Steele. *The Blue and the Gray*. New York: Fairfax, 1982.

Cornish, Dudley Taylor. *The Sable Arm: Negro Troops in the Union Army, 1861–1865*. New York: W.W. Norton, 1966.

Cox, Clinton. *Undying Glory: The Story of the Massachusetts 54th Regiment*. New York: Scholastic, 1991.

Davis, William Watson. *The Civil War and Reconstruction in Florida*. New York: Columbia University, 1913.

Dennett, Tyler. *John Hay: From Poetry to Politics*. New York: Dodd, Mead, 1934.

Denny, Robert E. *Civil War Medicine: Care & Comfort of the Wounded*. New York: Sterling, 1994.

_____. *The Civil War Years: A Day-by-Day Chronicle*. New York: Gramercy, 1992.

Draper, John William. *History of the American Civil War*. New York: Harper's, 1857–1870.

Duncan, Russell. *Where Death and Glory Meet: Colonel Robert Gould Shaw and the 54th Massachusetts Infantry*. Athens: University of Georgia Press, 1999.

Dyer, Frederick. *A Compendium of the War of the Rebellion*. New York: Thomas Yoseloff, 1959.

Eaton, Clement. *A History of the Southern Confederacy*. New York: Collier, 1954.

Edwards, William B. *Civil War Guns: The Complete Story of Federal and Confederate Small Arms; Design, manufacture, identification, procurement, issue, employment, effectiveness, and postwar disposal*. New York: Castle, 1978.

Bibliography

Faust, Patricia L. *Historical Times Illustrated Encyclopedia of the Civil War.* New York: Harper Perennial, 1986.
Foote, Shelby. *The Civil War: A Narrative.* New York: Random House, 1958.
Fox, William Freeman. *Regimental Losses in the American Civil War 1861–1865.* Albany, N.Y.: Albany, 1889.
Garrison, Webb. *Friendly Fire in the Civil War.* Nashville, Tn.: Rutledge Hill, 1999.
Johns, John Edwin. *Florida During the Civil War.* Gainesville: University of Florida Press, 1963.
Johnson, Clint. *Bull's-Eyes and Misfires: 50 People Whose Obscure Efforts Shaped the American Civil War.* Nashville, Tn.: Rutledge Hill, 2002.
Kettell, Thomas Prentice. *History of the Great Rebellion.* Hartford, Ct.: F.A. Howe, 1865.
Livermore, Thomas Leonard. *Numbers and Losses in the Civil War in America 1861–1865.* Bloomington: Indiana University Press, 1957.
Lossing, Benson J. *Our Country, A Household History For All Readers From The Discovery of America to the Present Time, volume 2.* New York: Henry J. Johnson, 1879.
McAulay, John D. *Civil War Breech Loading Rifles: A Survey of the Innovative Infantry Arms of the American Civil War.* Lincoln, R.I.: Andrew Mowbry, 1991.
McMaster, John Bach. *Our House Divided.* Greenwich, Ct.: Fawcett, 1961.
McPherson, James M. *The Negro's Civil War: How American Negroes Felt and Acted During the War for the Union.* New York, N.Y.: Pantheon, 1965.
Marvel, William. *Andersonville: The Last Depot.* Chapel Hill: University of North Carolina Press, 1994.
Nulty, William H. *Confederate Florida: The Road to Olustee.* Tuscaloosa: University of Alabama Press, 1990.
Olustee Battlefield Citizens Support Organization. *The Battle of Olustee and The Olustee Battlefield Site: A Brief History.* Olustee, Fl.: Renaissance, 1992.
Parish, Peter J. *The American Civil War.* New York, N.Y.: Holmes & Mier, 1975.
Price, William H. *The Civil War Centennial Handbook.* Arlington, Va.: Prince Lithograph, 1961.
Quarles, Benjamin. *The Negro in the Civil War.* Boston, Ma.: Little, Brown, 1953.
Robertson, James I. Jr. *Soldiers Blue & Gray.* New York, N.Y.: Warner, 1988.
Roman, Alfred. *The Military Operations of General Beauregard in the War Between the States 1861–1865, Including a Brief Sketch and Narrative of Service in the War With Mexico.* New York, N.Y.: Harper and Brattens, 1884.
Schiller, Herbert M. *Sunter Is Avenged! The Siege & Reduction of Fort Pulaski.* Shippensburg, Pa.: White Mane, 1995.
Schmucker, Samuel M. *The History of the Civil War in the United States.* Philadelphia, Pa.: Jones Brothers, 1865.
Smith, John David. *Black Soldiers in Blue: African American Troops in the Civil War Era.* Chapel Hill: University of North Carolina Press, 2002.
Tenney, W.J. *The Military and Naval History of the Rebellion in the United States*

Bibliography

with Biographical Sketches of Deceased Officers. New York, N.Y.: Appleton, 1867.

Tomes, Robert, and Benjamin G. Smith. *The War with the South: A History of the Great American Rebellion.* New York, N.Y.: Virtue & Yorston, 1862–1867.

Trudeau, Noah Andre. *Like Men of War: Black Troops in the Civil War 1862–1865.* Boston, Ma.: Little, Brown, 1998.

Victor, Orville J. *The History, Civil, Political, and Military, of the Southern Rebellion, From Its Incipient Stages to Its Close, 2 volumes.* New York, N.Y.: James D. Torrey, 1861–1865.

Warner, Ezra J. *Generals in Blue: Lives of the Union Commanders.* Baton Rouge: Louisiana State University Press, 1960.

_____. *Generals in Gray: Lives of the Confederate Commanders.* Baton Rouge: Louisiana State University Press, 1959.

Wertz, Jay, and Edwin C. Bearss. *Smithsonian's Great Battles & Battlefields of the Civil War: A Definitive Guide Based on the Award Winning Television Series by MasterVision.* New York, N.Y.: William Morrow, 1997.

Wiley, Bell Irvin. *Embattled Confederates.* New York, N.Y.: Bonanza, 1964.

Williams, George Washington. *A History of the Negro Troops in the War of the Rebellion 1861–65.* New York, NY: Bergman, 1968.

Secondary Sources, Magazines and Periodicals

Civil War History
Civil War Times Illustrated
  June 1962
  April 1972
  January 1978

INDEX

Abbott, Col. Joseph C. 86, 87, 88, 90, 191
Abell's Artillery, C.S.A. 39, 192, 195
Alachua County, Fla. 10
Ames, Gen. Adelbert 156, 164, 165
Anderson, Gen. Patton, C.S.A. 161, 167
Anderson, Col. Robert 167
Antietam 21
Appleton, Maj. John 25, 27
Army of Northern Virginia 3, 180, 184, 185
Army of Tennessee 2, 167
Asboth, Gen. Alexander 58

Bailey, Capt. Romanzo 96
Baldwin, Fla. 29, 39, 40, 41, 42, 43, 45, 46, 47, 50, 54, 55, 60, 61, 62, 69, 72, 97, 139, 154, 160, 164, 173
Ball's Bluff 4
Barbers, Fla. 47, 53, 55, 57, 73, 75, 76, 120, 127, 140, 153, 154, 160, 164
Barton, Col. William B. 34, 75, 104, 105, 111, 114, 115, 165, 169, 170, 192, 193
Battery Wagner 3, 11, 21, 29, 112, 120, 131, 133, 146, 159, 172, 186, 191
Beauregard, Gen. P.G.T., C.S.A. 9, 30, 31, 32, 33, 57, 58, 61, 73, 109, 150, 160, 164, 167
Bell, Col. Louis 164
Bird, Maj. Pickens, C.S.A. 192
Bogle, Maj. Archibald 98, 126, 127, 128, 150
Bragg, Gen. Braxton, C.S.A. 7, 9

Camp Beauregard 37
Camp Cooper 43, 48
Camp Finegan 35, 36, 37, 38, 39, 41, 43, 45, 49, 159

Camp Milton 164
Camp Shaw see Camp Finegan
Camp William Penn 84
Cannon, Capt. Henry A., C.S.A. 103, 192
Cezar, Sgt. Garnet 120
Chambers, Capt. W.E., C.S.A. 62, 63, 163
Charleston, S.C. 2, 7, 9, 17, 21, 30, 31, 50, 57, 58, 150, 160
Chase, Capt. James M. 132
Chase, Salmon 14, 182
Chatham Artillery, C.S.A. 61, 68, 76, 98, 99, 104, 109, 192, 194
Chickamauga, Battle of 3, 134
Chickasaw Bayou, Battle of 11
Clark, Lt. James 73, 105, 111, 153, 154
Clinch, Col. Duncan L., C.S.A. 135, 192
Coan, Major W.B. 114, 191
Colquitt, Gen. Alfred H., C.S.A. 30, 61, 64, 65, 67, 74, 76, 78, 79, 81, 84, 86, 98, 99, 100, 101, 107, 109, 128, 134, 138, 157, 182, 183, 184, 192, 194
Colquitt, Lt. Hugh H., C.S.A. 110
Cooper, Gen. Samuel, C.S.A. 30
Custer, Gen. George Armstrong 22

Dahlgren, Admr. John 23, 54
Dana, Capt. Gustavus 45, 121, 129, 130, 144, 155, 162
Dancy, Lt. James M., C.S.A. 102, 103, 168
Dancy, Lt. Robert F., C.S.A. 102
DeGroff, Lt. Nicholas 107, 111
Department of the Gulf 11, 58, 59
Department of the South 58, 160
Dickison, Capt. John, C.S.A. 57, 68, 176
Duren, Lt. Charles 131

215

Index

Eddy, Lt. George E. 93, 94
Egan, Sgt. Patrick 137, 169, 177
18th South Carolina Infantry, C.S.A. 166
8th United States Colored Troops 5, 20, 24, 34, 60, 61, 81, 87, 88, 89, 90, 91, 92, 93, 94, 95, 96, 97, 98, 104, 105, 140, 144, 150, 178, 180, 193
Elder's Horse Battery 20, 24, 81, 105, 137, 165, 193
11th South Carolina Infantry, C.S.A. 155
Emilio, Capt. Luis 123, 124
Evans, Col. J.W., C.S.A. 78

Fernandina, Fla. 1, 7, 29, 43, 61, 156, 167, 181
5th Florida Cavalry Battalion, C.S.A. 168, 192, 195
5th Georgia Cavalry, C.S.A. 68, 166
55th Massachusetts Infantry 17, 154, 165
54th Massachusetts Infantry 3, 5, 20, 21, 22, 23, 24, 25, 27, 28, 32, 72, 116, 117, 118, 119, 120, 121, 122, 123, 124, 125, 126, 128, 129, 130, 131, 132, 133, 137, 154, 157, 158, 165, 170, 178, 180, 186, 191, 193
59th Virginia Infantry, C.S.A. 166
Finegan, Gen. Joseph, C.S.A. 4, 31, 32, 33, 36, 37, 40, 51, 52, 53, 57, 63, 65, 66, 67, 68, 74, 75, 76, 80, 65, 109, 134, 135, 138, 144, 145, 149, 150, 151, 157, 160, 161, 162, 163, 167, 180, 181, 182, 183, 184, 185, 192
1st Florida Infantry Battalion, C.S.A. 31, 67, 108, 109, 117, 192, 195
1st Georgia Regular Infantry, C.S.A. 44, 53, 63, 64, 67, 73, 74, 76, 102, 103, 107, 166, 192, 195
1st New York Engineers 175
1st North Carolina Infantry (35th United Stated Colored Troops) 34, 116, 118, 122, 125, 126, 127, 128, 129, 131, 132, 143, 165, 178, 191, 193
1st U.S. Artillery, Battery B 22
1st U.S. Artillery, Battery M 105, 191, 193
Florida Railroad 65
Flynn, Pvt. James 147
Fort, Lt. John, C.S.A. 103
Fort Pulaski, Ga. 12, 108
Fort Sumter, S.C. 21
40th Massachusetts Mounted Infantry 20, 24, 34, 48, 51, 56, 57, 62, 89, 116, 141, 147, 153, 165, 191, 194

48th New York Infantry 24, 29, 34, 72, 105, 107, 108, 112, 113, 114, 115, 165, 176, 177, 191, 193
47th New York Infantry 34, 105, 115, 121, 165, 191, 193
Foster, Gen. Robert 156, 164
4th Georgia Cavalry, C.S.A. 64, 68, 77, 101, 142, 192, 195
4th New Hampshire Infantry 164, 165
Fraser, Philip 13
Freeman, Lt. Stinson, C.S.A. 103
Fribley, Colonel Charles 60, 90, 91, 92, 93, 98, 144, 145, 146, 191
Furness, Capt. William 97, 172, 173

Gainesville, Fla. 15, 61, 62, 68
Gamble, Capt. Robert H., C.S.A. 78, 192
Gamble's Artillery, C.S.A. 76, 78, 84, 98, 104, 192, 194
Gardner, Gen. William, C.S.A. 31, 33, 58, 145, 160, 161, 162
Garfield, Gen. James A. 16
Gettysburg, Battle of 3, 134
Gillmore, Gen. Quincy 11, 12, 16, 17, 18, 19, 20, 27, 29, 30, 43, 46, 50, 53, 54, 59, 60, 61, 68, 69, 70, 164, 174, 176, 184
Gilmer, Gen. Jeremy, C.S.A. 31, 58
Goodling, Cpl. James 123
Gordon, Gen. Thomas, C.S.A. 15
Grace, Capt. James W. 170
Grant, Lt. M.B., C.S.A. 66, 133
Graybill, Col. Tully, C.S.A. 192
Grossman, Lt. Frederick 151
Guerard, Capt. John M., C.S.A. 192
Guerard's Battery, C.S.A. 67, 109, 124, 192, 195
Guss, Col. Henry 29

Hall, Lt. Col. James 175
Halleck, Gen. Henry 18, 19, 27, 59
Hallowell, Col. Edward N. 28, 32, 118, 119, 120, 122, 125, 137, 178, 191
Hamilton, Capt. John 47, 93, 94, 95, 96, 98, 191, 194
Hamilton's Battery 81, 93
Harrison, Col. George P., C.S.A. 67, 76, 100, 101, 102, 108, 109, 128, 134, 167, 182, 183, 192, 195
Harrison, Maj. Robert, C.S.A. 44, 48, 50

216

Index

Hawley, Colonel Joseph R. 34, 56, 75, 78, 79, 81, 83, 86, 87, 88, 104, 120, 165, 191, 193
Hay, John 17, 20, 55, 71, 171
Henry, Lt. Col. Guy V. 34, 37, 38, 40, 46, 47, 52, 62, 75, 76, 78, 95, 165, 191, 194
Hill, Gen. Daniel H., C.S.A. 32
Hilton Head, S.C. 29, 164
Holcombe Legion, C.S.A. 166
Holland, Maj. W.T., C.S.A. 192
Hooper, Lt. Col. Henry 123, 125, 131
Hopkins, Lt. Col. C.F., C.S.A. 109, 192
Huggins, Lt. Col. James H., C.S.A. 192
Hunter, Pvt. Sam, C.S.A. 104

Independent Massachusetts Battalion 20, 24, 28, 34, 165, 191, 194

Jacksonville, Fla. 7, 15, 25, 26, 27, 29, 31, 32, 34, 43, 50, 53, 68, 69, 75, 87, 97, 153, 156, 158, 164, 173, 176
Jenkins, Capt. C.S., C.S.A. 192
Johnston, Gen. Joseph E., C.S.A. 167
Jones, Charles 128, 167
Jones, Gen. Samuel, C.S.A. 14
Jordan, Pvt. James, C.S.A. 143

Keely, Capt. John, C.S.A. 110
Kiawah Island, S.C. 61

Lake City, Fla. 44, 45, 50, 54, 55, 59, 63, 64, 68, 69, 70, 74, 75, 87, 102, 168
Lang, Sgt. Henry 112, 113
Langdon, Capt. Loomis L. 81, 191
Langdon's Battery 81, 84, 105, 165
Lay, Maj. John F., C.S.A. 15
Lewis, Capt. DeWitt 44
Lincoln, Abraham 2, 12, 16, 17, 71, 181, 182, 185
Lincoln Cavalry 147
Little, Lt. Henry 133, 155
Littlefield, Col. M.S. 165
Lofton, Lt. Col. John T., C.S.A. 192

Madison, Fla. 45, 65
Majer, Surgeon Adolph 97
Marshall, Capt. G.E. 57, 62
McClellan, Gen. George B. 22
McCormick, Lt. Col. A.H., C.S.A. 36, 37, 42, 77, 78, 192
McCrea, Lt. Tully 22

McMullen, J.J. 103
Mercer, Gen. H.W., C.S.A. 166
Meriam, Frank B. 27
Merrill, Sgt. Otis A. 88
Metcalf, Lt. Henry H. 137, 191
Middleburg, Fla. 62
Milton Florida Light Artillery 68, 78
Montgomery, Colonel James 34, 55, 116, 117, 120, 122, 124, 125, 165, 183
Moore, Col. Henry 83, 115, 191
Morris Island, S.C. 61, 178
Mosby, Col. John S., C.S.A. 57
Myrick, Lt. H. 93, 94

Neal, Col. James H., C.S.A. 192
Newell, Capt. Robert 117, 118, 130, 159, 160
97th Pennsylvania Infantry 29, 43, 156
19th Georgia Infantry, C.S.A. 67, 78, 84, 99, 104, 110, 115, 117, 123, 124, 148, 192, 194
Northrup, Col. L.B. 9
Norton, Lt. Oliver 91, 144

Ocean Pond, Fla. 3, 5, 37, 63, 65, 66, 80
Okefenokee Swamp 65
Olustee, Fla. 3, 4, 5, 46, 63, 64, 69, 70, 72, 75, 76, 96, 104, 109, 125, 128, 133, 134, 135, 137, 142, 146, 147, 150, 154, 156, 158, 170, 171, 172, 174, 175, 178
Olustee Station, Fla. 149
115th New York Infantry 26, 34, 38, 42, 73, 105, 110, 111, 113, 114, 121, 122, 153, 165, 179, 191
157th New York Infantry 165
169th New York Infantry 165
112th New York Infantry 165
Osborn, Col. Francis 61
Otis, Col. J.L. 156

Palatka, Fla. 50, 60, 61, 69, 169, 176, 177, 179
Palmer, Abraham 72, 73
Penniman, William Frederick 64, 65, 77, 85, 142
Pennypacker, Maj. Galusha 43
Port Hudson, Battle of 11, 146
Pyles, Lt. Col. Louis G., C.S.A. 62

Rambo, Lt. Drury, C.S.A. 78
Reed, Lt. Col. W.N. 98, 126, 191
Rice, J.C. 143

Index

Roach, Joab 143
Roberts, Marshall O. 16
Rosecrans, Gen. William 7

St. Augustine, Fla. 1, 7, 16, 29, 61, 69, 156, 167, 181, 182, 186
St. John's River 18, 25, 177
St. Mary's River 47, 48, 53, 60, 61, 69, 178
Sammon, Col. Simeon 111, 114, 191
Sanderson, Fla. 50, 51, 52, 55, 57, 112, 141, 153, 160
Savannah, Ga. 31, 65, 66, 108, 113
Scott, Maj. G.W., C.S.A. 161, 192
Seabrook Island, S.C. 30
2nd Florida Cavalry, C.S.A. 36, 44, 48, 49, 62, 68, 76, 78, 105, 134, 138, 157, 176, 192, 195
2nd Florida Infantry Battalion, C.S.A. 80, 104
2nd South Carolina Infantry (Union) 20, 24
17th Connecticut Infantry 165
7th Connecticut Infantry 20, 22, 24, 29, 34, 56, 78, 79, 80, 81, 82, 84, 85, 86, 88, 89, 98, 100, 137, 140, 165, 177, 181, 193
7th New Hampshire Infantry 20, 24, 34, 56, 62, 81, 86, 87, 89, 90, 104, 105, 132, 147, 155, 159, 165, 193
75th Ohio Infantry 165
Shackelford, Cpl. Henry, C.S.A. 99, 123, 143
Shiloh, Battel of 3, 134
Shimmelfenig, Gen. Alexander 30
6th Florida Infantry, C.S.A. 63, 67, 76, 115, 117, 128, 192, 194
6th Georgia Infantry, C.S.A. 45, 67, 76, 78, 84, 101, 104, 107, 108, 109, 117, 183, 192, 194
64th Georgia Infantry, C.S.A. 31, 67, 76, 78, 84, 98, 102, 115, 117, 192, 195
Smith, Col. Caroway, C.S.A. 77, 78, 138, 192, 195
South Mountain, Battle of 21
Stanton, Edwin 19, 59, 178
Stevens, Sgt. George 118
Stickney, L.D. 16
Suwannee River 15, 46, 54

Tallahassee, Fla. 4, 15, 58, 59, 74, 149
Ten Mile Station, Fla. 157

Tenth Connecticut Infantry 156
Terry, Gen. Alfred 57
Thayer, Eli 16
3rd Rhode Island Artillery 24, 93, 137, 159, 164, 165, 169, 177, 191, 194
3rd South Carolina Infantry (Colored) 20, 165
3rd U.S. Artillery, Battery E 191, 194
3rd United States Colored Troops 24, 60, 165
32nd Georgia Infantry, C.S.A. 63, 67, 76, 85, 100, 101, 103, 104, 107, 108, 117, 128, 192, 195
Tilghman, Col. Lloyd 165
Tourtellotte, Jerome 80, 181
Trimmer, William H. 39, 40, 41
28th Georgia Artillery Battalion, C.S.A. 192, 195
28th Georgia Infantry, C.S.A. 63, 67, 76, 78, 102, 104, 115, 192, 194
21st Massachusetts Infantry 128
24th Connecticut Infantry 61
24th Massachusetts Infantry 165
27th Georgia Infantry, C.S.A. 108, 110, 117, 128, 143, 192, 194
26th Virginia Infantry, C.S.A. 166
23rd Georgia Infantry, C.S.A. 67, 104, 117, 192, 194

U.S.S. *Cosmopolitan* 25, 178
U.S.S. *General Hunter* 25, 27
U.S.S. *Island City* 44
U.S.S. *Maple Leaf* 25, 27
U.S.S. *Norwich* 25, 27
U.S.S. *Ottawa* 25
U.S.S. *Perry* 44
U.S.S. *St. Mary's* 27

Villepigue's Battery, C.S.A. 166
Vogdes, Gen. Israel 164

Welles, Gideon 18, 23, 171
Wheaton, Capt. John F., C.S.A. 98, 192
Wheaton's Battery, C.S.A. 98, 148, 166
Wilson, Pvt. Joseph T. 118, 127
Wilson's Creek, Battle of 4
Wise, Gen. H.A., C.S.A. 30
Wood, Gen. D.P., C.S.A. 10

Zachry, Col. Charles T., C.S.A. 192

www.ingramcontent.com/pod-product-compliance
Ingram Content Group UK Ltd.
Pitfield, Milton Keynes, MK11 3LW, UK
UKHW041955140426
5217IPUK00015B/810